DEVELOPING
A STRATEGIC BUSINESS PLAN WITH CASES:
An Entrepreneur's Advantage

Robert P. Crowner

IRWIN

Homewood, IL 60430
Boston, MA 02116

ISBN 0-256-08636-2

Printed in the United States of America.

2 3 4 5 6 7 8 9 0 ML 7 6 5 4 3 2 1

TABLE OF CONTENTS

[handwritten margin notes: "explain on marketing", "Bus. Do plan", "Bus. Do plan", "1 or 2 bullet. Do not develop proforma financial But do rudimentary breakeven or other analysis. Sensitivity on volume"]

v

DEVELOPING
A STRATEGIC BUSINESS PLAN WITH CASES:
An Entrepreneur's Advantage

Robert P. Crowner

CHAPTER 1

INTRODUCTION

This book is about how to develop a Strategic Business Plan. It is written with the intent of helping students, entrepreneurs, and business people prepare such plans both initially and on an ongoing basis. Strategic planning encompasses the process of integrating an organization's mission, major goals, objectives, and policies along with the strategies to accomplish them into a cohesive whole with a common focus. In addition, strategic planning must consider the tactics or implementation of the strategies if is to be feasible, practical and workable.

Of necessity, strategic planning deals with the future. Although decisions can only be made in the present, they can be made with the intention of bringing about some desirable future result. In order to do such planning successfully, it is necessary to identify key factors and methods that could be employed. It is not, as many may believe or assume, meant to replace managerial intuition or judgment. On the contrary, it incorporates these key subjective attributes into the planning process. It puts flesh on the skeleton and provides the wherewithal to accomplish the firm's mission.

There seems to be a natural bias against planning latent within many of us. Perhaps we like spontaneity, dislike discipline or are just plain lazy. Thus planning involves some amount of self-discipline in exchange for accelerated and orderly growth. Entrepreneurs and owners of small businesses may think of themselves as driving a speedboat which they can "turn on a dime." They see themselves able to change course and thus outwit the ponderous lake freighter with its vast inertia and resistance to change. They believe that they can manage in a reactive mode and more than catch - up with the advantage of quickness gained from small size and the absence of the bureaucracy present in so many large companies. In a large measure they are right! However, the larger competitor has vast resources due to size alone that may allow it to outlast the fuel supply of the "speedboat." Think what the small company could do with the ability to change rapidly if strategic planning were also done.

Another enemy of strategic planning is the fact that operating problems tend to diminish or supplant planning efforts. Many owners and entrepreneurs may have become successful and gained their reputation from being adept at solving current operating problems in a previous employment situation. While this ability was desirable then, a new organizing skill is needed in running a successful small business and that involves longer-range planning. Planning does not take the fun out of life but may provide more time for fun by avoiding learning by making costly mistakes.

Strategic planning presupposes change or the need for change. Change is more acceptable if it is understood and accepted by those affected by it and better yet if they had a part in planning and creating it. Therefore, it is important to get the active involvement and commitment of others in the organization. This begins by creating a dialogue with them. After all, they have a stake in the business also.

WHY DO STRATEGIC BUSINESS PLANNING?

Most people think the reason for making a Strategic Business Plan is to help convince someone to invest money into the business. While this is an important reason, for few potential investors would invest money in a business without first seeing a business plan, it is not by any means the only or even most important reason for all existing businesses need a Business Plan! However, it is an important selling tool.

A business plan provides direction and marshals resources toward specific goals and objectives, for if you don't know where you are going, you may well end up someplace else. It minimizes sub-optimization of parts of the business at the expense of the whole. It provides a framework for coordinating all parts of the organization. It focuses attention on major issues that can affect the survival and growth of the business.

Developing a business plan, if done properly, must generate a thorough analysis of the external and internal environment of the firm or what is generally called a situation analysis. This analysis is also called a SWOT analysis for Strengths, Weaknesses, Opportunities, and Threats. Such an analysis in and of itself is extremely valuable to the owner or entrepreneur. Chapter 2 will deal with the development of this precursor to the business plan at some length.

Once completed, the business plan becomes a measuring stick for judging performance of the firm and appraising its management. True, the proverbial bottom line, net profit, is highly regarded as a measure of performance and logically so. However, there are other qualitative factors whose measurement is facilitated by business planning. These factors include such things as quality, creativity, innovation, motivation and knowledge. Planning not only encompasses timing but provides for the evaluation of it also. Common commitment can flow from the plan and in turn be measured against it.

The above discussion should make it evident that developing a Business Plan is not a one-time event perhaps required by potential investors. Rather it is a continuing process. The original plan should cover a three-to five-year period and be updated and extended each year. Once into the habit, planning loses its stigma and becomes part of the normal business.

WHO DOES STRATEGIC PLANNING?

Developing a Strategic Business Plan is the job of the CEO, Chief Executive Officer, and undoubtedly his most important job. In most small businesses, the CEO is the owner. While the CEO must prepare the plan himself, that does not mean he should not seek the help of others, such as key people in his own organization or professional consultants. Often these people bring a different perspective to the discussion and by simply asking questions may stimulate the mind of the owner to think of other options previously overlooked. Thus the CEO must set the climate for effective planning including the value system he wishes the firm to have.

In order for the CEO to develop and write a Business Plan he must allow sufficient time for the process, which the first time through always takes more time than expected. Since there are only sixteen usable hours in a day, this means that priorities must be set by the CEO. Therefore, some operational duties and responsibilities must be delegated to others at least temporarily. He should focus his thinking and the majority of his time on pinpointing four to six key issues.

OUTLINE OF BOOK

Before discussing the actual preparation of the Business Plan in Chapter 5, several tools for use by the owner in writing a Business Plan need to be presented and developed which are necessary for thorough preparation for the writing task. Chapter 2 deals with making a Situational or SWOT Analysis as mentioned earlier. Chapter 3 deals with various tools for Financial Analysis including income statements, balance sheets, ratios, and breakeven analysis which helps evaluate risk. Chapter 4 discusses Strategy Development, for this is a key factor in the Plan. Chapter 5 describes how to write the Business Plan. Chapter 6 presents the case, Gal-Tech Corporation, and a sample Business Plan for this case. Chapter 6 is followed by a group of business cases suitable for discussion or written analysis or developing a business plan.

CHAPTER 2

SITUATION OR SWOT ANALYSIS

In preparing to develop your business strategy, it is particularly helpful to make a situation analysis or what is commonly called a SWOT analysis for Strengths, Weaknesses, Opportunities and Threats. Stated another way a SWOT analysis looks at the internal environment (strengths and weaknesses) and external environment (opportunities and threats) of the firm. Such an analysis is needed because it is always easier and more effective to build on a firm's strengths and opportunities than it is to have to fix or shore - up all of the weaknesses and counteract all of the threats. Of course, in actual practice a strategic business plan will do some of each but emphasize the positive side.

EXTERNAL ENVIRONMENT -- *Threats and Opportunities*

The preferred place to start is the external environment the firm will be functioning within or, in the case of an existing firm, is functioning within. By beginning with the threats and opportunities facing the firm, it is easier to relate the strengths and weaknesses of the firm to this external situation. Also, it is convenient to begin with the threats and then develop the opportunities that are often the opposite side of a potential threat or at least may flow from a potential threat.

Several factors impinge on the industry a business proposes to enter. These are, in order of their importance: competition, technology, economic conditions, and political and social factors. Actually there is often a close interrelationship among these factors so they need to be examined with that in mind.

Competition

Competition, both existing and potential, and the new firm's reaction to it may well determine survival, much less success of the firm. Competitors always seem threatening and intimidating to the new firm. Yet, they can offer opportunities, as one competitor seldom covers all aspects of the market providing opportunity for "niching" by the new firm. Undoubtedly, the classic material that has been written on the subject of competition is that by Michael E. Porter in his two books, *Competitive Strategy* and *Competitive Advantage*, both by Free Press, 1980 and 1985. Much of the following material is attributable to him.

Those companies operating within a given industry can perceive the entry by a new firm as a threat because the new firm will increase total capacity and will try to gain market share, which will lower prices or inflate costs, thus lowering profits for existing companies in the industry. Members of the industry may take refuge behind several barriers to entry as noted below:

1. Economies of scale -- decline in unit costs as volume increases.

2. Product differentiation -- brand identification and customer loyalties from past advertising or customer service.

3. Capital requirements -- including those up-front costs for product development and advertising as well as facilities, inventories, customer credit and start-up losses.

4. Switching costs -- one-time costs the buyer faces when switching from one supplier to another.

5. Access to distribution channels -- favorable ties based on long range or exclusive relationships or high-quality service.

6. Cost disadvantages independent of scale -- such as proprietary technology, favorable access to raw materials and location, government subsidies, and learning and experience curves.

7. Government policy -- including licensing, limiting access to raw materials, and standards for product testing and pollution control.

The end result may be expected retaliation and entry-deterring prices.

The intensity of rivalry is another factor in the competitive environment and is the result of the following factors:

1. Numerous or equally balanced competitors.

2. Slow industry growth.

3. High fixed or storage costs.

4. Lack of differentiation or switching costs.

5. Capacity augmented in large increments.

6. Diverse competitors.

7. High strategic stakes.

8.   High exit barriers.

The third competitive factor outlined by Porter is pressure from substitute products, which may create a price ceiling. The secret for the new firm is to offer a product or service that can perform the same function but has some subtle enhancements or advantages. The industry in turn may react by collective actions such as heavy advertising.

The fourth factor is the bargaining power of buyers who may be able to force down prices, demand higher quality and more services, or play one supplier against another. A buyer's or group of buyers' strength is influenced by the following factors:

1.   Purchases of large volume relative to the seller's sales.

2.   Products or services purchased represent a significant part of the buyer's costs.

3.   Products purchased are standard or undifferentiated.

4.   Buyer faces few switching costs.

5.   Buyer earns low profits.

6.   Buyers pose a credible threat of backward integration.

7.   Industry's product is unimportant to the quality of the buyer's products or services.

8.   Buyer has full information.

The final factor is the bargaining power of suppliers. Suppliers can exert bargaining power over an industry by the threat of lowering profits through threatening to either raise prices or reduce the quality of products or services. Labor is a supplier that can exert control through scarce, highly skilled employees or through tightly unionized labor. The potential of suppliers is enhanced by the following conditions:

1.   Supplier group is dominated by a few companies and is more concentrated than its customers' industry.

2.   Limited substitute products or services are available.

3.   Purchasing industry is not an important customer of the supplier group.

4.   Supplier's product is important to buyer's business.

5.   Supplier's products are differentiated or switching costs have been built up.

6.   Supplier poses a credible threat of forward integration.[1]

The analysis of competition should include a detailed look at immediate competitors as well as likely future competition. Competitors should be analyzed to determine the strengths of each one that sets them apart in some way. These may include their product, quality, manufacturing effectiveness, reputation, service capabilities, advertising effectiveness, and technological position. Potential weaknesses should be determined so that the new firm can target any vulnerable positions.

The present objectives, goals and strategies used by current competitors should be noted. These factors are often stated in company reports or information given to employees and are thus in the public realm. More subtle inferences can often be determined by observing the actions a competitor is currently taking. Changes in strategy on the part of competition can often be determined well in advance of it becoming effective by closely monitoring changes in product, advertising, etc., all of which do not require espionage.

Technology

Certainly, most people are aware of the increasing pace in the advance of technology. Change in some fields, such as computers, seems to be following a geometric progression with increasing power and speed being accompanied by decreasing costs for the performance obtainable. Nor is technological change limited to computers. Even relatively stodgy industries such as steel are experiencing changes that allow relatively small companies to compete effectively. The legendary ascendancy of the Japanese automobile manufacturers was made possible by applying technological change not only in manufacturing but also in management.

This accelerating technological change has occurred in the materials used in products and in their manufacture. An example of this is the use of melanin to coat sunglasses as described in the "Gal-Tech" case in the case section of this book. Jim Gallas, the founder of Gal-Tech, hopes to develop a new business based upon this technology.

Another area of technological change is the manufacturing process. For instance, Nucor Corporation has completed a thin-slab plant to make a very thin piece of steel at much lower costs. Such a plant should produce a competitive advantage for Nucor in supplying part of the automobile and appliance industries. Another area of the

---

[1] The above material is based on Michael E. Porter, *Competitive Strategy* (New York: Free Press, 1980), pp. 3-33.

manufacturing process, in which the Japanese have been innovators, is the JIT, Just-In-Time, method of scheduling and minimizing inventory. Innovative equipment often accompanies or triggers the change in the manufacturing process.

The use of labor can be dramatically affected by technology reducing the amount required while substantially upgrading the skills and education needed. An example of this kind of change is the emphasis now being placed upon SPC, Statistical Process Control, which calls for each worker to calculate and chart the performance of his own function, thus predicting problems and facilitating corrective action before the problem actually adversely affects the product.

Finally, rapid change can affect the use of products. An example of this is the simple over-the-counter pharmaceutical aspirin. Although the use of aspirin as a preventer of heart attacks is still controversial, many doctors personally have quietly begun a regimen.

Two contrasting strategies can be employed by different companies in regard to technology, being a leader or being a follower. Both work for individual firms under the right circumstances. Being there "the fustest with the mostest" can give the firm a lead on competition that is difficult for others to overtake. Many pharmaceutical firms operate under the maxim that a two - year lead in technology will often keep them ahead for the long pull. Such a strategy, however, does involve a continuing commitment of considerable time and money with the always-present risk of failure to produce a viable product. Few firms can afford to do basic research any more but instead concentrate their limited resources on applied research. The case "Hines Industries, Inc." in the latter part of this book illustrates the use of this type of strategy.

The second technological strategy of being a follower or "Number Two" can work also. This strategy provides for learning from and capitalizing on "Number One's" mistakes and efforts to develop a product. Reverse engineering can yield substantial results, often allowing the follower to pull ahead of the leader in the long run. An example of this strategy that worked was the case of Zenith in the early days of color television. RCA, an arch rival of Zenith, with the leadership of General Sarnoff, the Chairman of the Board, pioneered the development of compatible color television with no audience to enjoy it and no sponsors for color broadcasts. At an estimated cost of $120 million without any profits, RCA succeeded in developing the product and subsequently subsidizing color broadcasts on its subsidiary NBC. In the early days, RCA made all of the various brands of color television that were made except Zenith, because Zenith said color television was not ready and might never be. Once color television became a viable product, Zenith entered the race and soon was the leader by learning from RCA and perfecting its quality well beyond RCA's. The same strategy on the part of Zenith was used in printed circuit board technology with similar favorable results.

9

Economic Conditions

Economic conditions both in the United States and internationally are an important external environmental factor. While a small business owner might perceive himself to be helpless in regard to the economy because of the firm's small size, it is important to consider this area in deciding the best response to make. Economic conditions can threaten a firm and/or offer opportunities at the same time. Likewise, the international economy with its increasing dominance can be threatening or offer an opportunity. The old adage of is the "glass half empty or half full" seems to apply -- are you a pessimist or an optimist.

Specific factors to be considered in this broad area of economic conditions include real economic growth versus simply inflation. Extensive data is available through government agencies providing statistics nationally, regionally and by specific industry. Private sources for similar data are also available. Inflation also affects interest rates which are an important consideration for a new firm, which must secure funds. Interest rates also affect savings and consumption, sometimes in dramatic ways such as housing starts.

Another important factor is employment and productivity. Employment affects both the supply of labor and the ability of consumers to purchase goods and services. Productivity is a paramount consideration when developing cost projections, for a firm can afford to pay higher wages if they are accompanied by higher productivity. Again much statistical information is available in most libraries from government bureaus, particularly the Department of Labor.

The final significant factor to be considered under economic conditions is demographics. Once again this factor can affect both the marketing and operations of the firm. For many years the fertility rate in the United States had fallen, which along with the increasing life expectancy led to the "graying of America." These phenomena adversely affected the soft-drink industry and others that catered to younger segments of the population. On the other hand, the pharmaceutical firms benefitted from the increasing older age group. The legendary "baby boomers" and "yuppies" have had a dramatic effect on many industries as the "orange progressively moved through the snake." Now the echo boom is having an effect and the fertility rate itself seems to have bottomed out and may even have turned up at last, for the United States was not reproducing itself. Counter to these internal trends is the increase in population in the less-developed parts of the world. This growth offers opportunities for exporting.

Political and Social Factors

The political climate for businesses is affected by all three levels of government: local, state and federal. While the federal government is often considered to be the most important, for individual situations either or both of the other two can be most significant.

Therefore, it is important for the small business owner to follow developments at all three levels on a regular and continuing basis.

The power of business to pressure or lobby the government is usually directly proportional to its size. Thus small companies, much less beginning companies, have little clout at the federal or state level. However, if many small companies band together under the auspices of a trade group or small business group, their clout is enhanced. On the contrary, at the local level the opposite can be true. The small business in a small town can be a "big fish in a little pond" able to exert considerable influence. Often this influence is enhanced if the owner is personally well known and respected. In fact, big business in a small town is often seen as an outsider and someone to be distrusted if not feared.

Government at all levels has a propensity to regulate and to regulate business in particular. Somehow government officials and legislators seem to think they become more intelligent and honest when they come to Washington, D.C.

INTERNAL ENVIRONMENT -- *Strengths and Weaknesses*

When analyzing the Internal Environment of the firm, it is desirable to begin with the strengths present and then look at the weaknesses. In the case of a start-up situation, the internal environment becomes the individuals involved and the resources they bring to the company including such things as product ideas, marketing expertise, engineering and product development concepts, manufacturing or service ideas and expertise, human resources, management expertise, and financial resources. It is preferable to begin with marketing followed by engineering, operations, management and finance because products and marketing drive the firm.

Marketing

Marketing is frequently divided into the four "P's", standing for Product, Price, Place and Promotion. An analysis of internal marketing strengths and weaknesses begins with the products or services being offered or, in the case of a new venture, to be offered. Throughout this section, the term products will be used to represent products or services in the case of a firm providing a service rather than a specific product. First, the actual products should be examined followed by proposed or potential products.

Product

The company's products should be compared to products offered by competitors, which were examined in the External Environment analysis, in terms of quality and features. Unique attributes that are important to customers should be identified and highlighted. The products should be considered from the physical standpoint, for size and appearance can be important attributes.

Functionality is particularly important since everyone seems to be rushing and short of time. Hence, the concept of being user-friendly, which was coined by the computer and software industry, has become descriptive of customers' desires. Serviceability is important to many customers particularly if servicing is required on a regular basis and the customer intends to do it himself. Even if the service is to be routinely done by others, if the item can not be conveniently serviced the word gets back to the owner either by complaints from the service person or through higher costs of servicing.

Along the same line, packaging can be an important feature in enticing the purchaser to examine the product and ultimately buy it. Packaging, if well done, may expose key attributes to the customer or at least call attention to key features through pictures or written messages. If it is not possible or desirable to allow the customer to physically examine the product, the next best thing is to be able to see it through the package. Still another consideration is the ease of unpacking the product. We are all familiar with the problems of unpacking recorded audio tapes, for instance. In this instance, security considerations make it important to minimize theft but unfortunately the solution too often seems to have been the creation of a large and hard-to-open package with the attendant disposal problems of the plastic packaging materials.

Another consideration is the potentiality for new applications for existing products, such as the use of baking soda to remove odors from refrigerators. Related to this is the issue of providing "specials" for customers. This idea can be an important competitive factor in some industries such as the medical device field. Often, a physician will wish to try a variation of a standard product that is thought to provide an advantage in a particular procedure. "Specials" are expensive to make but the regular product business to a hospital may hinge on satisfying a particular physician. Deliberately offering customized products may be important as is the case with options in the automobile industry where customers can choose what they wish.

Potential products and services beyond those presently being offered or initially planned are an important consideration. Often, these additional or related products in the same product line can broaden the customer base or even attract entirely new customers. New products that are unrelated to the present product line should be considered for the same reasons.

The *perceived* reputation and quality of the firm and its products or services are particularly important. It is of little consolation to believe that your quality is better than customers think, since they make their buying decisions based upon their *perceptions*, not what you say is the case. Certainly, this idea is evident recently in the case of the quality image of General Motors' automobiles. Although General Motors believes its quality has improved, its sales record would seem to indicate the customer's perception is otherwise. Beyond the image it is important to objectively qualify and quantify the reputation and quality of the company and its products as the company itself sees them and measures them. Having done this, the difference between the company's view and the customer's view, if one exists, must be defined and explained so that unfavorable gaps can be closed.

The product mix or intended mix should be examined in some detail. Does the company offer competing or overlapping products internally? Given the circumstances internal competition can be useful or a diffusion of resources. Is a full range of sizes or services offered? Should the variety of products or the number of models present or contemplated be reduced or expanded? Are or should replacement parts or subassemblies be sold? While no single right answer to these questions applies in all cases for a given firm or venture proposal, it is important to raise these issues.

Pricing

Sequentially following Product considerations in the four "P's" of marketing is Pricing. Once the products or services to be offered have been established, pricing is the next key issue. Ultimately, competition exerts a strong influence on pricing if it does not actually control or determine it. Product differentiation can moderate or minimize the influence of competition but it never can completely insulate the company from competition. Every product, even a monopoly, has some form of competition from substitute products. Pricing needs to take into consideration features offered compared to competitive products and the *perceived* value by the customer. In general, customers seem to be willing to pay more for superior quality as *perceived* by them. Finally, as pricing is being finalized, a Break - even Analysis, which is developed in Chapter 3, should be performed in order to maximize profitability. It is important to realize that a product that is at least covering its variable costs and contributing something toward overhead and profit is valuable and should not be dropped without first replacing it with a product that contributes more toward fixed overhead and profit. Thus, while costs do not set prices, they must be determined and are an important consideration in setting product strategy.

Place

The third "P" in marketing is Place or Distribution. Many small businesses do not have to worry about distribution much because they are retailers and thus at the end of the distribution chain. However, even a retailer is concerned about its supplier as far as reliability and timing as well as services provided. Manufacturers have to be concerned with Distribution since it provides the ultimate path to the customers. Options to be considered are distributors, wholesalers, dealers, brokers, and manufacturer's representatives. Each path offers particular advantages and disadvantages for a given firm considering its position in the product life cycle and its size and marketing clout.

Another factor to consider in the area of distribution is the use of regional warehousing versus shipping direct to the customer. Storage and handling costs are compared to delivery time factors. JIT (Just-In-Time) is not only a "buzz word" now, but can effect real savings for the ultimate customer and, thus, is a significant consideration. Still another distribution issue is the use of common carriers for delivery versus delivery by the firm's trucks. The above factors are examples of things to be considered and is not an exhaustive listing.

Promotion

Promotion, the final "P," is most commonly identified with advertising. Advertising has a dual purpose of informing the customers and inducing them to buy the product being advertised. Some advertising may be of the institutional or image type designed to promote the company in a general way, but this type is not as common. The theme to be used in the advertising is important as is the media to be used. The amount and kind of advertising being done by competition is particularly important since it can even be a barrier to entry in a given industry. Once advertising is begun and competition follows the lead, it may be difficult to scale down or stop advertising. Thus, the cost of advertising needs to be carefully determined before committing resources which could become a serious drag on profitability with little benefit to sales levels because of similar moves by competition. Of course, advertising should be legal and tasteful, which raises the important issue of ethics to be discussed later.

Other methods of promotion include the use of trade shows and promotions such as in-store displays, coupons, and discounting. Trade shows are particularly important in some industries such as machinery. Discounting and coupons are important forms of promotion at the retail level.

Selling carried out by an internal sales force, rather than using agents or brokers, is important for a small manufacturing company if it is financially strong and can handle the administration of a sales force, if its products are similar and use the same marketing channel, if sales territories are concentrated, and if it wants to retain primary control of distribution. Other issues to be considered are the use of specialists versus generalists as salespersons and the assignment of territories which may be exclusive, overlapping, or unassigned. The number of accounts to be assigned to an individual salesperson must be determined as well as the use of house accounts. In turn, compensation could include a salary, commission, or some combination of the two. Incentives seem to be popular now with the increased emphasis on individual achievement.

Market Research is yet another factor to be examined. Obviously, the small firm does not have the resources or expertise to do its own market research. However, some research will be required initially from published material by the government and other sources. If specialized research seems indicated, it can be contracted from a reputable market research firm; however, the cost can be substantial.

Engineering and Product Development

Certainly the key factor in this function of the company is creativity. Often the owner or entrepreneur is a particularly creative and imaginative person. This fact seems to either preclude gathering similar people into the firm or actually encourage the hiring or internal development of such people. In any event, the owner is usually creative in only one or two functional areas of the business and, therefore, needs creative help in other areas. A key internal factor then is how creative are the employees and other members of the management group or proposed management group. One thing that supports creativity is recognition and rewards to motivate employees. It also helps if a systematic approach is taken to creativity. Unfortunately this is not necessarily the typical approach taken by entrepreneurial owners. They may favor a more "seat-of-the-pants" approach.

Another key factor in the engineering area is to design with ease of manufacturing a key consideration following after functionality for the customer and low maintenance cost. The cost to manufacture the product, whether it is done in-house or contracted out, must be considered in designing for quality, price, and function. Engineering needs to have a direct input to quality considerations and the control of quality. Finally, does or should engineering support service to the customer?

Operations

The Operations function of the firm, as used here, includes manufacturing, if it's done, or provision of a service activity. In both cases, the technical skills possessed by employees and management are significant. Are there unique or unusual expertise or technical skills present? If the company does not have these skills, some way must be provided to obtain them as needed.

Operational *facilities* must be assessed. Capacity constraints should be identified both as to plant size and configuration. Existing equipment should be assessed or equipment that must be provided should be identified. One issue to be resolved is general purpose versus special purpose equipment.

Flexibility in the Operations function is a key factor to be considered and included whenever possible given the fast-changing, competitive environment of business today. Not only is the usual domestic competition present but even more dynamic foreign competition is a major factor to be considered.

Flexibility needs to be considered in *facilities location*. Ideally, facilities should be located near markets with favorable transportation costs. Labor availability with the required skills and favorable wage costs are important but may conflict with market considerations. In any event, these cost factors require examination and trade-offs must be made.

Plant layout can be another strength or weakness. Process layouts, which are also called functional layouts or job shops, are characterized by process departments or groupings of like machines with products being transported from department to department as required by the operations to be performed. The process layout is the most flexible but induces scheduling and work-in-process inventory control problems. Specialization of labor is common unless higher skilled, more versatile labor is employed which in turn raises the cost of labor. Lot sizes as processed through this kind of layout are relatively small. The Japanese have fine tuned this kind of layout by using group technology with some redundancy in equipment to make it very cost effective.

Product-based layouts, in which assembly lines are commonly employed, are fixed according to the order of operations required for the product to be made. Work-in-process inventory is minimized but so is flexibility. Typically, higher volumes are required for this type of layout to be cost effective. Relatively low skill levels are required for employees. Automation is often a consideration in this type of layout.

The third type of layout is material based. People, material and equipment are brought to a central location where the product is being fabricated. This type of layout is used to make large heavy machinery that is built in small quantities. It is used relatively infrequently.

The cost accounting structure for the firm should facilitate the determination of direct costs of manufacturing and the contribution to overhead and profit for each product. The system most suitable for these requirements is a direct costing system. Under this system the variable costs are determined as the direct material, direct labor, and variable overhead (fringe benefits) used to make the product, which vary directly with the volume produced. Semi-fixed and fixed overhead are accumulated and compared against a predetermined budget. Overhead is not absorbed against products except for government reporting purposes. When it is possible to allocate some items of overhead to particular products, this is done to facilitate differential profit analysis.

The presence or desirability of *backward integration* in production should be examined. Sometimes cost advantages can be gained by integrating backward toward producing the product, if the firm is a retailer only, or producing the materials used in manufacturing. The current wisdom in many industries, given the inflexibilities present in union contracts, is to avoid or even divest integrated manufacturing activities.

Another strength or weakness to look for in operations is *maintenance*. Good maintenance can minimize downtime, delayed shipments and poor quality. High quality seems to mandate preventative maintenance. Many firms continue to do maintenance on demand, that is when breakdowns or shutdowns occur. This method would seem to require more inventory to accommodate unplanned shutdowns of unknown duration. However, continuous inspection using statistical process control can predict and determine when repairs and maintenance are needed.

Material procurement and inventory control can be an important strength or weakness. It is concerned with single versus multiple sources of supply, pricing versus quantities purchased, known and reasonable lead times that are reliable, and satisfactory incoming quality and quantity levels. Inventory levels for raw materials, work-in-process, and finished goods are important to cover contingencies that may arise but need to minimized within those parameters.

Production planning and scheduling can be another key factor and raises several questions to be answered. What planning and control techniques, that are being used, need to be reviewed? Are bottlenecks - there always are some - a problem and are material shortages a problem? Is much overtime required and who works it? How are batch sizes determined and are schedules being met?

Quality assurance and control is the last key area in Operations to be evaluated. The level of scrap and rework should be determined or planned. Statistical process control techniques have become virtually mandatory if quality is to be assured. Finally, the level and nature of customer complaints should be evaluated.

Human Resources

Human resources do not fit neatly into a particular functional activity within a firm but are important enough to require a separate category. Skills and expertise are important as far as availability , flexibility, and depth are concerned. Of related importance is the ability to recruit and train employees as needed and required for general as well as specialized occupations.

Wages and employee benefits that are paid or will need to be paid are a major consideration. Of course, these items are related to the skills required but competition for employees in the area of the firm may be even more significant in establishing a floor for wages and benefits.

Training and employee development often provide the competitive edge for a firm. If the skills required are not available on the market, it may be essential for the business to train its own "experts." If done properly, training may also give employees an added sense of loyalty.

Work methods and working conditions are important. Questions to be asked include: Is work simplification practiced and are incentives used? How efficient and effective are operations? What is the safety and health record of employees and how frequent are sick days? How much employee turnover is there and what is causing it? Is the internal and external labor pool sufficient to sustain the production level needed? What is the status of employee relations? Is there representation by a union and, if so, what caused the employees to seek a union?

Management

Although management is part of human resources in a broad sense, its key role in the success of a firm, particularly a small business, warrants a separate close examination. Of key importance is flexibility, for small business typically has to be more flexible than a large business if it is to survive. Therefore, management must have a strong tolerance for risk although it should not be foolhardy. In addition to appropriate and adequate experience and education to succeed and grow, management should have appropriate expectations and determination to succeed. Intuition and judgment are major factors for a successful management team.

The cultural climate, values and ethics within a firm are of major significance since they provide an atmosphere within which everything else takes place. Survey after survey has shown that the ethics of a firm are basically set by the owner or CEO. It is not so much what he says or perhaps preaches, but rather it is what he does that employees use as a model. Saying or doing nothing regarding ethics and values for the firm does communicate a message that ethics are not important. This, in turn, may cause employees to make their own decisions based on the situation and expediency. The top management reporting to the owner or CEO must help in this important area.

Finance

For the small business availability of funds is always an important consideration. Most businesses experiencing trouble have experienced or are experiencing cash flow problems. This is particularly true, yet often unexpected, for growing and successful ventures. The first source of funds is the level of cash that can be expected to be generated internally from profits and depreciation as well as minimizing assets. The gap between these internal sources and the funds required can be filled by borrowing from banks. Interest rates to be paid are important as well as the future capacity for borrowing from this important source of funds. Finally, the use or availability of venture capital is important to determine.

Financial control systems are very important for a small business and are often neglected by the owner in his enthusiasm to get started. The main control device used is a budget. It should be put in place first and should be compared regularly with timely monthly reports to the actual figures generated by the firm. The use of personal computers and inexpensive accounting software packages make this relatively easy to do without requiring the regular services of an accountant. There should be participation of other key employees in the budget process so that a sense of ownership is developed. Flexibility should be built into the budget process through the use of supplemental budgets, alternative budgets ("Plan B"), and variable expense budgets. Capital expenditure budgets are needed to plan for future growth and facilitate the acquisition of funds. Net working capital needs are important to budget for particularly in the case of a rapidly growing firm.

Profitability and return on investment are key measures to be made of any small business. In addition to having fun, owners typically have making a profit as a goal. Making an adequate profit in the early years often eludes a small business but is not necessarily a bad sign if it was anticipated and planned for. Not only is the level of profitability important but even more so is the trend in profitability. The cause of whatever trend is there must be determined. Good trends are just as important as poor ones since they help identify good things that can be applied in other parts of the business where poorer results may be evident. Finally, the return on investment is most significant as a measure of the business's success in rewarding the investors.

SUMMARY

This chapter has discussed the Situation Analysis or SWOT Analysis. This analysis should be made when preparing for the start-up of a new small business, the purchase of an existing small business or for building a Strategic Plan for a growing business. Both the External Environment with its Opportunities and Threats and the Internal Environment with its Strengths and Weaknesses needs to be examined.

External Environment

A. Competition

    1. Threat of entry.

        * Economies of scale.
        * Product differentiation.
        * Capital requirements.
        * Switching costs.
        * Access to distribution channels.
        * Cost disadvantages independent of scale.
        * Government policy.

    2. Intensity of rivalry.

        * Numerous and equally balanced competitors.
        * Slow industry growth.
        * High fixed or storage costs.
        * Lack of differentiation or switching costs.
        * Capacity augmented in large increments.
        * Competitors diverse in strategies.
        * High strategic stakes.
        * High exit barriers.

    3. Pressure from substitute products.

4. Bargaining power of buyers.

  * Purchases large volume relative to the seller's sales.
  * Products or services purchased represent a significant part of the buyer's costs.
  * Products purchased are standard or undifferentiated.
  * Buyer faces few switching costs.
  * Buyer earns low profits.
  * Buyers pose a credible threat of backward integration.
  * Industry's product is unimportant to the quality of the buyer's products or services.
  * Buyer has full information.

5. Bargaining power of suppliers.

  * Supplier group is dominated by a few companies and is more concentrated than its customers' industry.
  * Limited substitute products or services are available.
  * Purchasing industry is not an important customer of the supplier group.
  * Supplier's product is important to buyer's business.
  * Supplier's products are differentiated or switching costs have been built up.
  * Supplier poses a credible threat of forward integration.

B. Technology

  1. Rapidity of change.

    * Materials.
    * Manufacturing process.
    * Equipment.
    * Labor.
    * Use of products.

  2. Being the leader.

  3. Being a follower.

C. Economic Conditions

  1. Real growth.

  2. Interest rates.

3. Inflation.

4. Employment.

5. Productivity.

6. Demographics.

D. Political and Social Factors.

1. Political climate.

    * Local.
    * State.
    * Federal.

2. Relative power of company.

3. Propensity of government to regulate.

Internal Environment

A. Marketing

1. Actual products and services.

2. Potential products and services.

3. Reputation and quality.

4. Product mix.

5. Pricing.

6. Distribution.

7. Promotion.

8. Internal sales.

9. Market research.

B.   Engineering and Product Development.

   1.   Creativity.

   2.   Designing for ease of manufacturing.

   3.   Supporting customer service.

C.   Operations.

   1.   Technical skills.

   2.   Operational facilities.

   3.   Flexibility.

      *   Plant location.
      *   Plant layout.
      *   Cost structure.
      *   Backward integration.
      *   Maintenance.

   4.   Material procurement and inventory control.

   5.   Production planning and scheduling.

   6.   Quality assurance and control.

D.   Human Resources.

   1.   Skills.

   2.   Wages and employee benefits.

   3.   Training and development.

   4.   Work methods and conditions.

   5.   Turnover.

E.   Management.

    1.   Flexibility.

    2.   Risk tolerance.

    3.   Depth.

    4.   Experience.

    5.   Expectations.

    6.   Intuition and judgment.

    7.   Cultural climate, ethics, and values.

F.   Finance

    1.   Availability of funds.

    2.   Financial control systems and budgets.

    3.   Profitability and return on investment.

CHAPTER 3

TOOLS FOR FINANCIAL ANALYSIS

Financial analysis is an essential tool in analyzing a business situation. It is a *means* to an end. The symptoms for the major problem as well as other problems facing the business are typically evident in the income statement, balance sheet and comparison ratios for the company and the industry. The student or prospective owner will benefit by following the lead of most business consultants who first "run the numbers" on a company before determining the problems facing the company and the value of the company. Financial analysis will also determine constraints within which management must operate. The use of pro forma statements and budgets as well as comparison to the industry is equally significant for the proposed new business . This chapter will cover the use of vertical and horizontal analyses of income statements and balance sheets, the use of ratios in comparing a firm to its industry, the construction of comparative balance sheets and income statements, and breakeven analysis.

USE OF FINANCIAL STATEMENTS

Income Statement

An Income Statement presents the revenues and costs of a firm over a particular time period in order to determine the net profit achieved. The typical time periods used for income statements are a month, quarter, or year. The net profit as determined minus any dividends paid is carried over to the Balance Sheet as retained earnings. The Retained Earnings account is thus the connecting link between the two financial statements.

A vertical analysis of the income statement is an essential step in financial analysis. A vertical analysis is simply stating all items in any one year in the income statement as a percent of net sales as noted in Table 1. By looking at the Cost of Sales over the three-year period, it can be seen that it is dropping as a percent of sales particularly in 1987.

A horizontal analysis should be performed at least on the Net Sales figure on the income statement. The horizontal analysis is simply calculating the percent change from year to year related to each previous year's net sales. In Table 1, the net sales have been increasing about 35 percent per year at an increasing rate. It is often useful to do a complete horizontal analysis of the entire income statement.

Having determined that net sales are growing about 35 percent per year and that the cost of sales, selling expenses and administrative expenses are all decreasing as a percent of sales, the question about why these things are happening has still to be answered. Given the nature of fixed expense and knowing that there are some elements of fixed expense in all of the three categories noted as decreasing as a percent of sales, it seems logical to deduce that these changes are a result of an increasing sales level. However, the significantly low percent of Cost of Sales in 1987 remains to be explained by examining the company itself either through internal records or through discussion with the owner and employees. Answers that might be anticipated are favorable material purchases, productivity increases through automation or the installation of an incentive plan and the spreading of semi-fixed and fixed elements of manufacturing overhead over a larger volume base.

Table 1

Vertical Analysis

	1987 $	1987 %	1988 $	1988 %	1989 $	1989 %
Net Sales	150	100	200	100	275	100
Cost of Sales	100	67	130	65	165	60
Gross Profit	50	33	70	35	110	40
Selling Expense	20	13	23	12	33	12
Administrative Expense	10	7	12	6	13	6
Profit Before Taxes	20	13	33	17	62	22
Taxes	10	7	16	8	30	11
Net Profit	10	6	17	9	32	11

Horizontal Analysis

	1986 $	1986 %	1987 $	1987 %
Sales Change	+50	+33	+75	+37

Another useful analysis technique, especially during periods of inflation, is indexing. To index a series of data, a convenient base year is selected and established as 1. By simply dividing all of the other numbers in a horizontal time series by the base year number, an index number is created such as 1.05, etc. By comparing this number to an index of inflation, which is published monthly by the government, it is possible to measure the change in the company over time in real terms.

Balance Sheet

A Balance Sheet is a "snapshot" or picture of the assets and liabilities of a company at a given moment in time. Because of the dynamic nature of some of the accounts shown on the balance sheet such as cash, accounts receivable, inventory and accounts payable, the balance sheet changes every day or even every hour. As noted earlier, the retained earnings account is the connecting link between the income statement and balance sheet. It should be noted that retained earnings is simply an accounting entry and does not represent cash. Therefore, retained earnings can *not* be spent.

The same techniques described for analyzing income statements -- vertical and horizontal analyses and indexing -- can be used on balance sheets as well. For instance, if the ratio analysis showed that net working capital for the company was decreasing as compared to the industry, horizontal analysis would show how the components of working capital, such as cash, receivables, inventory and payables are changing over time. Reference to company data should then be made to determine the causative factors for the observed changes.

USE OF RATIOS

The use of ratios to compare the company to the industry in which it operates is particularly useful in establishing benchmarks. If several years' data are available, trends for the company and industry also become evident and assist in the analysis.

It is imperative that continued references be made to the original data behind the ratios, so that the ratios are meaningful and not artificial. In any case, there are certain drawbacks in the use of ratios that should be noted, such as the following:

1. Different companies sometimes use different accounting methods. When this happens, it is obvious that the data will vary.

2. Methods of recording and valuing assets, write-offs, costs, expenses, etc., vary from company to company and industry to industry. An example of this is the method of handling intangible assets such as goodwill. Because of the difficulty of evaluating intangibles, they are frequently eliminated in determining net worth or equity. It is recommended that tangible net worth be used in calculating ratios. Tangible net worth is net worth minus intangible assets.

3. Financial statements are historical and as such reflect past performance. They can serve as a basis for projecting the future, but only if specific strategies are developed to make the projected results materialize.

4. Comparable data are not always available for a particular industry or company.

5. The industry data used are industry medians and some of the groups are fairly small.

6. Mergers and diversification have made ratios less useful in comparing single product companies to industry numbers.

A series of ratios for key manufacturing, wholesale, and retail business groups are published annually by *Dun's*. *Robert Morris & Associates* also publishes an annual listing of ratios for service business groups as well as the three groups published by *Dun's*. A comparison of the kinds of ratios given by these two sources is shown in Table 2 below. Other sources for this information are industry periodicals for the industry in question. Still another technique used is to get the financial data for several typical single product or service competitors and create a set of industry statistics.

Table 2

Financial Ratios Published

	Dun's	Robert Morris
Profitability	NP/NW	PBT/NW
	NP/NS	PBT/NS
	NP/TA	
Liquidity	CA/CD	CA/CD
	(CA-INV)/CD	
	FA/NW	
	CD/INV	
Leverage	TD/NW	TD/NW
	CD/NW	
Turnover	NS/TA	
	NS/NWC	NS/NWC
	NS/INV	CS/INV
	COL. PER.	NS/REC

NP = Net Profit	CD = Current Debt
NW = Tangible Net Worth	FA = Fixed Assets
NS = Net Sales	INV = Inventory
NWC = Net Working Capital	TA = Total Assets
CA = Current Assets	TD = Total Debt
PBT = Profit Before Taxes	CS = Cost of Sales
REC = Receivables	COL. PER. = Rec./Avg. Daily Sales

The median, upper quartile and lower quartile are given for each ratio. The median figure from the business group is normally used in making company comparisons. It is important to keep in mind that the median given is the median of each ratio and not the ratios of the median company. Therefore, some inconsistencies among ratios can be expected, particularly if extremely accurate correlation among ratios is attempted. Ratios should be used to discover and analyze basic trends and not to establish precise magnitudes of their individual components.

CONSTRUCTION OF FINANCIAL STATEMENTS FROM RATIOS

A very useful tool that can be used to understand financial relationships is a comparative or mock balance sheet and income statement. This tool, which was originally developed by Thomas L. Powers while he was teaching at Eastern Michigan University, can be utilized to understand the financial relationships within a company and its relationships to another company or industry figures.

To utilize this technique, a balance sheet must first be visualized in its most basic elements, namely, total assets, total debt and net worth or equity as shown in Figure 1. The next step is to set both sides of the balance sheet equal to 100. The 100 can be thought of as dollars to understand relative magnitude or as a percent to understand certain relationships within the company.

FIGURE 1

Total Assets	100	Total Debt + Net Worth	100

The model in Figure 1 then forms the basis for all future analysis. In order to proceed with the analysis, assume a set of ratios for the company and its industry as shown in Figure 2. In analyzing ratios, it must be remembered that a ratio is a function of two figures, the numerator and denominator, which may act independently of each other or may be interrelated such as TD and NW and CA, CD and NWC. Since both the company and industry ratios are to be examined, the complexity of changes and the possibility of erroneous assumptions and conclusions are readily seen and highlight the need for careful, systematic analysis. Throughout this analysis the abbreviations used in the formulas and tables are consistent with the definitions listed at the bottom of Table 2.

FIGURE 2

	Company	Industry
NP/NW	18%	13%
NP/NS	6%	6.5%
CA/CD	1.7	1.9
(CA-INV)/CD	1.0	1.2
FA/NW	100%	125%
TD/NW	55%	78%
CD/NW	23.4%	21.4%
NS/NW	3.0	2.0
COL. PER.	20 Days	20 days

Referring to the ratios in Figure 2, a number of questions can be asked relative to the company and the industry.

1. What is the relative capital structure of each?

2. Which has the greater working capital?

3. Which has the greater profit versus sales and net worth?

4. Which has the greatest relative sales?

These questions are the beginning of a number of questions that can and will need to be answered.

To proceed in the analysis, a mock balance sheet and income statement can be made for both the company and industry by following the basic steps below.

1. Determine the relative amounts of TD and NW for the company.

   Given: TD/NW = .55   TD + NW = 100

   By using algebra, NW and TD can be determined as follows:

   .55NW = TD = 100 - NW
   1.55NW = 100
   NW = 64.5
   TD = 35.5

   In a similar manner, the industry TD and NW can be determined.

   .78NW = TD = 100 - NW
   1.78NW = 100
   NW = 56.2
   TD = 43.8

   The balance sheet for the company and industry are shown in Figure 3.

FIGURE 3

	Company		Industry	
	Total Debt 35.5		Total Debt 43.8	
	Net Worth 64.5		Net Worth 56.2	
Total Assets 100		100	Total Assets 100	100

2. Determine the relative amounts of CD.

Company	Industry
Given: CD/NW = .234	Given: CA/CD = 1.9
CD = .234(64.5)	CD = .214(56.2)
CD = 15.1	CD = 12.0

3. Determine the relative amounts of CA.

Company	Industry
Given: CA/CD = 1.7	Given: CA/CD = 1.9
CA = 1.7(15.1)	CA = 1.9(13.0)
CA = 25.7	CA = 22.8

4. Determine the relative amounts of INV.

<table>
<tr><td>Company</td><td>Industry</td></tr>
</table>

Company

Given: Quick Ratio = 1.0
$(CA - INV)/CD = 1.0$
$25.7 - INV = 15.1$
$INV = 10.6$

Industry

Given: Quick Ratio = 1.2
$(CA - INV)/CD = 1.2$
$22.8 - INV = 14.4$
$INV = 8.4$

5. Determine the relative amounts of FA.

Company

Given: $FA/NW = 1$
$FA = 1(64.5)$
$FA = 64.5$

Industry

Given: $FA/NW = 1.25$
$FA = 1.25(56.2)$
$FA = 70.3$

6. Determine the relative amounts of Net Sales.

Company

Given: $NS/NW = 3.0$
$NS = 3.0(64.5)$
$NS = 193.5$

Industry

Given: $NS/NW = 2.0$
$NS = 2.0(56.2)$
$NS = 112.4$

7. Determine the relative amounts of Trade Receivables.

Company

Given: COL. PER. = 20 days
$20 = REC/(NS/365)$
$REC = 20(193.5/365)$
$REC = 10.6$

Industry

Given: COL. PER. = 20 days
$20 = REC/(NS/365)$
$REC = 20(112.4/365)$
$REC = 6.2$

8. Determine the relative amounts of cash (and prepaid expenses).
Assuming cash is the residual of CA - (REC + INV)

Company

Cash = CA - REC - INV
Cash = 25.7 - 10.6 -10.6
Cash = 4.5

Industry

Cash = CA - REC - INV
Cash = 22.8 - 6.2 - 8.4
Cash = 8.2

9. Determine the relative amounts of Long Term Debt.

Company	Industry
Given: TD = CD + LTD	Given: TD = CD + LTD
35.5 = 15.1 + LTD	43.8 = 12.0 + LTD
LTD = 26.4	LTD = 31.8

10. Determine the relative amounts of Other Assets.

Company	Industry
Given: TA = CA - FA - OA	Given: TA = CA - FA - OA
100 = 25.7 - 64.5 - OA	100 = 22.8 - 70.3 - OA
OA = 9.8	OA = 6.9

11. Determine the relative amounts of Net Profit.

Company	Industry
Given: NP/NW = .18	Given: NP/NW = .13
NP = .18(64.5)	NP = .13(56.2)
NP = 11.6	NP = 7.3

12. Determine the relative amounts of Costs.

Company	Industry
Given: NP = NS - COSTS	Given: NP = NS - COSTS
11.6 = 193.5 - COSTS	7.3 = 112.4 - COSTS
COSTS = 181.9	COSTS = 105.1

13. Determine the relative amounts of NWC.

Company	Industry
Given: NWC = CA - CD	Given: NWC = CA - CD
NWC = 25.7 - 15.1	NWC = 22.8 - 12.0
NWC = 10.6	NWC = 10.8

The balance sheet and income statement for the company and industry reflecting the values calculated above are shown in Figure 4.

FIGURE 4

Balance Sheet

Company				Industry			
Cash	4.5			Cash	8.2		
REC	10.6			REC	6.2		
INV	10.6			INV	8.4		
CA	25.7	CD	15.1	CA	22.8	CD	12.0
FA	64.5	LTD	20.4	FA	70.3	LTD	31.8
OA	9.8			OA	6.9		
		TD	35.5			NW	56.2
		NW	64.5				
TA	100		100	TA	100		100

NWC = 10.6	NWC = 10.8

Company		Industry	
NS	193.5	NS	112.4
COSTS	181.9	COSTS	105.1
NP	11.6	NP	7.3

In summary, it is now possible to determine what is causing various ratios to be high or low by assessing the relative magnitude of each element in the ratios.

NP	-	Company exceeds industry by 59%
NS	-	Company exceeds industry by 72%
NW	-	Company exceeds industry by 15%
CD	-	Company exceeds industry by 26%
INV	-	Company exceeds industry by 26%
REC	-	Company exceeds industry by 71%
NWC	-	Company is below industry by 2%
Cash	-	Company is below industry by 45%
FA	-	Company is below industry by 8%

The final step in determining **WHY** the elements of the ratios are high or low is returning to the business itself to look for causal factors.

A Final Word of Caution

The industry ratio figures as published by *Dun's* and *Robert Morris & Associates* are the median ratios for each category and are not the ratios of the median company. Therefore, if the median ratio NP/NW comes from a different company than the median ratio NP/NS, the Net Profit, which is common to both ratios, would not be equal if each ratio was used to calculate it as previously outlined. The technique described in this section is useful in developing approximate balance sheets and income statements but should not be expected to produce perfectly correlated results. Furthermore, all figures are based on a percent of Total Assets. If there is a large difference in the asset base, distortions in this kind of analysis will be evident.

BREAKEVEN ANALYSIS

The purpose of the Breakeven Analysis is to determine the quantity at which a product or group of products will balance the costs and the revenue so that the product or company breaks even -- it does not make a profit or loss. This kind of an analysis is useful in establishing pricing as well as the effect of changing pricing, and determining the effect of changes in costs on profitability. It can be calculated by using formulas or it can be displayed graphically.

There are three cost elements that should be considered in determining a breakeven point: variable costs (VC), semi-fixed costs (SFC) or semi-variable depending upon whether you are a pessimist or an optimist, and fixed costs (FC). Many people do not use the semi-fixed category because it represents considerably more effort to sort out this refinement but it is important as will be seen.

Variable costs are those costs that vary directly with the *quantity produced*. This category includes direct material and direct labor used to produce the product and variable overhead. Variable overhead includes expenses which vary directly with the quantity produced. Certainly included in variable overhead are fringe benefits paid to direct labor which are usually applied as a percent of direct labor in the range of 20 percent to 40 percent depending upon the benefit package. Also included would be the part of utilities directly used to run machinery to produce the product.

Semi-fixed costs are costs that vary in increments of production rather than directly. These include such items as indirect material, indirect labor, supervision, some utilities not charged to variable or fixed overhead, expendable tooling, maintenance, manufacturing support activities such as material control, scheduling, engineering, and quality assurance. These costs typically look like an irregular stairway when they are graphed.

Fixed costs are costs that do not change with the quantity produced unless the manufacturing facility is shut down. These include depreciation, security, rent, utilities such as heat and general lighting, real estate taxes, and general building maintenance.

As the quantity *produced* increases, there should be a lowering of the cost of goods sold as a percent of sales because the fixed overhead costs and some of the semi-fixed costs are spread over a larger volume base and thus the costs per unit *produced* should decrease as a percent of sales. If this relative decrease in costs does not occur it represents a real danger sign. Either the variable costs are increasing faster than sales or new increments of semi-fixed or fixed costs are being added faster than anticipated by sales growth. Conversely, as the quantity *produced* declines, unit costs can be expected to rise as the semi-fixed and fixed costs are spread over a smaller volume base.

Another factor that will affect the cost of goods sold, as determined by an absorption system of accounting for overhead, is whether inventory is being increased or depleted. Building inventory inflates the quantity *produced* and thus lowers the unit costs by spreading fixed and semi-fixed manufacturing overhead costs over a larger base while depleting inventory has the opposite effect.

The general equation for determining profit is:

P (Profit) = S (Sales) - C (Costs) where sales is price times volume and costs include all three categories.

P = S - (VC + SFC + FC)

In order to simplify the calculation, the quantity sold is assumed to be equal to the quantity produced as it would be in the long run assuming no planned change in inventory.

If profit is set equal to zero, as is the assumption in a breakeven calculation, the equation becomes:

S = VC + (SFC + FC)

By substituting the variable cost per sales dollar (p) times the sales $ for the total variable costs, the equation becomes:

S = (p x S) + (SFC + FC)   or
S x (1 - p) = (SFC + FC)

It should be noted that the SFC will vary indirectly with volume produced; therefore, a series of trial and error calculations are needed around the estimated breakeven point to determine their effect on breakeven. The common practice is to assume that all costs other than variable costs are fixed costs, which simplifies the equation even further.

The breakeven analysis lends itself to a graphic presentation because it is easier to show the effect of semi-fixed overhead. Figure 5 shows a graphic breakeven presentation based upon the data shown in Table 3 below with breakeven occurring at a quantity of 260. Breakeven in Table III occurs at $120,000 in revenue.

Table 3

Qty	Price	Revenue	VC	TVC	SFC	FC	TC
0						$20,000	$ 20,000
100	$400	$ 40,000	$200	$ 20,000	$30,000	20,000	70,000
200	400	80,000	200	40,000	34,000	20,000	94,000
300	400	120,000	200	60,000	40,000	20,000	120,000
400	400	160,000	200	80,000	46,000	20,000	146,000
500	390	195,000	200	100,000	55,000	20,000	175,000
600	390	234,000	200	120,000	60,000	20,000	200,000
700	390	273,000	200	140,000	65,000	20,000	225,000

SUMMARY

Financial analysis of a company is a means for identifying the problems facing the company, establishing financial constraints within which the company must function, placing a value on a company, and planning for a new venture The consistent, early use of financial analysis will shorten the time needed for the total analysis of a business situation.

Vertical and horizontal analysis of the income statement and balance sheet, indexing of the income statement and balance sheet, the use of business ratios and the construction of mock financial statements were discussed as useful techniques in performing the financial analysis. The factors to consider when doing a Breakeven Analysis were discussed along with the mathematical calculation of a solution and a graphic solution.

FIGURE 5

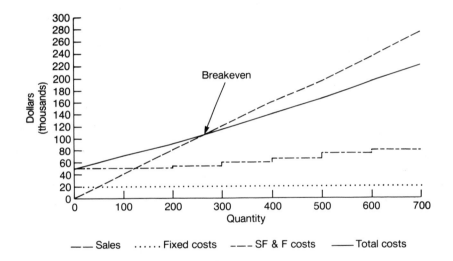

CHAPTER 4

STRATEGY DEVELOPMENT

Before writing the actual Business Plan, some time should be spent in developing potential strategies. The overall business strategy includes product, marketing, and manufacturing elements. Again strategy formulation begins with the products or services to be provided followed by the other elements of marketing -- price, place (distribution), and promotion. Once these factors are established, operations strategy is considered. In every case it is important to consider alternatives both down-side and up-side. Too often the potential down-side risks are recognized but the up-side is considered a lucky event rather than a risk. However, an up-side alternative can be a risk if not anticipated and planned for because it carries with it financial demands for working capital and cash for fixed assets.

PRODUCT

Although Product is one of the four "P's" of Marketing, it is discussed independently and first because of its paramount importance to the firm. The firm may be dealing with new or existing products or services. Usually, in entrepreneurial situations, there is at least some new feature to the product if it is not completely new. It is particularly common now to see small businesses seek some particular niche or focus to their product line. "Niching" by its nature tends to restrict the breadth of the line and limit the overall demand of the firm's product. But "niching" can increase the firm's demand because the firm may be extremely strong viz-a-viz competition in the particular specialized line, while weak within a broader product line. Unique features tend to increase brand loyalty, which can allow improved gross margins. However, these unique features may bring about some increases in costs.

Also of importance is the amount of product overlap to be considered. The following questions are worth asking:

1.   Should the firm offer competing lines? If so, should different levels of quality be considered and should different names be used then?

2.   Should private brands or labels be considered and to what extent will these detract from the primary brand?

3.   Should products or services be offered to retail consumers as opposed to retailers?

4. Should products for original equipment manufacturers (OEM) be produced or should the replacement market be the focus or both?

5. Should "specials" or customized products be a part of the product strategy?

MARKETING

Having considered Product in some depth, the remaining three "P's" of Marketing (Price, Place or Distribution, and Promotion) should be examined. The order indicated is logical to use because of the sequential nature of the three elements.

Pricing

Once product strategy has been thought through, pricing is the next issue to be decided. There seems to be a real proclivity for small business owners to use "penetration" pricing, presumably thinking this low pricing strategy is necessary in order to compete against large firms and capture market share or else thinking the small firm has lower costs because of its lack of bureaucracy and more favorable labor costs. The latter assumption may or may not be true. Perhaps the larger manufacturing firm has lower costs because of economies of scale as in the case of the automobile industry.

Another penetration pricing strategy to be considered is to be aggressive in pricing lower, based upon the assumption of getting down the learning curve faster by pushing volume produced up through lower prices. If a firm can in fact get down the learning curve faster, it may obtain a substantial lead on competition and forestall competitors from catching up in costs and thereby discourage them from reducing prices.

Another pricing strategy is bundling or unbundling. In the case of bundling, items that were formerly optional are included in the base price, usually at a somewhat lower price than when priced separately. This practice encourages the purchase of items that the customer would not have bought separately. Unbundling is the opposite of bundling.

Still another pricing strategy is "skimming," or charging higher prices initially while some customers are willing to pay more to be among the first to have the product. This pricing strategy, if carried out too long, will limit the market size unduly. Another side effect of this strategy may be to discourage those early buyers who see prestige in being first from buying early again if they believe they were overcharged in the past.

Distribution

Choosing the distribution channel or channels to use is important to the marketing strategy and deserves frequent review for change as the product goes through its cycle and as other dynamics in the external and internal environments change. Distribution can be intensive through many channels, which would be quite typical of many consumer items that are purchased by individuals such as power hand tools by Black & Decker. The opposite approach provides for selective or even exclusive distribution. This pricing strategy would be found where there are major differences in the product, when the product is technically complex, where brand loyalty is high, when pricing tends to be high, and infrequent or one-time purchases are made. Timing, such as the JIT concept,has become a major factor in distribution beyond the physical move itself. Furthermore, the physical flow and transactional flow are not coincidental or together in many instances.

Promotion

Advertising with a choice of five types of media and other forms of promotion are important elements of strategy that must be considered when developing the overall strategy. It can be an important element in a "niching" strategy, for instance. By focusing on a particular buyer group or groups, advertising helps inform and encourage sales. Another focus could be a relatively narrow geographic market that could be reached more effectively and at a lower cost than by advertising to a large geographic market. Domino's Pizza in its earlier years was an example of this advertising strategy, since it was a regional business and used primarily local newspapers for its advertising.

Other forms of promotion that should be considered for part of the firm's marketing strategy include in-store displays, the use of coupons, rebates, discounting, and special sales events. Special incentive programs such as vacation trips to exotic places for dealers, wholesalers, and manufacturer's representatives can be effective as part of the overall strategy. As mentioned earlier, it is difficult for a small company to justify its own sales force when it is just beginning. In fact, a company must be quite large to be able to support a sales force. Attendance at trade shows can be particularly effective for companies producing equipment to be used by other companies to produce their products.

OPERATIONS

The consideration of potential strategies for products and marketing is followed by operations or manufacturing in the case of a company making its own products. Many of these factors to be discussed are applicable for either providing a product or a service. The term product will be used for convenience.

Facilities

Wickham Skinner of Harvard Business School coined the term "focused factory" in order to describe the need for modern manufacturing facilities to focus on their relative competitive advantage and not try to be all things to all people.[1] The emphasis for manufacturing facilities presently is to pay attention to technology and, of course, quality. The perfection of manufacturing techniques by the Japanese, originally learned from others, has forced all others to reevaluate their manufacturing if they expect to continue to exist. The way to unprofitability or outright failure is strewn with those who did not heed the lesson. The idea that it is impossible to have too high a quality level, which the Japanese embraced, is being assimilated by others in order to be competitive.

Manufacturing facilities and the equipment used to manufacture products not only need to be modern and technologically current, but they need to be *flexible*. The drive has been not only to decrease inventory toward zero but also to reduce lot sizes while still reducing costs. While it is not yet practical to produce things one at a time, with flexibility in equipment and plant layout and a certain amount of redundancy it is possible to produce small lot sizes at a reasonable cost. The use of group technology has played an important role in machinery selection and plant layout.

Facilities location, while always important from the viewpoint of reducing shipping costs and labor costs, has taken on new meaning with the widespread use of JIT inventory techniques. While the U.S. does not have suppliers in close proximity as does Japan, U.S. firms have found it possible to minimize shipping time with careful planning. Certainly, the siting process for new plants must take into consideration the location of major customers and suppliers in addition to factors previously considered. For instance, can manufacturing plants supplying beer and soft drink producers are often located nearby.

Human Resources

After many years of struggling with unions and worker boredom, management finally seems to have learned its lesson. People, particularly their mental abilities, are the most important resource a firm has. It only makes sense to use this talent to solve problems and improve operations of the business or what is popularly called participative management. In order to carry out this style of management, the acquisition of talented employees must occur. Subsequently, both basic and specialized training must be carried out. Following these key steps, appropriate work assignments must be made and follow-up occur.

Purchasing

The biggest single cost now in the Cost of Goods Sold is direct material, far exceeding the cost of labor. Yet material cost has proven to be relatively intractable for

---

[1] Wickham Skinner, *Manufacturing The Formidable Competitive Weapon* (New York: John Wiley & Sons, 1985), pp. 71-82.

many firms. Certainly, manufacturing strategy must consider ways to reduce this important cost element. The beginning point is product design or redesign. The most effective way to minimize the cost of production, whether it is done in-house or contracted out, is to design the product for ease of production. This requires a cooperative effort on the part of product development, marketing, and manufacturing or vendor. Value analysis is a useful technique to use.

The next step is the "make or buy" decision. This decision uses techniques similar in many ways to a breakeven analysis. The incremental costs that will be incurred to manufacture a product are balanced against the incremental cost of purchasing the product. Included in the incremental costs are the direct costs of manufacturing, any incremental semi-fixed or fixed overhead costs, and any capital expenditures required to produce the product in the anticipated quantity. A discounted cash flow analysis can then be used to determine the relative advantage of making versus buying.

Other subjective factors to be considered when buying are the reliability of the vendor regarding delivery and quality and the availability of other sources of supply. Subjective factors for consideration, if making the product, are the availability of skilled employees and equipment, the quality attainable, and the stability of short and long term demand in regard to other production requirements including seasonal factors.

Inventory Control and Scheduling

Several techniques that should be considered for the scheduling of production or procurement of material are available when developing manufacturing strategy. Materials Requirement Planning (MRP) is a comprehensive, sophisticated system for planning the procurement of material to support production and the scheduling of production itself. It requires a great deal of internal discipline, a complete bill of material for all products, a computer to operate the system, and a strong commitment from top management to make it work. MRP has its greatest potential in a process based plant layout.

The use of Pareto's Law, otherwise known as the ABC method or 80-20 rule, should be considered in inventory control. It is a management by exception tool which provides for concentrating on 30 percent of the items (A & B) that constitute 95 percent of the value in inventory. This, coupled with a simple two-bin system for controlling the ordering of the C items, provides an adequate system for controlling inventory in a small firm that is not manufacturing.

Another technique to be considered is the use of an Economic Order Quantity (EOQ) system for determining the quantity of material to order or an Economic Production Quantity (EPQ) for determining the lot size to be produced. These systems are simpler than MRP and can work well in a small business with limited items to inventory. It is also necessary to determine lead times and forecast sales demand.

As discussed previously, JIT should be considered no matter what system of scheduling and inventory control is being used. Although it may be more difficult for a small business to use JIT than a large company given the current logistical conditions, JIT should examined and utilized to the extent practical. An inventory turn every two weeks for a manufacturing facility is attainable in most situations if the proper effort is put into the system.

SUMMARY

The development of a business strategy requires attention to three main factors in a business: product, marketing and operations. The product strategy is influenced by "niching" and the degree of product overlap. The following questions relate to product overlap.

1. Should the firm offer competing lines?

2. Should private brands or labels be considered?

3. Should products or services be offered to retail consumers?

4. Should products be produced for OEM or aftermarket?

5. Should "specials" or customized products be sold?

In the Marketing area, strategy should consider pricing, distribution, and promotional factors. The three strategies discussed, which are not the only possible strategies, were low base pricing, aggressive pricing based upon the learning curve, and "skimming."

Distribution requires consideration of an internal sales force versus the use of wholesalers, dealers, and manufacturers' reps. Each has its peculiar advantages, depending upon the product line, geographic area, and quantity being sold.

Promotion includes advertising, in-store displays, coupons, rebates and incentives for salespeople and distributors who do personal selling. Advertising is another activity which can facilitate "niching." Personal selling is critical for big ticket or technical products.

Operations strategy must consider the following factors:

1. Facilities including flexibility, technology, and JIT.

2. Human resources including selection and training of employees and participative management.

3. Purchasing including product design and value analysis and "make or buy" decisions.

4. Inventory control and scheduling including MRP, EOQ, EPQ, ABC, and JIT techniques.

CHAPTER 5

WRITING THE BUSINESS PLAN

Having completed the SWOT analysis (Chapter 2), the Financial Analysis (Chapter 3) and thought through the potential strategies (Chapter 4), the *owner or entrepreneur* is prepared to write the actual Business Plan. Certainly, one of the main reasons for writing a Business Plan is, like a personal resume or advertising, to attract the attention of potential investors and secure a subsequent interview to begin the process of securing funds. Since a firm usually gets only one chance for securing funds from a given individual or organization, it is important that the Plan be not only well written and the right length so as to create some excitement and enthusiasm for the situation, but it should be well packaged. Appearance is the beginning point of interest, which is analogous to dressing well for an employment interview. Since the Plan will hopefully bring about a subsequent interview, it must be easily explainable orally in the interview.

Entrepreneurs and small business owners tend to be optimistic and their plans usually reflect this. After all, you would not want a pessimistic salesperson! Investors, on the contrary, are more likely to be pragmatic realists who see many investment opportunities and must evaluate the risks involved versus the opportunities for gain. Investors, particularly venture capital firms, look for a favorable "return on invested capital" and are interested in relatively short-term commitments in the three-to seven-year range expecting to get their appreciation in their invested capital within this time frame. Banks are primarily interested in getting the principal sum of the loan back as agreed upon with interest, of course.

What do investors look for in businesses that they consider attractive for making investments? As has become evident to many now through the work of Tom Peters and Robert Waterman in their book, *In Search of Excellence*, a focus on the customer is critical to success and this truth is well-known to potential investors.[1] If the business has some proprietary position in a product or service such as a patent, trademark, copyright, or even some "know how" that is not easily obtained by others, investing becomes more attractive. Along with these factors, investors always appreciate the small business person's knowledge of and interest in the needs and goals of the investors. Conversely, investors are not impressed with unrealistic growth projections that deviate significantly from industry norms unless very convincing evidence is presented.

The Business Plan should be comprehensive and succinct. The maximum length should be 40 pages, including key exhibits and charts, depending upon the complexity

---

[1] Thomas J. Peters and Robert H. Waterman, Jr., *In Search of Excellence* (New York: Harper & Row, 1982), pp. 156-199.

of the business. A second volume can be prepared to include detailed schedules, exhibits and literature if necessary. A neat-looking cover should be used. The body of the plan should be typed or done on a word processor. Remember that a plan that is too elaborate can actually hurt its acceptance. The following format should be used for the Business Plan.

TITLE PAGE

The Title Page should contain the name of the business, its address, and phone number. Many like to include the names of the principals of the business since these will typically be the contact persons. The date of the Plan should be stated. Many like to consecutively number each copy for psychological reasons of exclusivity.

EXECUTIVE SUMMARY

The Executive Summary should not exceed two pages in length and is placed immediately after the Title Page in the Plan. It is very important since some will only read this part of the Plan and all will form critical first impressions after reading it. The contents of the Executive Summary will be discussed at the end of this chapter since it must be written *after* the Plan is completed.

TABLE OF CONTENTS

The Table of Contents should show the major elements of the Business Plan divided into Sections as shown in this chapter with the beginning page number of each section. Headings of subsections may be shown if desired.

SECTION A -- THE COMPANY

1.   Definition of the Company or Mission Statement

This subsection is designed to state the general nature and purpose of the company, such as a manufacturer, wholesaler, retailer or service business. It should state the primary products or services offered by the firm, the primary target markets and customer groups served and functions provided, the channels of distribution and technology used to serve the customers, any geographic factors involved in marketing or operations, product development activities if done by the firm, and operations factors as conducted by the firm. The primary values and ethics of the firm should be included.

2.   Origins of Firm and Owners

A brief summary of the origins of the firm, if it is not a new venture, should be placed here. A brief description of the principals of the firm should be written, keeping in mind that the Management Team will be discussed at some length in Section F.

3. Key Goals and Objectives

Key goals are time-oriented and can be described as long-term and short-term. Long-term goals generally cover a three-to five-year time frame. While they are broad statements of purpose, they also need to be specific. They cover key areas such as profitability, marketing and competitive position, manufacturing and productivity, product development and technological leadership, and human resources. These long-term goals give further meaning and direction to the Mission Statement. Short-term goals are yearly in time frame and should be very specific.

Objectives are specific statements of what will constitute goal accomplishment. They bridge the gap between the present and the long-term goals. Objectives must not only be specific but should provide for flexibility to cover unanticipated events, often in the external environment of the firm. Objectives must be measurable over time with results that can be quantified and evaluated. They should be motivating with some "stretching" required, yet attainable. They must be understandable to those who will act on them, which can be attained by having them participate in the setting of the objectives. Participation has the advantage of getting commitment for implementation. Finally, there must be an interrelationship between objectives for the firm so that they are not mutually exclusive. It would be appropriate to establish objectives in the functional areas of the firm so as to be complementary to the goals.

SECTION B -- PRODUCT/SERVICE

1. What It Is

Because readers of the Plan may not have the same level of knowledge or sophistication as the owner or entrepreneur, it is important that the description of the product or service be stated in clear and simple terms without putting down the reader. This section should describe the firm's products or services, including development activities that are presently under way. Particular attention should be given to the readiness of the products to be marketed in the case of a new venture. Photographs, catalog sheets, brochures or drawings are useful to include, as pictures tell the layman more than words.

2. How It Works

A brief description or diagram as to how the product actually works to fulfill the customer's needs should be included. Product performance data can be included here if it is pertinent.

3. What It Is For

The various uses for the products or services should be outlined pointing out

51

factors that give it appeal. Any unique features that will give the product or service a high potential for success should be highlighted. Such appeal could be based on accomplishing things faster, as in the case of personal computers using the "386" chip, or more effectively than competing products. Or appeal could be based on appearance or quality. It may be helpful to list some prior users if the product is technical in nature.

4. Proprietary Advantages

If there are proprietary advantages to the product or service such as patents, trademarks, copyrights or "know how," they should be outlined here. Investors are always interested in anything that gives a firm a unique advantage.

SECTION C -- MARKETING

1. Present Market

This subsection must establish the need or demand for the product or service, which in turn confirms the potential for the business to succeed and therefore is critical to the Plan. The key factors to be considered are listed below.

a. Prospective Customers

Prospective retail customers should be identified as to income level, sex, age, place of residence, education, type of employment, intelligence, sensitiveness to price and quality, economic and political persuasion, and other psychological characteristics. Prospective wholesale and corporate customers should be identified as well.

b. How Many There Are

The number of customers in the present market as defined above should be quantified by type if indicated.

c. Market Growth Rate

The market growth rate should be quantified based upon historical data and calculated trends. Sources for this kind of data include trade associations, trade literature, industry studies, government data and opinions of industry "experts."

2. Competition

Major competitors, including three to six of the most important, should be listed and briefly discussed in regard to market share and unique competitive advantages each may have.

3. Industry Trends

Industry trends beyond the market growth determined previously should be identified. These might include anticipated technological changes, changes in consumers' product or service requirements.

4. How the Firm Will Compete

Having looked at the competition and industry trends, the Plan must establish what strategies the firm will use to provide user benefits which set its products or service apart from the competition.

a. User Benefits

As stated earlier, investors are tuned into the concept of customer orientation. For this reason as well as its importance to the firm itself, user benefits need to be outlined. These might include such factors as improved product performance, improved product appearance or convenience, higher quality, fewer rejects or breakdowns, lower costs and improved efficiency, more rapid inventory turnover, user friendliness, and increased productive capacity.

b. Specific Target Markets

First, the Plan must establish that there is a market for its products beyond being just another "me too" competitor if it is to interest investors and ultimately be successful as a business. Specific target markets need to be identified which want the user benefits noted above. The concept of "niching" as developed in Chapter 4 might be a useful approach depending upon the product and industry. The market could be segmented any number of ways, for instance by age, income, sex, to name a few. Letters and comments from users in the targeted sectors can be useful in demonstrating that a specific target market is viable.

c. Planned Marketing Strategy

This subsection defines the Marketing Strategy which the firm will employ to reach its target markets given the presence of competition as identified previously. It is important that the reader of the Plan understand in a general way how the firm plans to market its product or service.

(1) Pricing

Factors to consider in developing a pricing strategy that were discussed in Chapter 4 include penetration pricing, "skimming," and bundling or unbundling. Bundling strategies can be effective as evidenced by option packages for automobiles which are examples of both bundling into an option and unbundling from a standard car.

(2)   Selling Methods and Distribution

As discussed earlier, having your own sales force while often considered first is seldom practical for small businesses unless the product or service is highly technical and carries a high price tag. A variation of this concept is used by some firms or in selective situations where the executives of the firm do the selling. This works well where high level personal contacts are important and where the price for the product or service is quite high. In the $1,000 to $10,000 price or order range, manufacturer's representatives are commonly used by small firms. These independent contractors handle non-competing products in the same or related industries on a commission basis. The selection of representation is important to the investor from the standpoint of the quality of the contacts the reps have and how much time they will devote to the firm's product. The plan should include evidence indicating which reps have agreed to represent the firm.

Products or services priced under $1,000 are most often handled through wholesalers or dealers to retailers, to retailers direct, or through catalogs. Securing adequate distribution can be a stumbling block for the small business and needs to be documented carefully in the Business Plan.

(3)   Sales Support

Sales support can be external as in the case of supplying outside sales agents with product literature and publicity articles. Or it can be internal such as processing orders, prompt shipping, managing the sales force or distribution network, providing sales incentives, and providing sales leads and referrals. The Plan should state specifically how these support activities will be provided and what they will cost

(4)   Promotion

Promotional strategies including advertising and other techniques were outlined in Chapter 4 and will not be repeated here. It should be noted that these activities are most important to the potential investor in the firm and should be thoroughly covered in the Plan.

5.   Projected Sales And Estimated Market Share

Projected financial performance will be provided in Section G so the material to be inserted here includes sales forecasts by time period such as quarterly in order to show any seasonal patterns and trends over time. A qualitative discussion of the forecasts is helpful to the potential investor with three forecasts being commonly provided: expected, optimistic, and conservative. The three forecasts require quite different levels of working capital and other resources with the optimistic forecast typically being the most demanding in this regard. Sales breakdowns by major product groups if there is more than one product group and by customer groups are useful to include. Finally, an estimate of the market share the firm plans to obtain over time should be included. This estimate is particularly significant if considered with the strength and intensity of competition.

SECTION D -- PRODUCT DEVELOPMENT

1.   Present

A section in the Business Plan on product development or the development of a service activity may not always be required or even appropriate. If a going business is being purchased or enlarged and the same products or services are to be continued, then this section can be omitted. Even in the case of a new product or service, it is wise to keep this section simple in its language so that non-technical people can read and understand it. Tangible products should be discussed rather than theoretical concepts.

2.   Future

It is very important to clearly state the *current* status of future products or services. In dealing with future product development, it is often useful to stress the technical team rather than try to explain the technology itself. The qualifications, experience and previous accomplishments of the team may say more to the potential investors than trying to explain a difficult research concept.

SECTION E -- OPERATIONS

Operations are present in any company. In the case of a firm which makes products, it is called manufacturing. In the case of a firm which sells but does not make its products, operations are limited to the activities of purchasing, inventory control, displaying and stocking merchandise, shipping and receiving, and facility maintenance. The operations strategy and plans should cover a five year time horizon because facilities and equipment often have long delivery cycles.

1.   Facilities

Physical facilities can be subdivided into several categories for ease in describing and understanding. Because they can be one of the most costly items in a start-up situation or their replacement in an existing company, it is important that the needs be thoroughly covered in a way that can be understood by the potential investor.

a.   Physical Facilities

Important factors to be considered include the location, size and future expansion capabilities of the physical facility whether it is a plant, warehouse, store, or office. Other physical features that may be significant such as air conditioning, ceiling height, special clean rooms, and lighting should be included. The proximity to means of transportation such as truck, rail, water and air should be stated. Locational relationships to key customers or suppliers should be noted if significant.

b.   Production Process

A description of the production process or processes which will be used should be included. This might be a product or process layout or some combination. Often a flow chart or some form of illustration may be clearer than a verbal description. Make or buy factors can be included here. The degree of mechanization or automation to be used at different time stages of the Plan should be noted also.

c.   Machinery and Equipment

The types of machinery, equipment and tooling to be used to manufacture or handle the products that are made or sold by the firm should be included here. The capabilities of the equipment in terms of precision and quality as well as the capacity of the equipment should be listed. Consideration should be given as to how future growth will be handled. Vendors and suppliers of the equipment that are expected to be used should be stated.

d.   Maintenance

Because of quality considerations in manufacturing these days, it may be significant to describe the provisions being made for maintaining machinery and equipment. These could include preventive maintenance, periodic qualification of equipment to ensure that parts being made are still within acceptable tolerances, and tooling replacement.

e.   Cost of facilities

The estimated costs of capital equipment and related extraordinary expense associated with installation and make-ready activities should be included along with the timing of the expenditures. These figures are particularly important in determining the financial requirements and are of obvious interest to the potential investor. Ongoing expenses for operating, maintaining, and replacing tooling and equipment should be stated also.

2. Materials

Materials often account for 50 percent or more of the cost of a product and thus deserve a thorough description in the Plan. This is particularly true or should be true of new ventures where initial capital costs are to be minimized by buying the product or significant parts of it from vendors. Later, as the firm grows, the purchase of the entire product or subassemblies from outside sources may change to manufacturing these items in-house.

a. Sources

Sources of supply for key materials or components should be included with attention given to back-up sources and their reliability. Capacity limitations for particularly vulnerable items should be explored in terms of continuity of supply and future growth. Quality is very important and consideration should be given to qualifying vendors using statistical methods.

b. Availability

Material availability should be discussed in terms of normal lead times and expedited times should rapid increases in quantities be required. The use of long-term contracts with periodic quantity releases should be considered as part of a JIT strategy.

c. Price Volatility and Costs

Pricing of purchased materials and services should be discussed in terms of sensitivity to supply and demand, required delivery, and quality requirements. Price breaks based on volume can be important in making purchasing commitments and in costing products and services at expanded volume. Consideration should be given to price sensitivity to inflation and other economic factors.

3. Staffing

Staffing of employees at all levels in the organization is extremely important and particularly so in the case of a small business or new venture. Typically a small business needs employees who are flexible and can "wear more than one hat" because the firm cannot afford an elaborate hierarchy or bureaucracy. The following categories should be included.

a.   Qualifications Required

Including a detailed description of each position will usually not be possible, given the length constraints of a Business Plan. A general description of the education, skills and experience needed for key positions should be placed here. An evaluation of the supply of people available within a reasonable distance of the need can be helpful.

b.   Quantity Required

A determination of the quantity of each type of employee needed over the time frame of the Plan should be made and included.

c.   Wages

The anticipated wages to be paid by type of position should be stated. Reference should be made to competitive wages in the area and how these wages may impact the firm now and in the future. Fringe benefits to be provided should be included here also. The method for handling overtime, holiday, and sick pay should be stated.

4.   Quality

Quality issues are very important to the firm and particularly to potential investors in the firm. Without quality a firm is doomed to failure or at best a mediocre existence. If quality assurance laboratories are to be provided, mention should be made about them. Statistical control techniques such as statistical process control, charting, qualification of vendors, incoming sample verification, and accelerated life testing should be covered in the Plan. The reporting relationship of this important function should be clearly stated along with the number of employees involved.

5.   Manufacturing Engineering Support

Manufacturing Engineering Support for the manufacturing firm begins as the product or products are being developed by Product Development people. This support is needed whether product development is done in-house or contracted out. Sometimes in a small firm the two activities are combined and may even be one person. However, the viewpoints needed for development versus manufacturing are somewhat different while having many things in common. Certainly one common element is the need and ability to design for ease of manufacturing and producing the product at a reasonable cost to maximize sales and profits. Manufacturing Engineering determines the process to be used in manufacturing, the plant layout to be used, the machinery and equipment required, the arrangement and work of production employees, the standard times for producing the products, and the costs of producing the products.

Manufacturing Engineering support is needed on an ongoing basis to refine and fine tune the manufacturing process. Bottlenecks and "best" methods are all relative in that, when one bottleneck is eliminated, another takes its place by definition. A constant vigil must be maintained in this activity lest the firm suffer a quality or cost disadvantage. The provisions to carry out these activities should be outlined here in the Plan.

SECTION F -- MANAGEMENT TEAM

The Management Team that will manage and operate the business is of paramount importance to the success of the firm and, therefore, of major interest to potential investors. One-man bands are not popular with investors although many entrepreneurs seem inclined to like that role personally. Issues such as management style need to be addressed for different styles can be effective in different situations. Participative management is "in" but autocrats can be effective too, particularly if they are also benevolent. Another factor is the flexibility to be expected from management, which is particularly important in start-up situations or in the early period of a new, small business.

1.   **Composition**

The composition of the team should be briefly stated here with more detailed biographical sketches included in an appendix.

a.   Founders and Principals

Potential investors are always interested in the background of the entrepreneurs, founders, and principals of the business. These people normally have an equity stake in the firm.

b.   Key Employees

Key employees are those who have a significant influence on the business, often in the technical, manufacturing or marketing areas. They often do not have an equity position in the firm. If employment contracts have been negotiated with them, that fact should be stated as well as their method of compensation.

c.   Directors and Consultants

Directors and/or consultants may play a significant role in the formation of a new venture and in an ongoing situation. Although working on a part-time basis, they may provide "value added" by contributing specialized or unique talent to the organization as contrasted with friends or neighbors.

2. Organization

A choice can be made between a verbal description of the organizational structure of the firm or a visual chart depicting the organization. Still another approach could be to put the chart in an appendix with a brief reference to it in the Plan here.

3. Compensation

The compensation of the Management Team is very significant for the firm and potential investors. Motivation is always a key factor in the success of managers in a company. Financial incentives or opportunity for future financial gain are two popular ways to motivate key managers. A bonus based upon measurable, superior performance is perhaps the best approach initially, since most owners are reluctant to issue stock that might dilute their own ownership and control. It is important to make the bonus at least partly if not largely contingent upon long-term performance. The compensation of the Management Team including its base salaries and incentive plans should be stated here.

SECTION G - FINANCIAL ANALYSIS

Financial projections are really a summation in financial terms of the Business Plan. They must include projections for a five-year period of the Income Statement, the Cash Flow Statement, and the Balance Sheet, as well as the most recent four years if the company is not a start-up situation. The projections need to be reliable and congruent with the narrative of the Business Plan. In order to show the sensitivity of the projections, it is helpful to have alternate scenarios showing the conservative and optimistic projections as well as the expected situation. To this end, it is very important to state a set of assumptions for each scenario, especially the key ones. Finally, a Breakeven Analysis should be presented. In the case of an existing company, similar historical data for the last three years of operation should be presented. Sample statements by quarters are provided after all statements have been discussed here.

1. Income Statement

The Income Statement should be presented in a monthly format for the first two years and quarterly for the next three years. The Income Statement should be presented in the format that follows in Figure 1, including at least that much detail.

2. Cash Flow Statement

The Cash Flow Statement, as shown in Figure 2, should be projected over the same time intervals as the Income Statement, i.e., by month for two years and quarterly thereafter. The Cash Flow Statement is extremely important for new ventures and very important for all small businesses, particularly those experiencing rapid growth. It is more significant than the Income Statement in new ventures and differs from it in a number of respects.

The Cash Flow Statement reflects the receipt and disbursement of cash from *all* sources including changes in debt position, changes in equity, and changes in assets. Receipts from sales through cash or collection of receivables and disbursements for expenses actually paid are included. Depreciation is not a cash flow and, hence, is not included. Of course, cash is included in net working capital (current assets minus current liabilities) but is especially critical since it could decrease rapidly while other elements of current assets such as receivables and inventory were being built up. Typically in start-up situations this very thing happens, and expenditures for fixed assets which also create a severe cash crunch and even insolvency. Cash projections are essential in establishing the level of working capital required.

3. Balance Sheet

The Balance Sheet, as shown in Figure 3, should be projected by quarters for the five-year period beginning with the current balance sheet.

4. Financial Ratio Comparison

Although not essential, it may be useful to present a series of key ratios for the company and the industry within which it operates. As outlined in Chapter 3, four categories of ratios can be utilized: profitability, liquidity, leverage, and turnover. At this point in the Plan, this kind of a comparison could be shown in tabular form by quarter over the time period of the projected statements.

5. Breakeven Analysis

A Breakeven Analysis should be included to demonstrate at what point the company will cover its full costs. This can be related to the time frame when the required sales level will be reached. Probably the most convenient way to present this analysis is in chart form as outlined at the end of Chapter 3. No further discussion or illustration will be made here.

6. Capital Budget

A schedule of capital expenditures required or anticipated by year over the next five year period should be included.

FIGURE 1

COMPANY NAME
Pro Forma Income Statement
Years Included
(In thousands of $)

	January	February	March	April

SALES REVENUE
  Less Sales Allowances
NET SALES REVENUE

COST OF GOODS SOLD
  Material
  Labor
  Overhead
    TOTAL

GROSS MARGIN

OPERATING EXPENSES
  Selling
    Salaries
    Advertising
    Other
      Total
  General & Administrative
    Salaries
    Depreciation
    Research & Development
    Other
      Total
TOTAL OPERATING EXPENSE

Income (Loss) from Operations
Interest Income (Expense)
Profit Before Taxes
Provision for Taxes
NET PROFIT

Net Increase (Decrease) to
Retained Earnings

FIGURE 2

COMPANY NAME
Pro Forma Cash Flow Statement
Years Included
(In Thousands of $)

	January	February	March	April
BEGINNING CASH BALANCE				
Receipts				
Collections				
Interest Income				
Long-Term Debt				
Equity Funds				
TOTAL RECEIPTS				
Cash Disbursements				
Direct Materials				
Direct Labor				
Manufacturing Overhead				
Less Depreciation				
Operating Expenses				
Capital Expenditures				
Long-Term Debt				
Interest Expense				
Income Tax Expense				
TOTAL DISBURSEMENTS				
NET CASH FLOW				
Cash Before Short-Term Loans				
Short-Term Borrowing				
Short-Term Repayments				
ENDING CASH BALANCE				

FIGURE 3

COMPANY NAME
Pro Forma Balance Sheet
Period Ending
(In Thousands of $)

	Current	Quarter	Quarter	Quarter
ASSETS				
Current Assets				
Cash				
Accounts Receivable				
Less Doubtful Accounts				
Net Accounts Receivable				
Notes Receivable				
Inventory				
Prepaid Expenses				
Total Current Assets				
Fixed Assets				
Land				
Buildings				
Equipment				
Less Depreciation				
Total Net Fixed Assets				
TOTAL ASSETS				
LIABILITIES				
Current Liabilities				
Accounts Payable				
Notes Payable				
Taxes Payable				
Other				
Total Current Liabilities				
Long-Term Debt				
TOTAL LIABILITIES				
EQUITY				
Common Stock				
Preferred Stock				
Capital in Excess of Par Value				
Retained Earnings				
NET EQUITY				
TOTAL LIABILITIES & EQUITY				

SECTION H -- FINANCIAL STRUCTURE

This final section will discuss the legal form of organization such as sole proprietorship, partnership, or corporation and the means for securing initial and ongoing funds. The potential investors will be most interested in the legal form of the business since it will impact their liabilities, rights and potential for recovery of their investment.

The initial and periodic, ongoing capital requirements of the firm can be developed from the figures presented on the Balance Sheet and Cash Flow Statement. These should be summarized briefly by time period, probably in tabular form.

The proposed sources of capital should be laid out next, which would include the investment to be made by the entrepreneur or owners followed by funds from external sources. External sources typically might include term loans from banks or individuals, a line of credit from a bank which allows a fluctuating debt balance, debt convertible into stock, and sale of preferred or common stock to outsiders. Venture capital firms often want a combination of debt and some form of equity participation that would lead to capital gains if the firm is successful or to assuming control of the firm if it proves to be unsuccessful. A summary should also be provided of the uses of the proceeds of the financing.

In general, the entrepreneur or small business owner does not wish to relinquish any control of the firm to outsiders or even to key employees. At the same time, the owners may wish to minimize their investment. While this is a favorite wish, it is seldom feasible to accomplish both of these goals simultaneously, given the large sums of money that may be required and the inherent risk involved. If debt without ownership participation is of first priority for a source of funds, the owner must be prepared to contribute a reasonable amount of equity initially. Often the potential lender will wish to have an option to secure an equity position if certain conditions regarding working capital and profitability are not met and maintained. While the Plan will outline the proposed capitalization of the firm, the owner must expect that negotiation will occur and flexibility is required in establishing the final deal.

NOW IT IS TIME TO WRITE THE *EXECUTIVE SUMMARY*

As stated previously, the Executive Summary must be written after the Business Plan is completed and is placed immediately after the Title Page. It should not exceed two pages in length and must succinctly state the essence of the Business Plan. Many potential investors use the Executive Summary to screen firms as far as their interest in investing in the firm. The Summary should create some excitement in the reader and generate interest in learning the details of the Plan. The writing style, however, should be businesslike, crisp and concise.

Typically, the Executive Summary should include the following items.

1. **Current Status of Firm**

2. **Mission Statement & Key Goals**

3. **Products and/or Services Provided**

4. **Market Potential**

   a. Potential customers.

   b. Benefits to customer of firm's products or services.

4. **Distinctive Competence**

   Brief summary of unique factors which firm will possess in regard to meeting its mission, goals and objectives.

5. **Financial Summary**

   a. Brief five-year summary of the key items on the Income Statement.

   b. Funds required and their sources.

   c. Benefits and their timing for investors.

CHAPTER 6

SAMPLE BUSINESS PLAN

This chapter will present a case, "Gal-Tech and Melanin: A Case of Technology Transfer" followed by a sample Business Plan for this start-up firm. Gal-Tech is about an entrepreneur, James Gallas, who has formed a company to commercialize his new invention, melanin concentrate. Students should first read the case in detail several times and then prepare their Business Plan for the firm. Sufficient information is presented in the case to prepare a complete Plan.

GAL-TECH AND MELANIN: A CASE OF TECHNOLOGY TRANSFER

It had been a rough day. Jim Gallas leaned back in his office chair and tried to relax, but thoughts of his current research problems kept plaguing him. For more than five years now, he had been trying to develop an efficient solar energy heat exchanger. To do this he needed a near-perfect solar energy absorber. His efforts had met with frustration.

Then he had decided to try melanin.

Melanin is a natural substance found in the skin and eyes of most animals. In humans, melanin darkens the skin when exposed to the sun, thus protecting us from the sun's radiation. In the back of the eye, melanin forms a "black box" that absorbs much of the harmful radiation coming into the eye.

Gallas hoped that melanin would prove to be the perfect energy absorber so he began to research melanin extensively. After several experiments, he found that while melanin absorbed light, it did not generate enough heat for practical energy production. These experiments revealed however, that melanin had some interesting properties; it absorbed the sun's rays that were most damaging to the human eye. Melanin absorbed virtually all of the ultraviolet light, much of the blue light, and some of the blue-green light. As a result of these experiments, melanin's solar energy prospects did not look good, but Gallas wondered if melanin could be useful in another way.

As Gallas tried unsuccessfully to push the frustration of not finding a good energy absorber out of his mind, he glanced down at his desk at some glass slips with melanin on them. The thought struck him that melanin might make a good sunglass coating. The glass, if covered with melanin, would protect the human eye by absorbing the harmful radiation of the sun. The phone rang, and he was jarred back to more pressing problems. The following week he continued his search for a perfect colar absorber. Then while he was working, the thought of coating sunglasses with melanin surfaced again. Where had this idea come from? Oh, yes, he remembered, he had thought of it the prior week! The thought dwelled with him; nelanin did have exactly the right properties to block the harmful rays of the sun. Maybe melanin could be a commercial product. But how could melanin be coated onto something like glass or plastic?

Gallas's interest in melanin increased. It seemed to have more potential as a filter against harmful sunlight than as a heat absorber within solar heaters. Although there are substances other than melanin that will block some of the harmful effects of the sun, none are natural, and none will do the job as efficiently or effectively as melanin does. Other substances block the ultraviolet or blue or green or red light, but none block the harmful effects of the sun in the optimum proportion and over the entire light spectrum, as melanin does.

Wherever it was important to block the harmful effects of the sun, melanin could be useful. Some of the products that might utilize melanin came immediately to mind: sunglasses, eyeglasses, contact lenses, and protective coatings for auto, home, and office windows, even paint. Also, Gallas hypothesized that adding melanin to plastics would help protect the plastic from the sun's damage and keep it from decomposing. He believed in melanin's great potential, so he continued his research.

Gallas set about the task of mixing melanin, a water-soluble substance, with plastic. First he tried to melt the plastic and mix it with melanin, but this only resulted in a messy glob. Using various techniques, he tried for six months to mix melanin and plastic, but was unsuccessful. As a result of these experiments, Gallas realized that melanin and plastic would have to be mixed at the molecular level.

Mel Eisner, a fellow physicist, became interested in the problem and began to work with Gallas. Mel suggested that a melanin precursor might mix with a plastic monomer. Gallas conducted several more experiments with the advice and help of a chemist, Frank Feldman, and eventually the process worked. He had invented a melanin concentrate that would mix with plastic or could be formed into a film and applied to glass. For their help in developing the process, and with the understanding that they would continue to be active in the development of melanin concentrate into a commercial product, Gallas promised Eisner and Feldman each 15 percent of the future business income from the invention.

GOING FOR A PATENT

Gallas prepared a detailed description of his process and applied for a U.S. patent. The patent authorities rejected his application, because they did not believe that the process he described constituted a true discovery. Gallas rewrote his request and resubmitted, again with no success.

Gallas now wondered what to do. He had a process that he had discovered, and he was convinced the process was unique and therefore patentable. Also, he knew that a patent was absolutely necessary for his invention to become a successful product.

Determined to get a patent, Gallas decided to use a patent attorney. He wanted a law firm with an experienced patent attorney, an excellent reputation, and offices in both Houston and Washington, D.C.. He also wanted a firm that believed he could obtain the patent and would fight to get it. He decided to use a well-known patent law firm in Houston, Texas that met all of his requirements. He was impressed that several attorneys on the staff of the firm were former attorneys at the U.S. patent office.

Since Gallas could not afford to pay the fees that the patent attorneys required in order to file the patent request, he convinced them to accept as payment 15 percent of the final benefits that would be derived from the patent. The patent attorneys accepted his offer and a staff attorney from the firm was assigned to file the patent request. The application was filed for the third time but the request was again rejected by the U.S. patent office this time on the basis of "obviousness" because another patent had recently been awarded for putting melanin into a skin cream.

Another year passed but Gallas did not give up. He decided that if he gave a senior attorney at the law firm, Mr. Barnes, a 5 percent interest in the patent, Barnes would be more motivated to get the application accepted. The patent application was rewritten again. A clear description of the Gallas process showed that melanin-treated lenses designed to protect the human eye were significantly different from melanin-treated skin cream, and that no one had a patent to incorporate melanin onto transparent plastic or glass. This argument convinced the examiner, and the patent was granted October 6, 1987.

The patent abstract reads: "Optical lens system incorporating melanin as an absorbing pigment for protection against electromagnetic radiation." The patent protects the process of applying melanin to surfaces such as plastic and glass from duplication. Gallas retained the patent attorneys to protect and defend his new patent. Knowing how important the patent was, he estimated an expense of $10,000 per year for attorney fees to protect the patent once the product was commercialized.

BECOMING A BUSINESSMAN

Once he had a patent which would protect his invention, Gallas went about developing his new technology into a business. The patent was owned by a "partnership" of Gallas 50 percent, Eisner 15 percent, the law firm 15 percent, Mr. Barnes 5 percent, and Feldman 15 percent.

The patent attorneys helped Gallas to incorporate under the name of Gal-Tech Corporation, which was chartered in December, 1987, as a C Corporation. Two thousand shares of stock were authorized, and one thousand issued. Stock was to be divided using the same percentages as the patent ownership, with each of the final stockholders receiving their stock at $1.00 par value. However, Gallas recognized that rights to the patent did not necessarily carry over to the corporation.

The attorneys had talked of giving their top partner, Mr. Sliplock, 5 percent, which Gallas assumed would come out of the firm's 15 percent. Only later, when negotiations were under way to develop the actual production company, Gal-tech, did he discover that the attorneys had meant an additional 5 percent. Gallas argued that since Mr. Barnes would receive 5 percent of the company, Mr. Sliplock's percentage should be included with the law firm's 15 percent; they agreed. Because Frank Feldman could no longer give time to the project, Gallas felt that his percentage should be lowered. Feldman agreed to trade his 15 percent of the patent for 2 percent ownership in Gal-Tech. Another chemist was brought in, Robert Williams, who was given 3 percent of the stock, and Feldman's remaining 10 percent was given to Gallas. Gallas was uncomfortable with the Houston law firm owning such a large percentage (10 percent) of the company, and offered to pay them $65,000 for their remaining ownership, payable as soon as the corporation was capitalized. This stock was then divided between Gallas (7 percent) and Eisner (3 percent). In addition, Gallas had promised Mel Eisner $25,000 and Frank Feldman $10,000 for their past work. Eisner and Feldman were willing to take notes with interest-only annual payments at 10 percent, and the principal due at the end of five years. Gallas, who had invested several years and a great deal of his own money, was willing to take a similar note for $100,00. In this way, the patent became the property of Gal-Tech Corporation, and could be amortized over its remaining life. The final stock ownership was Gallas, 67 percent; Eisner, 18 percent; Barnes, 5 percent; Sliplock, 5 percent; Feldman, 2 percent; and Williams, 3 percent.

Gallas knew that before anyone would invest in Gal-Tech, he would have to develop a market for melanin concentrate. While he was applying for the patent, he had been contacted by the television network CNN. Not wanting to discuss his discovery before receiving the patent, he had put them off. Once the patent was issued he contacted them and arranged for a television interview. After the interview aired, several other media representatives contacted him for interviews and/or articles. While visiting Monterrey, Mexico, Gallas read an article about himself and his process in a local newspaper and realized that his discovery was beginning to gain widespread press coverage. Prompted by the publicity about melanin and its potential, several large companies contacted Gallas about the process, but because he did not have a marketing strategy nor a definite commercialization plan, few maintained their interest.

Gallas began to research possible markets for his discovery. He quickly learned that the ophthalmic industry includes eyeglasses, sunglasses, contact lenses, and surgically implanted intraocular lenses. However, FDA approval would be needed before contact lenses and intraocular lenses could use melanin. The most obvious potential user of the melanin concentrate seemed to be the sunglasses industry. He manufactured a few pairs of melanin-treated sunglasses as prototypes. With their amber-colored lenses, the glasses made eye-catching samples to show to prospective investors.

Gallas learned that the sunglass industry already offered lenses that block a specific portion of the light spectrum. Ultraviolet absorbers block a significant percentage of the UV range. Nationwide, optical labs report coating 13 percent of eyeglasses with UV protection, which is the state of current technology for eye protection. Blue-blockers blocked out all of the blue light, but sacrificed color vision. Gallas felt that melanin would be the logical next step because melanin would block the harmful effects of UV, blue, and blue-green light.

Convinced more and more of the commercial significance of his discovery, Gallas began contacting firms that he thought would be interested in melanin. As a physicist, he would ask to speak to the person in charge of technical development, and proudly explain his discovery and its uses to this person. Time after time, he was surprised to hear negative comments about incorporating melanin into their products using his process. Perhaps the greatest turning point in the development of his product was when he realized that the real value of the melanin process was not its technical attributes, but the perception of value by the consumer. This led Gallas to talk to the marketing departments of the companies that he was contacting. He was surprised when he received a much stronger response from the marketing managers than he had from the scientists.

Also, instead of contacting only manufacturers, he began to contact distributors and those companies that manufacture and market their own sunglasses. The marketing managers in these firms brought much more positive responses, and a few firms began to show genuine interest in using melanin.

After many interesting inquiries, two large sunglass manufacturer/distributors began serious talks with Gallas. One represented the high end of the market, the other represented the low-end. Gallas believed that the high end might offer a contract before the end of the his first year, paying a licensing fee of $200,000 and a 50 cent royalty per pair sold. Because the low end company's sales were more seasonal, they would probably not produce melanin sunglasses until the second year. Gallas estimated that they would then pay a licensing fee of $100,000, and also pay a 50 cent royalty per pair sold. The high end distributors estimated that they could sell 1,140,000 pairs of melanin-treated sunglasses the first year. Between the two distributors, sales would double the second year, and increase by 50 percent the third year. Sales would be recorded at the time the concentrate was shipped; receivables could be expected to equal six weeks' sales.

The sunglass firms that had contacted Gallas had excellent name recognition, well-established distribution channels, and promotional and advertising capabilities that little Gal-Tech could not possibly match. Because of this, Gallas decided that he should negotiate an agreement to let the sunglass firms advertise his product along with their own, instead of attempting to reach the consumer himself. Still, Gallas knew that advertising, promotion, travel, and entertainment would consume $100,000 of Gal-Tech's first-year budget and at least 10 percent of gross income thereafter.

The closer Gallas got to commercializing his product, the more questions he had concerning the structure of his company and the manufacture of melanin concentrate. He had initially planned to license the manufacture of the melanin concentrate, but he realized that allowing others to produce the concentrate might endanger his control of the process and weaken his patent. Gallas decided that Gal-Tech would have to produce the melanin concentrate itself. He reviewed the manufacturing operations of his company. The sunglass lenses would be coated with 10 microns of the melanin concentrate. Assuming the average diameter of a lens is about 6 centimeters, each pair of sunglasses would require .085 grams of melanin concentrate. It would therefore require about 85 kilograms of melanin to produce the tint for 1 million pairs of sunglasses. Actual production of concentrate should include an additional 20 percent to account for losses and defects in the process of coating the lenses, plus 10 percent to be used for internal research and development. Therefore, it would take about 115 kilograms of melanin concentrate to support the sales of one million pairs of melanin-coated sunglasses.

The melanin concentrate could initially be produced in twenty-liter containers in a batch process that takes place over a 24-hour period and yields about 75 grams of melanin per container. Assuming 250 days of production per year, each twenty-liter vessel would yield about 19 kilograms of melanin per year. Because of this short production cycle, only a two weeks' supply of chemicals will be kept on hand; also, a finished inventory of two weeks' sales will be kept.

The raw materials used in the production of melanin concentrate are peroxides such as benzol peroxide, solvents such as chloroform and methanol, and the melanin precursors such as catechol and L-Dopa. These raw materials are readily available from several suppliers in quantities necessary to produce all projected requirements. Substitute raw materials are also available. The raw materials cost approximately $1.00 per gram of melanin concentrate produced, a cost which is not expected to change within the next three years.

There are no physical properties of melanin concentrate that limit transportation or distribution. Shipping expenses will be about $4,000 the first year.

Personnel will be divided into three important functions at Gal-Tech: production, sales and marketing, and administration and finance. Each function needs a director; production also requires two technicians and a shipping clerk, and administration requires

72

a secretary/bookkeeper. The production chief will be in charge not only of production, but also research and development, and will need to have a Ph.D. in physics or chemistry. His/her salary will be included in cost of sales. Gallas estimates that the kind of people necessary to make Gal-Tech a success would require annual salaries of: Chairman of the Board $20,000; President $55,000; Production Manager $40,000; Sales and Marketing Manager $30,000; Administrator $25,000; Shipping Clerk $15,000. Individual salaries are not expected to change over the following three years, but Gallas estimates that at the beginning of the third year, they will have to hire two more technicians, one more shipping clerk, and one more secretary to help the marketing chief. Gallas budgets an additional nine percent for payroll taxes, up to the legal limits. Health and workmen's compensation insurance should be about $8,000 per employee for the first year of operations and increase 5 percent each year.

Dr. Gallas feels that the firm will need room to grow. Five thousand square feet of office/warehouse space is available at 50 cents per square foot per month, which includes common area maintenance and property taxes. Finish out will be accomplished by the landlord, including inside walls and HVAC. One month's rent is required as a deposit. Annual insurance should be about one dollar per square foot of space. Furniture and fixtures required and their costs are: lab furniture and fixtures $12,000; vent hoods (2) $18,000; scale $10,000; microscope $10,000; ovens $10,000; chemicals $10,000; glassware $5,000; lab computers $5,000; office furniture and equipment $20,000; office computer, software $6,000; and office supplies $2,000. These costs will be depreciated over five years, using straight-line depreciation. If sales increase according to plan, $100,000 will have to be borrowed at the beginning of the third year to purchase additional equipment. Dr. Gallas hopes to then negotiate a note to be payable over five years, at an interest rate of 12 percent. He knows that any investors will require audited financial statements, and is prepared to pay $5,000 per year for this and other accounting services.

In order to stay a viable company, Gal-Tech will have to invest in itself through research and development. The first year of operation, $200,000 will need to be spent, and 20 percent of gross revenue thereafter for R & D.

BECOMING A GOING CONCERN

Dr. Gallas has made an appointment with a venture capitalist, and plans to ask for $250,000 to capitalize Gal-Tech. James Gallas has the vision needed to make his discovery a profitable company. He has a patent and a solid knowledge of how his business will operate. What he doesn't have is the formal structure and financial projections required to attract the capital necessary to bring his vision to life. He needs a formal plan, incorporating all that he knows about his target markets, proposed operations, and financial commitments, including pro forma financial statements for three years.

A NOTE ON THE SUNGLASS INDUSTRY

The sunglass industry is composed of three basic components: prescription sunglasses, high-end sunglasses (over $20.00 per pair), and low-end sunglasses (under $20.00 per pair). The non-prescription sunglass market is growing steadily. In 1985, 160 million pairs were sold, and 175 million pairs were sold in 1986. Bausch and Lomb's Consumer Products Division estimates that total sales for the industry were $1.3 billion in 1987, a 16 percent increase over 1986. From 1986 to 1987 the under-$20 market segment increased 9 percent, and the over-$20 market segment, which accounts for 40-45 percent of the total sunglass market, increased 22 percent. There are over 250,000 locations that sell sunglasses in the USA, according to Bausch & Lomb, with nearly 55,000 locations selling sunglasses that retail at $20 or over. Many traditional optical retailers are now displaying sunglasses separately and setting up kiosks from which to sell sunglasses.

Brand awareness and glamour are important factors in the sunglass business, and sales are often influenced by celebrities' use of a particular brand. The perception of value by the consumer is also important in the marketing of sunglasses. Vuarnet claims its sunglasses "not only protect your eyes and make a fashion statement, they also help your visual performance and through that your physical performance." This perception of quality is apparently well received by consumers, who purchased $50 million in sunglasses from Vuarnet in 1987.

A BUSINESS PLAN FOR GAL-TECH

The Business Plan shown below was developed by John P. McCray and Juan J. Gonzalez from information provided in the case. The Title Page and Table of Contents have been omitted for convenience. Only three years, by year, are shown on the Pro Forma Statements to conserve space on the spreadsheets.

EXECUTIVE SUMMARY

Gal-Tech Corporation, chartered in Texas in 1987, has developed melanin as its principal product, which it plans to manufacture and market to manufacturers of glass and plastic products, specifically sunglasses. A patent is held on the process.

Melanin is a natural product found in the skin and human eye. It is the means for protecting the human eye from light radiation as it absorbs harmful light rays in proportion to their damaging effects. Competitors' methods of blocking the harmful effects of the sun are not only less effective, but sacrifice color vision.

Gal-Tech is now actively pursuing product manufacturers to incorporate melanin concentrate into their products. Firms in the sunglass industry have already shown an interest in melanin. This industry had sales in 1987 of $1.3 billion so the potential is great. The projected revenue from royalties and fees from sunglass manufacturers over the next three years is estimated to be $3,720,000. Sales beyond this initial three-year period are expected to grow rapidly as the public becomes more aware of the product and more uses are discovered for it.

Gal-Tech has a distinct competence in developing and manufacturing melanin concentrate. Dr. James Gallas and Dr. Melvin Eisner, who are both physicists, developed the concept and process over a five-year period and possess more knowledge and experience than anyone else at this point in time. Therefore, Gal-Tech is in a unique position to market this unique process.

The pro forma financial statements in Section G of this plan show that, over the three-year period, Gal-Tech will earn revenues of $3,720,000 and earn a net profit of $390,000 for a return on equity of about 30 percent per year. The cash flow, although negative in the startup year, is very positive in subsequent years. The company expects to breakeven part-way through the second year.

Funds required to begin commercial production and marketing of melanin are $250,000. These can be obtained either from debt or equity sources. In the third year of operation, another $100,000 will be required to fund further expansion.

A. -- THE COMPANY

Gal-Tech Corporation is a new venture firm whose mission is to develop, manufacture and market melanin concentrates to other manufacturers for incorporation into plastic or glass commercial products. The company continues to develop new formulations and applications for melanin. The original development of melanin and the patent that was subsequently secured were done by Dr. James Gallas and Dr. Melvin Eisner.

The current key goal of Gal-Tech is to secure initial financing either through debt or equity sources to purchase the patent, required capital equipment, and provide working capital. A second key goal is to sell melanin to sunglass manufacturer's. The third key goal is to further develop other formulations and uses for melanin.

B. -- PRODUCT

Melanin is a natural substance found in the skin and eyes of most animals. In humans, melanin darkens the skin when exposed to the sun, thus protecting them from the sun's radiation. In the back of the eye, melanin absorbs much of the harmful radiation coming into the eye. It absorbs virtually all of the ultraviolet light, much of the blue light, and some of the blue-green light. Potential uses for melanin are to coat sunglasses, eyeglasses, and various kinds of windows. A patent has been obtained.

The amount of melanin concentrate used to coat the lenses of sunglasses would be enough to provide a 10-micron coating over the entire surface of the lens. Assuming the average diameter of a lens is about 6 centimeters, each pair would require .085 grams of melanin concentrate. Thus, it will require about 85 kilograms of melanin concentrate to produce the tint for 1 million pairs of sunglasses.

C. -- MARKETING

The potential commercial market for melanin includes the ophthalmic, plastics, tinted glass and paint industries. As a result of receiving national recognition and publicity, Dr. Gallas has had inquiries from several manufacturers in the contact lens, paint, and window film ineusties.

Potential Market

For the present, the ophthalmic industry. which includes sunglasses, contact lenses, and intraocular lenses, is the most likely user of melanin. Firms in the sunglass industry are interested in melanin as a filter against the harmful effects of the sun's rays. Firms that sell contact and intraocular lenses are also interested, but Federal Drug Administration (FDA) approval is required before melanin may be used in these products and takes considerable time and testing to secure. Therefore, the principal focus of immediate marketing and research in on the sunglass industry.

The sunglass industry is composed of three basic components: prescription sunglasses, high-end sunglasses (over $20 per pair), and low-end sunglasses (under $20 per pair). Nationwide, optical labs report coating 13 percent of eyeglasses with UV protection,[1] which is the state of current technology for eye protection. The non-prescription sunglass market is growing steadily. In 1985, 160 million pairs were sold and in 1986 175 million pairs were sold. Bausch and Lomb's Consumer Products Division estimates that total sales for the industry were $1.3 billion in 1987, a 16 percent increase over 1986. From 1986 to 1987, the under-$20 market segment increased 9 percent and the over-$20 market, which accounts for 40 to 45 percent of the total sunglass market, increased 22 percent.[2]

There are over 250,000 locations that sell sunglasses in the United States, according to Bausch & Lomb, with nearly 55,000 locations selling sunglasses that retail at $20 or over. Many traditional optical retailers are now displaying sunglasses separately and setting up kiosks from which to sell them.[3]

Brand awareness and glamour are important factors in the sunglass business, and sales are often influenced by celebrities' use of a particular brand. The perception of value by the consumer is also important in the marketing of sunglasses. Vuarnet claims its sunglasses "not only protect your eyes and make a fashion statement, they also help your visual performance and through that your physical performance."[4] This perception of quality is apparently well received by consumers, who purchased $50 million in sunglasses from Vuarnet in 1987.[5] As a natural substance, melanin should be well received by buyers of sunglasses.[6]

Competition

While there is no direct competition for melanin coated sunglasses at the present time, when melanin enters the market through one or more manufacturers, other major

---

[1] Bennett, Irving, O.D. *1988 State of the Ophthalmic Industry*, Advisory Enterprises, New York, 1988.

[2] Bennett, p. 16.

[3] Bennett, p. 16.

[4] *Consumer Reports*, August, 1988, p. 504-509.

[5] Bennett, p. 16.

[6] Standard & Poors, October 13, 1988.

manufacturers can be expected to offer substitute coatings. Melanin's blocking power can be somewhat resembled by tintings, films, and dyes. Overlapping films and tints will provide a crude look-alike, but they can not duplicate the melanin protection and may decompose over time. Other manufacturers could only claim to have a "melanin-like" product due to the patent held by Gal-Tech which reads in part: "Optical lens system incorporating melanin as an absorbing pigment for protection against electromagnetic radiation."

User Benefits

Melanin is a natural substance found in the skin and eyes of most animals. It absorbs virtually all of the ultraviolet light, much of the blue light, and some of the blue-green present in light from the sun. It will provide to the users of sunglasses that are coated with melanin protection from virtually all of the harmful effects of sunlight on the eyes. This can be accomplished without diminishing the ability of the wearer to see true colors.

Target Market

Gal-Tech will initially target the sunglass industry. It is relatively easy to incorporate melanin into sunglasses, and there is an immediate demand for such a product. Active negotiations are currently underway with two major sunglass manufacturers who represent the high-end and low-end of the market. These firms have expressed an interest in using melanin concentrate in their products. Gal-Tech will manufacture melanin concentrate and supply it to firms upon their signing a licensing contract. It is proposed that the sunglass firms pay an initial licensing plus a royalty percentage of 50 cents per pair sold.

Marketing Strategy

Because of consumer brand loyalty, Gal-Tech will market directly to manufacturers. The manufacturer or distributor of melanin products will be expected to advertise the natural benefits of melanin to the general public. Advertising by manufacturers which use melanin will be encouraged through price breaks.

Initial penetration into the sunglass coating market will be achieved by securing a license agreement with one or more of the large manufacturers of sunglasses. With this license agreement in hand, cash flow will be generated to develop other markets. Gal-Tech will maintain control through on-site support. The advantages of this strategy are outlined below:

1. Low initial capital cost.
2. Name recognition within the industry of the manufacturer or distributor.
3. Already established distribution channels will be open to the product.
4. Promotional and advertising capabilities of the manufacturer or distributor exceed those of Gal-Tech.

Projected Sales

Production requirements for melanin concentrate are 85 kilograms for each one million sunglasses to be coated plus 20 percent overage to cover the additional material needed by manufacturers for losses and defects in their production process. An additional 10 percent is to be provided for internal research and development. Thus, about 115 kilograms of melanin concentrate will be required to support annual sales of tint for one million pairs of sunglasses. The high-end distributors estimate sales of 1,140,000 pairs of melanin-treated sunglasses the first year. With the advent of the second distributor in the second year, sales are expected to double and continue to increase by 50 percent in the third year. Thus melanin sales by Gal-Tech are expected to be 115, 230, and 345 kilograms, respectively, over the three-year period.

D. -- PRODUCT DEVELOPMENT

Product Development will be an ongoing effort by Dr. Gallas, Dr. Eisner and the Production Manager. The direction of future activities, in addition to further developments for the sunglass industry, will include applications for eyeglasses, windows and paints.

E. -- OPERATIONS

Facilities

The production process for melanin will consist of using 20 liter-containers in a batch process which takes place over a 24-hour period and yields about 75 grams of melanin per container. Therefore, it will require twelve 20 liter-containers to produce 230 kilograms of melanin annually, which is the initial production capacity.

Gal-Tech plans to lease 5,000 square feet in an office/warehouse development area. Interior finishing to Gal-Tech's specifications will be accomplished by the landlord including such things as inside walls and air conditioning. Initial equipment that will be purchased include the following:

Rent Deposit	$ 2,500
Lab furniture & fixtures	12,000
Vent hoods (2)	18,000
Scale	10,000
Microscope	10,000
Ovens	10,000
Chemicals	10,000
Glassware	5,000
Lab computers	5,000
Office furniture & equipment	20,000
Office computer & software	6,000
Office supplies	2,000
TOTAL	$ 105,500

Materials

Raw materials used in the production concentrate are peroxides such as benzol peroxide, solvents such as chloroform and methanol, and the melanin precursors such as catechol and L-Dopa. These materials are readily available from several suppliers in quantities necessary to produce all projected melanin requirements. Substitute raw materials are also available. Pricing is competitive and quite stable.

Distribution

The melanin concentrate will be shipped to buyers by the most cost-efficient means. There are no physical properties of melanin that limit transportation or distribution methods. A large inventory of melanin concentrate will not need to be maintained due to the short production cycle.

Staffing

Because of the simple production process only two technicians with a background in chemistry will be needed initially at a salary of $20,000 each. In addition a shipping clerk at a salary of $15,000 and a secretary/bookkeeper at a salary of $15,000 will be required initially. At the beginning of the third year the number of employees will be doubled to accommodate growth.

Quality

The quality level achieved in melanin production is very high. Because of time spent in the initial development of melanin and its production, the "bugs" have been worked out.

F. -- MANAGEMENT TEAM

The founders and principals of Gal-Tech are Dr. James Gallas and Dr. Melvin Eisner, both physicists who worked together on developing the melanin process since 1982. They will serve as Chief Executive Officer at a salary of $20,000 and President at a salary of $55,000, respectively.

The Production Manager will have a Ph.D. in chemistry or physics and will be responsible for the production activity as well as continue to research and develop new uses for melanin or methods for its production at a annual salary of $40,000.

The Sales/Marketing Manager will have previous experience in marketing of chemical products and an appropriate degree in business administration. This person will be responsible for contacting prospective customers and developing an advertising program as needed at a salary of $30,000.

The fifth management team member will be the Administrator at a salary of $25,000. This person will be responsible for supervising office personnel and providing financial budgets, data and reports.

The proposed Organization Chart for Gal-Tech follows.

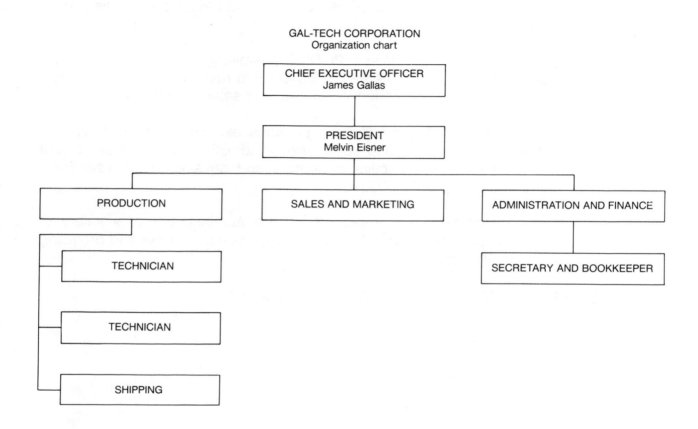

GAL-TECH CORPORATION
Organization chart

CHIEF EXECUTIVE OFFICER
James Gallas

PRESIDENT
Melvin Eisner

PRODUCTION

SALES AND MARKETING

ADMINISTRATION AND FINANCE

TECHNICIAN

TECHNICIAN

SHIPPING

SECRETARY AND BOOKKEEPER

G. -- FINANCIAL ANALYSIS

Following are the ProForma Income Statement, Cash Flow Statement, and Balance Sheet for Gal-Tech for a projected three-year period. The statements represent the expected sales levels and are thought to be conservative. Break even occurs at a royalty level of $920,000 (1,840,000 pairs of sunglasses) or 212 kilograms of melanin. This calculation does not include the initial licensing fees, which make it possible for the firm to generate a profit the second year. A small loss of $24,300 is anticipated the first year of operations.

Once the initial financing as outlined later is accomplished, cash flow for the first year of operations is negative. However, subsequent years' cash flow is strongly positive.

GAL-TECH CORPORATION
Pro Forma Income Statement
Three Years
(In Thousands of Dollars)

	Year #1	%	Year #2	%	Year #3	%
REVENUE						
Royalties	570.0	74.0%	1,140.0	91.9%	1,710.0	100.0%
License Fees	200.0	26.0%	100.0	8.1%		
Total	770.0	100.0%	1,240.0	100.0%	1,710.0	100.0%
COST OF SALES						
Chemicals	106.3	13.8%	212.6	17.1%	318.9	18.6%
Labor	95.0	12.3%	95.0	7.7%	150.0	8.8%
Shipping	4.0	0.5%	8.0	0.6%	12.0	0.7%
Total	205.3	26.7%	315.6	25.5%	480.9	28.1%
GROSS PROFIT	564.7	73.3%	924.4	74.5%	1,229.1	71.9%
OPERATING EXPENSES						
Acctg. & Legal	15.0	1.9%	15.0	1.2%	15.0	0.9%
Adv. & Promo.	100.0	13.0%	124.0	10.0%	171.0	10.0%
Amortization	13.0	1.7%	13.0	1.0%	13.0	0.8%
Depreciation	21.1	2.7%	21.1	1.7%	41.1	2.4%
Ins. - Prop.	5.0	0.6%	5.0	0.4%	7.5	0.4%
Ins. - Work. Comp.	8.0	1.0%	8.0	0.6%	12.0	0.7%
Ins. - Health	8.0	1.0%	8.0	0.6%	12.0	0.7%
Freight Out	2.4	0.3%	4.0	0.3%	6.0	0.4%
Rent	30.0	3.9%	30.0	2.4%	45.0	2.6%
Res. & Dev.	200.0	26.0%	250.0	20.2%	340.0	19.9%
Salaries	40.0	5.2%	40.0	3.2%	55.0	3.2%
Officer Salary	75.0	9.7%	75.0	6.0%	75.0	4.4%
Taxes - General	2.0	0.3%	2.0	0.2%	3.0	0.2%
Taxes - Payroll	18.0	2.3%	18.0	1.5%	24.3	1.4%
Other	38.0	4.9%	43.0	3.5%	59.0	3.5%
Total	575.5	74.7%	656.1	52.9%	878.9	51.4%
OPERATING INCOME	(10.8)	-1.4%	268.3	21.6%	350.2	20.5%
Interest Expense	13.5	1.8%	13.5	1.1%	25.5	1.5%
Income Before Tax	(24.3)	-3.2%	254.8	20.5%	324.7	19.0%
Income Taxes			66.6	5.4%	98.6	5.8%
NET INCOME	(24.3)	-3.2%	188.2	15.2%	226.1	13.2%

GAL-TECH CORPORATION
Pro Forma Cash Flow Statement
Three Years
(In Thousands of Dollars)

	Year 1	Year 2	Year 3
BEGIN. CASH BALANCE	184.1	27.0	176.1
Receipts			
Royalties	570.0	1,140.0	1,710.0
License Fees	200.0	100.0	
Less A/R Increase	71.2	71.3	71.3
TOTAL RECEIPTS	698.8	1,168.7	1,638.7
Cash Disbursements			
Direct Materials	114.5	218.9	326.1
Direct Labor	98.7	96.9	152.8
Shipping	4.0	8.0	12.0
Operating Expenses	541.4	622.0	824.8
Capital Expend.	105.5		100.0
Long-Term Debt			(80.0)
Interest Expense	13.5	13.5	25.5
Income Tax Expense		66.6	98.6
TOTAL DISBURSEMENTS	877.6	1,025.8	1,459.8
NET CASH FLOW	-178.8	142.9	178.9
Cash Before ST Loans	5.3	169.9	355.0
Short-Term Borrowing	19.8	6.2	29.5
Short-Term Repayments			
ENDING CASH BALANCE	27.0	176.1	384.5

GAL-TECH CORPORATION
Pro Forma Balance Sheet
Year Ending
(In Thousands of Dollars)

	Year 1	Year 2	Year 3
CURRENT ASSETS			
Cash	27.0	176.1	384.5
Acc. Receivable	71.2	142.5	213.7
Inventory			
Chemicals	4.0	8.0	12.0
Finished	7.9	12.0	18.0
Total Cur. Assets	110.1	338.6	628.2
FIXED ASSETS			
Plant & Equipment	105.5	105.5	205.5
Less Depreciation	21.1	42.2	83.3
Net	84.4	63.3	122.2
OTHER ASSETS			
Patents	200.0	200.0	200.0
Less Amortization	13.0	26.0	39.0
Net	187.0	174.0	161.0
TOTAL ASSETS	381.5	575.9	911.4
CURRENT LIABILITIES			
Accounts Payable	14.3	18.0	25.0
Accrued Pay. Taxes	3.0	3.0	3.0
Accrued Expenses	2.5	5.0	7.5
Current LTD			20.0
Total Cur. Liab.	19.8	26.0	55.5
LONG-TERM DEBT	135.0	135.0	215.0
TOTAL LIABILITIES	154.8	161.0	250.5
EQUITY			
Common Stock	1.0	1.0	1.0
Paid-in Capital	250.0	250.0	250.0
Retained Earnings	(24.3)	163.9	389.9
Total Equity	226.7	414.9	640.9
LIABILITIES & EQUITY	381.5	575.9	911.4

H. - FINANCIAL STRUCTURE

Gal-Tech is organized as a C-type corporation registered in Texas. Two thousand shares of common stock at $1 par value have been authorized and one thousand shares issued and held as shown below.

James Gallas	670 shares
Melvin Eisner	180
Barnes, attorney	50
Sliplock, attorney	50
Robert Williams	30
Frank Feldman	20

The patent upon which the melanin process is based is valued at $200,000 and is owned by James Gallas, 50 percent; Melvin Eisner, 15 percent; Barnes & Sliplock law firm, 15 percent; Frank Feldman, 15 percent; and Barnes, 5 percent. The proposed purchase of the patent by Gal-Tech would be accomplished by issuing notes payable in five years with interest only at 10 percent payable annually. These notes would be issued as follows: James Gallas, $100,000; Melvin Eisner, $25,000; and Frank Feldman, $10,000. The law firm would receive an immediate $65,000 payment for their interest in the patent once Gal-Tech is fully capitalized.

Gal-Tech will require initial funds of $250,000 to begin operations. Dr. Gallas is prepared to negotiate either debt or equity in exchange for the sum needed. The payback terms are also negotiable. The Pro-Forma Balance Sheet assumes that equity is used and that the 1000 shares are reapportioned rather than that additional stock is issued.

The funds received will be used to buyout the law firm's ownership in the patent, to provide capital equipment and provide working capital. No additional external funding is planned until the third year when $100,000 would be borrowed for expansion.

CASES

The small business cases that follow in this book are suitable as the basis for writing a Business Plan, class discussion, or preparing a written case analysis. The cases are basically self-sufficient. If a Business Plan is to be written, the student may need to do some research work on the industry or local conditions.

SYNOPSES OF CASES

1.   Flint Specialty Die, Inc.

Flint is a family-owned manufacturer of carbide dies located in Flint, Michigan. It sells primarily to the automotive industry. It sells its products directly to its customers. Flint has been chronically short of working capital.

2.   Hines Industries, Inc.

Hines is an individually-owned manufacturer of dynamic balancing equipment located in Ann Arbor, Michigan. Hines sells to the automotive aftermarket, electric motor, fan and other industries who manufacture rotating equipment where balance is critical. It sells its products primarily through manufacturer's representatives.

3.   Research Equipment Corporation and the MONITOR.

Research Equipment, located in Charleston, South Carolina, is a start-up situation that plans to manufacture and market a new fire detection system. It needs to establish financing and marketing distribution in order to begin operations.

4.   Fowler Tool & Die, Inc.

Fowler Tool is a family-owned manufacturer of tooling located in Livingston County, Michigan. Fowler sells almost exclusively to the automotive industry through direct contact by the owner.

5.   Waverly Pharmacy, Inc.

Waverly is a retail pharmacy located in Waverly, Ohio, and owned by three pharmacists. In addition to a retail pharmacy and separate gift shop, Waverly supplies prescriptions to nearby hospitals and nursing homes on a contract basis using prepackaged dosage forms.

87

6.   Health & Beauty Products Company.

       H & B is a closely-held packager and marketer of over-the-counter diet aids located in Decatur, Illinois. H & B buys its products in bulk and packages them in various sizes for sale to pharmacy chain stores as well as retail pharmacies. It was purchased by the present three owners under a leveraged buyout arrangement from a large conglomerate. After a rough beginning, H & B has recently experienced rapid growth. Heavy rebates are used as a basic marketing strategy.

7.   Miller Stamping & Die, Inc.

       Miller Stamping is a family-owned company selling to the automotive industry. It is faced with an ethical dilemma concerning the primary owner that threatens the very existence of the company.

8.   Thompson Products Company.

       Thompson Products is a family-owned wholesale pet food and supply company located in Maumee, Ohio. Thompson sells to retail pet stores in the northwestern Ohio southeastern Michigan area. The company has had a mixed record of profitability and is experiencing cash flow problems.

9.   How Do You Get Apples From An ELM?

       ELM Group, which was individually owned, was the manufacturer's representative for Apple Computer for the state of Michigan before Apple decided to use their own sales force. The company is faced with developing a new strategy as a result of Apple's change in marketing strategy. Some ethical issues are also presented in the case.

10.   Encore.

       The last case.

FLINT SPECIALTY DIE, INC.

As Bill Brewer thought about the continuing cash flow and negative net working capital problems facing the company, he reminded himself that these problems had existed from the beginning. Bill's father, Fred, who was President of Flint Specialty Die, Inc., began his association with the company in 1960 as a manufacturer's representative. He also represented fifteen other accounts. In March, 1967, one of the two partners who owned Flint died and Fred bought his half of the company from the estate. The balance sheet at the final closing of the sale unexpectedly showed working capital had been depleted and thus the problem began.

In 1971 Flint Specialty Die, Inc., bought out the other original partner's half so that Fred Brewer owned all of the 6,250 outstanding shares. In 1980 Bill Brewer, who was the Vice President, bought 375 shares from his father. It was planned that he would buy or inherit the balance of the outstanding stock over the next several years. Thus in the long run Flint's problems as well as its many strengths would be Bill Brewer's concern alone.

The Product

Flint Specialty Die, Inc., was a tool and die shop located in Flint, Michigan, which specialized in machining carbide dies. Flint bought unfinished carbide die blanks, finished the carbide, and mounted the carbide dies into tool steel holders. These carbide dies were primarily used by Flint's customers to cold form large quantities of metal parts. Cold forming is forging done cold with a power hammer in a progressive manner in a series of dies. The company tried to specialize in areas other shops did not like to do or could not do. The dies for the transaxle for front-wheel drive cars were an example of this policy.

Flint purchased most of its unfinished carbide dies from General Carbide Corporation located in Greensburg, Pennsylvania. General Carbide's manufacturing process is shown schematically in Exhibit I. The final sintering at 2500° F. to 2750° F. consolidates the parts to near 100 percent density. A large degree of shrinkage occurs during the sintering process -- approximately 17 percent linearly and 45 percent volumetrically. The sintered parts are then provided to shops such as Flint for final sizing, grinding and polishing.

Carbides have several unique properties. Wear resistance to abrasion is very high, outlasting steel alloys by 3 to 1. Carbides have an extremely high modulus of elasticity or resistance to bending under load which is two to three times that of steel. Carbides

---

have a torsional strength about twice that of high-speed steel. Compressive strength is extremely high with carbides being used in pressing applications of over one million pounds per square inch (PSI). Corrosion resistance is also high. The main disadvantage to carbides other than its high cost is its brittleness in tension. This limits interference fits to .0005 inch.

Some of the sizes and shapes produced by General Carbide are shown in Exhibit II. Flint specialized in the machining for cold heading shown in the lower part of the exhibit. Quality and service were stressed by Flint. The final finish on the part was always better than that specified by the customer.

Flint provided the customer's finished part drawing to General Carbide who then designed its part oversize so that adequate material will be available in the sintered part to provide for Flint's machining operations. Flint checked the incoming parts from General Carbide to determine how much tolerance was available. This check was made by the operator doing the machining. If allowances beyond common practice were found, an adjustment in the price to Flint was made since carbides were very expensive to remake.

Manufacturing

A chart that indicates how the company functioned as an organization is shown in Exhibit III. Bill Brewer, who was 33 years old in 1982, assumed the Vice President position in 1971 and was responsible for all plant operations and in addition spent about 10 percent of his time selling jobs and 10 percent estimating jobs. He went through his apprentice training at Flint Specialty Die, and he also had taken several management courses at Flint Community College. He characterized his management style as participatory. He did all of the fixturing planning for the company.

Direct supervision of the machinists was carried out jointly by the two foremen, Jim Roeb and John Smitz. Each man had been with Flint for about fourteen years. Jim Roeb was strong in the area of advanced technology and setup while John Smitz was stronger in dealing with people. The foremen were responsible for hiring, firing and supervising employees, scheduling, and doing the processing for machining each job. They also did some direct labor work. Typically 400 jobs from 25 different customers might be in the shop at any one time. A typical job took 1 1/2 months to complete from the time the material was ordered and consisted of less than ten pieces.

Flint rented 6,200 square feet in an industrial park in Flint, Michigan. About 2,000 square feet were used for storage of tool steel, carbide, and tools and the balance for manufacturing. The manufacturing space was tightly filled with universal type machines as listed below.

Number	Description
1	Extrusion Hone
7	ID/OD Combination Grinder
2	OD Universal Grinder
1	ID Universal Grinder
1	Reciprocating Hone
2	Rotary Surface Grinder
5	Plane Surface Grinder
3	High Speed Polishing Lathe
3	19" Engine Lathe
2	Electric Discharge Machine (EDM)
3	Vertical Mill
2	Vertical Drill Press
1	Shaper
1	Cut-off Saw
1	350 Ton Hydraulic Assembly Press
1	650 Ton Hydraulic Assembly Press (due in 9/82)]

The company also had much special purpose tooling, gauging and quality control apparatus. All heat treating of tool steel parts that hold the carbide die inserts was performed by outside contract.

Employees did not belong to a union and a union had never attempted to organize the company. Employees had been with the company from 1 to 14 years. No one had ever quit voluntarily although five or six had been fired for various reasons. The company's policy was to pay above the average wage in the area based on word-of-mouth reports from employees and business associates. Wages ranged from $6 to $13.75 per hour depending upon skill and experience with an average of about $10.25 per hour. Fringe benefits included life, hospitalization, emergency accident, major medical and dental insurance, paid vacations, and paid holidays. Tuition was reimbursed if the subject was related to the employee's work. Interest-free loans up to the equivalent of one week's pay were made for tool purchases made by employees.

Pay raises were given as often as quarterly based upon merit if the company was doing well. A blanket raise was given once a year if the company was doing well. Seniority was only used to determine when an employee could take his vacation since only 20 percent could be gone at any one time. Layoffs were governed by the skills needed to do the work in the shop at that time.

Cost control was maintained manually. A 5" by 8" card as shown in Exhibit IV was used for each tool number. The secretaries filled in the data by summarizing the daily job cards made out by each employee. Subsequent orders for the same tool were shown on the same card.

An estimate form as shown in Exhibit V was developed for each job as it was estimated by either of the Brewers. The back of the form carried the detailed labor usage by individual employee. The labor groups shown on the Form consisted of the following:

Group 1 - Lathes, Mills
Group 2 - OD, ID, Form Grinders
Group 3 - Top & Bottom, Surface Grinders
Group 4 - EDM, Finish Polish

The form when completed provided a comparison between the actual costs and the price quoted for the job. Labor was priced at $13.00 per hour for estimating purposes and 100 percent of the labor figure was used to cover all overhead. Material and outside services such as heat treat were priced at cost. To the sum of all of these costs was added a percentage figure for profit based on what the traffic would bear. Sometimes the company "farmed out" an entire job to a small carbide shop, if not much precision was needed, and added 10 percent to cover Flint's profit and overhead.

A manually prepared shipping report was made out monthly showing the job number, customer, price, material, subcontracts, labor plus 100 percent and estimated profit. A summary of completed orders shipped by month for 1981 is shown in Exhibit VI. Note that this exhibit did not include the partially completed orders that were shipped. A final yearly summary report showing sales and profit by month was made for 1981.

Labor performance versus the original estimate was evaluated on a subjective basis. Bill Brewer had in mind developing standards of some kind to aid in this evaluation.

Marketing

Fred Brewer, the president, who was 70 years old in 1982, was in charge of marketing. He was assisted by a salesman, Robert Jones, who was hired in April, 1981. From January, 1981, through June, 1982, the company was represented by a manufacturer's representative in Ohio but this firm was dropped because of unsatisfactory results. Fred did most of the estimating for jobs although Bill did some.

Selling was done through direct sales calls. Bob Jones spent all of his time calling on customers. Fred Brewer did more of the long distance and preliminary calls often combining these with vacation trips. Leads for new customers were obtained by word-of-mouth and noticing where industry was locating, i.e., Texas. New industry ideas were followed up by using the Thomas Register to pinpoint the location of specific potential customers.

The company's advertising was limited to the Thomas Register, the Harris Book and the Society of Carbide Engineers' quarterly magazine. A color brochure describing the company's facilities and capabilities was used to promote sales. These brochures were usually handed out on a personal sales call.

The company had about eighty active customers who were primarily in the automotive field. Exhibit VII shows the company's major customers in 1981, which illustrates Pareto's Law at work. Bill believed "Price is the #1 consideration for the customer" although the company brochure says, "Our difference is service." The company's favorable sales growth during the severe recession in the automotive industry was due to "higher penetration." Bill said "competition is dropping the ball by not servicing their customers and their quality is down." Flint's three major competitors were located in Romulus, Harbor Beach, and Melvindale, Michigan. Flint tried to eliminate smaller jobs that seemed less profitable and avoided small "header shops." This policy resulted in no bad debts in 1981.

Got more good customers or fewer but larger.

Although pricing was currently very tight because of the recession, Bill believed Flint "could get more business even if the recession continued or got worse." Flint was currently seeking new customers in Ohio, particularly in the Dayton area, because the Brewers thought this was the coming technical/industrial area. They were also actively seeking jobs in Texas -- one new customer was Walker Manufacturing, who made mufflers for automobiles and trucks. General Magnetic, a producer of ferrite magnets that were formed from powdered metal, was another relatively new customer. In 1981 Flint made 1,280 quotes for approximately twelve million dollars and received two million dollars in orders, which illustrated the state of competition. The company did do rework jobs and was now marketing a polishing bit for die maintenance.

Cold-formed parts made from carbide dies could replace parts made on a screw machine if sufficient volume was available. Exhibit VIII shows the successive parts from a five-step progressive die made by Flint. The tooling cost of these dies was about $150,000 but the customer's labor costs were only one-tenth of that used for screw machines. This part was used in automotive steering gear in large volume.

Financial Condition

Flint retained a local firm of certified public accountants to prepare quarterly income statements, balance sheets, and analyses of manufacturing overhead and selling, general and administrative expenses. Exhibits IX, X, XI and XII show these statements for 1978 through the first half of 1982, respectively. Accounts receivable were pledged as collateral for the bank loan. Trade accounts payable represented approximately eight months' interest-free credit extension by General Carbide, Flint's major supplier of material.

Bill Brewer was currently stressing keeping cash in the company. After delivery of the new assembly press in September, 1982, which will cost $67,000, he said no more machine purchases would be made until cash flow improved. Expansion of the business was actively being considered as a way to increase sales and profits. Another 1000 square feet of shop space and 1000 square feet of office space for a design area was needed, but there was no room on the present site. Presently the customers did all design work, but, if the design space were available, a designer/sales engineer and two

Hold off on expansion?

93

purchase computer is ok

draftsmen would be needed to provide this new service. Also, more management people might be needed to achieve higher productivity or higher volume. Bill thought a small computer would be useful in maintaining financial data and particularly useful in estimating jobs and following their progress. Still another longer-range proposal was the establishment of another shop, six to nine thousand square feet of floor space, in the Dayton area, which was estimated to cost $170,000. The company presently does 42 percent of its business in the Dayton area.

As Bill thought of these longer-term moves, he pragmatically came back to the current cash flow situation and mused, "First things first." The first half of 1982 had brought some higher expenses. The increase in professional services had been due to legal fees over an employee discrimination suit alleging the employee handbook had not been followed in laying him off. He sued for $10,000 and Flint finally settled for $1,000 just before the trial because of the tremendous costs expended that far. Bill thought that "Since the company was right, it was a matter of principle" but "Standing up for principle can be costly." Bill also wondered what his financial needs would be to support a continued growth rate of 25 percent per year and how he would finance the new hydraulic assembly press arriving in September.

EXHIBIT I
FLINT SPECIALITY DIE, INC.

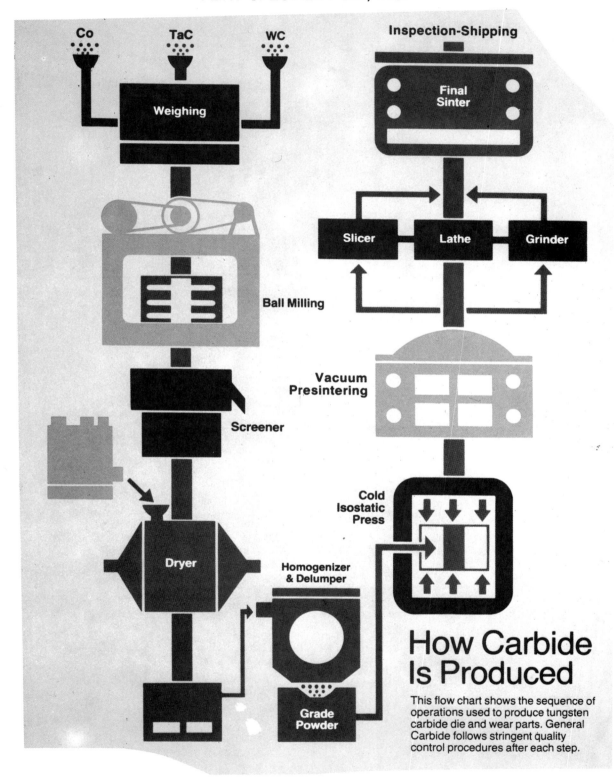

How Carbide Is Produced

This flow chart shows the sequence of operations used to produce tungsten carbide die and wear parts. General Carbide follows stringent quality control procedures after each step.

EXHIBIT II
FLINT SPECIALTY DIE, INC.

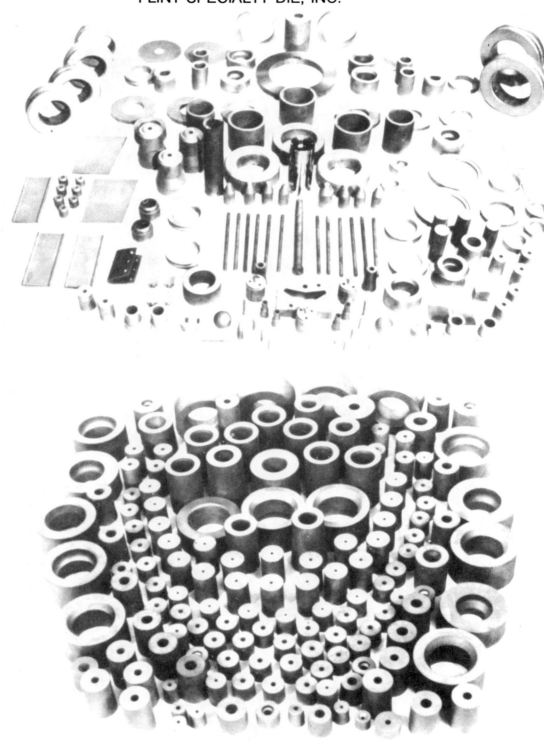

Included here is a selection of cold heading and cold extrusion die inserts

96

EXHIBIT V
FLINT SPECIALTY DIE, INC.
JOB ESTIMATE FORM

CUSTOMER _____ P.O. # _____ JOB # _____

PART # _____ QUANTITY _____ DATE DUE _____

UNIT PRICE _____ LOT PRICE _____ DATE OF SHIPMENT:

ESTIMATOR _____ PROJECT MANAGER _____

COST SUMMARY								
	HOURS				COSTS			
LABOR	UNIT	TOTAL	ACTUAL	VAR.	UNIT	TOTAL	ACTUAL	VAR.
GROUP 1								
GROUP 2								
GROUP 3								
GROUP 4								
TOTAL								

REVIEW COMMENTS:

MATERIAL				
O.S.				
TOTAL PRIME				
% O.H.				
B.E.				
% PROFIT				
BID				

DATE	PURCHASE-ITEMS (Vendor)	COST
		Total

DATE	OUTSIDE SERVICES (Vendor)	COST
		Total

99

DATE	OPERATIONS	NAME	HOURS	TOTAL HOURS	TOTAL HOURS

JOB # _____   LABOR DETAIL

EXHIBIT VI
FLINT SPECIALTY DIE, INC.
SUMMARY OF MONTHLY SHIPMENTS - 1981
(In Dollars)

Month	Completed Orders	Material	Outside Services	2 x Labor	Gross Profit
January	146,044	60,841	3,396	52,975	28,832
February	175,450	72,811	6,953	62,214	33,472
March	229,153	81,558	9,648	95,951	41,996
April	216,383	73,465	11,816	80,923	50,179
May	166,313	64,546	5,516	62,335	33,916
June	225,653	86,675	13,796	81,770	43,412
July	113,165	35,648	9,249	48,954	19,314
August	212,758	85,534	7,705	64,343	55,176
September	245,055	90,656	12,805	94,656	46,938
October	235,064	86,293	17,909	85,614	45,248
November	170,848	56,965	8,303	69,286	36,294
December	185,239	52,728	2,311	67,178	63,022
Total	2,321,125	847,720	109,407	866,199	497,799

1,053 Jobs

EXHIBIT VII
FLINT SPECIALTY DIE, INC.
CUSTOMER LIST - 1981
(In Dollars)

Customer	Sales	Profit	Percent
1. General Motors			
Plant A	339,620	53,660	15.8%
Plant C	161,153	26,371	16.4%
Plant E	144,688	99,799	69.0%
Plant T	112,934	18,781	16.6%
Plant Q	88,776	24,509	27.6%
Plant M	76,230	12,800	16.8%
Plant H	46,840	7,285	15.6%
Plant Y	41,766	5,716	13.7%
Plant Z	22,180	9,071	40.9%
Plant F	14,754	2,290	15.5%
Plant O	10,718	1,919	17.9%
Plant J	7,863	1,418	18.0%
Overseas	7,070	1,166	16.5%
Plant R	613	(188)	-30.7%
Total GM	1,075,205	264,597	24.6%
2. 1093	319,469	N.A.	
3. 1100	176,746	76,728	43.4%
4. Ford Motor	174,104	6,209	3.6%
5. 1246	147,191	34,536	23.5%
6. 1231	97,966	12,113	12.4%
7. 1052	96,128	9,895	10.3%
8. 1074	90,961	18,533	20.4%
9. 1150	87,995	24,093	27.4%
10. 1123	86,740	15,740	18.1%
11. Chrysler	61,326	6,400	10.4%
12. 1254	32,651	2,791	8.5%
13. 1182	21,813	2,731	12.5%
14. 1088	14,570	3,328	22.8%
15. 1205	14,378	4,390	30.5%
16. 1012	11,785	3,959	33.6%
17. 1034	11,654	(921)	-7.9%
18. 1121	11,331	3,698	32.6%
Subtotal	2,532,013	488,820	22.1%
Others (37)	111,311	(3,489)	-3.1%
Total	2,643,324	485,331	20.9%

EXHIBIT VIII
FLINT SPECIALTY DIE, INC.
PARTS FROM FIVE STEP CARBIDE DIE

EXHIBIT IX
FLINT SPECIALTY DIE, INC.
INCOME STATEMENT
(In Dollars)

	1978	1979	1980	1981	1982 (6 months)
NET SALES	1,413,379	2,035,178	1,988,865	2,546,963	1,568,769
COST OF SALES					
Materials	515,675	834,198	709,455	867,793	515,440
Subcontractors	66,725	124,680	145,203	187,940	136,293
Freight	2,871	4,546	5,293	8,561	5,582
Direct Labor	339,520	463,015	510,445	578,929	352,482
Mfg. Overhead	280,573	357,870	356,665	374,350	257,851
Total	1,205,364	1,784,309	1,727,061	2,017,573	1,267,648
GROSS PROFIT	208,015	250,869	261,804	529,390	301,121
SELLING & ADM. EXP.	184,500	218,449	232,520	368,198	243,213
OPERATING INCOME	23,515	32,420	29,284	161,192	57,908
OTHER CHARGES					
Interest	20,848	24,223	35,224	43,338	24,791
Gain on Sales of Fixed Assets		(1,250)	(35,000)	(6,250)	
Total	20,848	22,973	224	37,088	24,791
Income Before Taxes	2,667	9,447	29,060	124,104	33,117
Income Taxes less Investment Credit					
NET INCOME	2,667	9,447	29,060	124,104	33,117

Handwritten annotations include: "Sales growth = 17.3%"; "~20%"; "Cathy will talk about Cost control"; "Selling & Adm. 243,213 - 32.36%"; "assume no tax???"; ".21 .76 2.32 9.93 5.28"; "EPS .02 .075 .23 .99 .53"; ".21 275% 206.7% 33% till here -46.7%"; "267% Ann. L growth rate"; "Annual growth = 90%"; "125,000 shares"; "Annual growth = 126%"; "write (See p.66) put 5 for Lezmu"; "Anticipate Future ROE profitability figure"; "DO for Lezmu 1983-85"; "ROE = 3.4% 11.2% 24.9% 12.5% 13.2%"; "104"

EXHIBIT X
FLINT SPECIALTY DIE, INC.
BALANCE SHEET
(In Dollars)

	1978	1979	1980	1981	1982 (6 months)
CURRENT ASSETS					
Cash	266	1,164	6,765	16,075	10,049
Accounts Rec.					
Trade	87,103	172,426	250,599	221,781	257,963
Other		654	606		
Inventories	175,925	244,955	139,366	368,154	256,114
Prepaid Expenses			5,980		2,514
Total	263,294	419,199	403,316	606,010	526,640
FIXED ASSETS					
Machinery	494,145	588,651	590,170	688,944	798,535
Automotive Equip.	22,081	25,201	28,201	49,829	49,829
Office Equip.	5,679	5,679	8,718	12,120	12,936
Total	521,905	619,531	627,089	750,893	861,300
Depreciation	325,898	346,278	346,309	372,638	398,503
Net Total	196,007	273,253	280,780	378,255	462,797
Leasehold Improve.	821	3,106	4,650	4,650	4,650
Amortization		1,397	2,271	3,146	3,776
Net Total	821	1,709	2,379	1,504	874
Net Fixed Assets	196,828	274,962	283,159	379,759	463,671
OTHER ASSETS					
Deposits	5,250	5,250	5,250	7,750	7,750
Organ. Exp.	369	369	369	369	369
Cash Value of $200,000 Officers Life Ins. *	15,625	19,475	20,825	562	1,238
Total	21,244	25,094	26,444	8,681	9,357
TOTAL ASSETS	481,366	719,255	712,919	994,450	999,668

* less loan of $26,550 in 1981

EXHIBIT X
(continued)
FLINT SPECIALTY DIE, INC.
BALANCE SHEET
(In Dollars)

	1978	1979	1980	1981	1982 (6 months)
CURRENT LIABILITIES					
Notes Pay. - Bank (Secured by A.R.)	72,347	146,502	102,643	200,212	69,400
Officers Loan	6,250	13,750	13,750	16,250	16,250
Accounts Payable	223,055	374,305	392,416	421,970	532,466
Accruals					
Interest			2,000	2,940	6,190
Salaries & Wages	11,646	9,123	15,978	30,663	27,380
Taxes	3,222	7,605	6,543	4,836	1,903
Insurance				5,821	
Income Taxes	3,653	7,556	9,006	20,625	9,123
Current Portion of Long-Term Debt	23,750	22,536	22,536	44,651	34,792
Total	343,923	581,377	564,872	747,968	697,504
LONG-TERM DEBT	59,287	53,275	31,384	5,715	28,280
TOTAL LIABILITIES	403,210	634,652	596,256	753,683	725,784
EQUITY					
Common Stock ($10)	125,000	125,000	125,000	125,000	125,000
Retained Earnings	53,156	62,603	91,663	215,767	248,884
Subtotal	178,156	187,603	216,663	340,767	373,884
Treasury Stock 6,250 shares	100,000	100,000	100,000	100,000	100,000
Total Equity	78,156	87,603	116,663	240,767	273,884
TOTAL LIA. & EQUITY	481,366	722,255	712,919	994,450	999,668

[Handwritten annotations:] Use to help pay employee dividends other competition — Sell stock — 5% summary — EQUITY SALE — Retained earnings were to high. Use to pay some A R & L.T.D.

EXHIBIT XI
FLINT SPECIALTY DIE, INC.
ANALYSIS OF MANUFACTURING OVERHEAD
(In Dollars)

	1978	1979	1980	1981	1982 (6 months)
Plant Supervision	51,449	91,405	56,283	51,618	30,966
Supplies	59,393	73,225	60,992	91,334	47,820
Repairs & Maint.	14,579	22,391	15,439	12,015	6,272
Payroll Taxes	30,984	40,604	39,039	46,149	41,868
Employee Ins. Bfts.	28,549	34,235	35,189	44,862	36,336
Bonuses	3,487	2,688	94		
General Taxes	4,480	4,064	6,829	7,254	5,250
Janitor & Delivery	15,581	18,883	17,840	21,782	11,916
Shop Travel	1,550	1,895	2,425	2,455	246
Insurance	23,479	23,104	37,520	36,102	17,563
Laundry	1,951	1,697	2,056	2,318	1,440
Engrng. & Develop.	8,539	4,250	94	8,375	
Depr. & Amort.	10,616	23,538	27,356	36,079	22,054
Rent	21,375	22,500	22,500	22,500	11,250
Utilities	10,225	10,941	12,569	12,873	9,908
Inv. Decrease (Inc.)	(5,664)	(17,550)	20,440	(21,366)	9,168
Indirect Labor					5,794
Total	280,573	357,870	356,665	374,350	257,851

EXHIBIT XII
FLINT SPECIALTY DIE, INC.
ANALYSIS OF SELLING, ADMINISTRATIVE & GENERAL EXPENSE
(In Dollars)

	1978	1979	1980	1981	1982 (6 months)
Salaries					
—Officers	76,375	80,750	83,831	117,680	73,596
Office	14,880	14,729	15,004	11,865	6,024
Sales				19,430	13,675
Auto & Travel	14,041	18,569	22,033	27,916	21,701
Promotion & Advert.	22,585	42,346	46,601	55,304	25,458
Payroll Taxes	3,750	3,750	4,000	5,250	7,500
Commissions	12,969	10,945	2,854	30,573	15,725
Employee Benefits	5,309	4,866	8,050	23,631	
Retirement Payment			3,375	6,500	3,250
Depreciation	4,513	4,474	7,985	9,094	4,440
Supplies	3,662	5,861	5,415	6,371	4,891
Dues & Subscriptions	3,640	4,076	4,569	6,615	3,786
Officer's Life Ins.	3,295	3,388	5,887	(5,687)	3,076
Telephone	7,345	7,549	8,866	11,414	6,856
Prof. Services	4,031	11,496	8,124	14,976	43,360
Donations	446	431	625	1,150	419
State Taxes	5,625	5,000	5,000	25,000	8,750
Miscellaneous	2,034	219	301	1,116	706
Total	184,500	218,449	232,520	368,198	243,213

108

HINES INDUSTRIES, INC.

In June, 1984, Gordon Hines, the President of Hines Industries, Inc., reflected upon the first quarter of the 1985 fiscal year with mixed feelings. His marketing strategy of "niching" had been successful. He had started his second company in sixteen years when he began Hines Industries in 1979. The first three years were characterized by rapid growth in sales but the recession took its toll in 1983. Exhibits I, II, and III show the Balance Sheet, Income Statement, and Expense Statements for the fiscal year's 1981 through 1984. The first quarter of 1985 looked as if it would be near the entire sales of 1984 and a profit of 12 percent to 15 percent should be produced. Maybe this high growth rate would produce a new set of problems.

Gordon Hines is not new to the entrepreneur ranks. In February, 1968 he founded Balance Technology, Inc., in Ann Arbor, Michigan, which manufactures and markets balancing equipment and vibration instruments. Bal Tec grew rapidly, but Gordon lost absolute control of the company when he needed outside money, a mistake he is determined to not make again. Eventually he was squeezed out of the management and finally sold his stock at a considerable profit to an outsider who in turn squeezed out the management that followed Gordon.

Gordon Hines has an unusual background in relation to the businesses he founded. He has a degree in psychology and at one time was a social worker for the Chicago YMCA. Later, while selling insurance, he successfully sold policies to two partners in a balancing equipment company who really did not have the funds to buy insurance. They were so impressed by Gordon's sales ability that they made him an offer to enter their business. Gordon accepted and soon was successfully selling machines and became involved in redesigning and improving them as well.

Gordon, who is 54, has a natural aptitude for visualizing how things look and work and can quickly conceptualize his ideas. He is a problem solver. His father was an engineer and took Gordon into work on weekends with him so that Gordon learned early about machinery and the engineering behind machinery. He completed two years of engineering work at the University of Illinois before his intense interest in people drew him toward psychology.

It is certainly a fair statement to say that Gordon Hines is Hines Industries. His creativity is in evidence everywhere -- marketing, design, manufacturing and even finance.

PRODUCTS

Hines Industries presently has five basic product lines, which are shown in Exhibit V. These machines are known as hard-bearing balancing machines. They come in a number of different models with different features as shown in the exhibit. All of the lines are available with microprocessor analyzers. The DL, Drive Line Balancing Machine, and the HC, Hard Crankshaft Balancing Machine, were the products that were first developed. The HC500A model has been sold to more than 120 customers in 33 states and 4 foreign countries. The HC Balancer is sold primarily to the automotive aftermarket for high performance and racing cars.

The DL line is used to balance the drive shaft for cars and trucks. Because of the heavy weights and usage given to trucks, their drive shafts, unlike cars, have to be replaced about every 50-75,000 miles and, of course, require balancing at that time. Dana Corporation is the exclusive sales agent for the Dana High Tech Driveline Package. In September, 1983, Dana placed a large order for ten units totaling $600,000. Shipments against this order began in February, 1984, and $321,000 remains in backlog as of April 30, 1984. A second order from Dana for $600,000 was received in June, 1984.

The other three product lines, which are sold in several sizes, are the HO or Horizontal Overhung Machine, the HVR or Hard Vertical Rotator Machine, and the HVS or Hard Vertical Static Machine. Balancing is important in parts that rotate in order to minimize or eliminate vibration. Parts that are not balanced create noise and excessive wear. These machines are sold to industrial customers to balance fans, pump impellers, pulleys, etc. These machines sell for about $22,000 each, but the HVR machine can reach $66,000.

Basically balancing can be done in one or two planes, depending upon the size or shape of the part to be balanced. The balancing equipment finds the center of the mass and determines how much weight must be added to or removed from a determined point or points on the part to balance it. Elapsed time for balancing varies between 15 minutes to 1 1/2 hours in the case of engine balancing plus time for loading and unloading the part. The heart of a balancing machine is the microprocessor, which quickly senses and performs the necessary calculations. Exhibit IX shows a schematic diagram of a balancer.

ORGANIZATION

Hines Industries is organized along functional lines. Exhibit VII depicts the organization as of June, 1984. Gordon Hines is the President and sole owner of the company. There are 46 employees including 18 temporary or part-time employees. Temporary employees do not receive all of the fringe benefits and are subject to being laid off first should a cutback be necessary. Five of the key employees -- Ron Anderson, Ken Cooper, Joann Huff, Mike Myers and Len Salenbien -- were with Gordon Hines at

Balance Technology and came to Hines Industries at various times after Gordon organized his new venture.

MARKETING

Marketing is managed in an overall way by Gordon Hines through three employees. Joann Huff is responsible for the automotive aftermarket. She joined Hines in June, 1980, after being with Bal Tec in secretarial and sales positions for nine years. She supervises 20 manufacturer's representatives employing 45 salesmen who sell the products to the ultimate customers. Mike Myers is responsible for the Drive Line machines, which are sold through several manufacturer's representatives. Industrial sales are handled by John Ramer through 3 manufacturer's representatives and some direct sales to customers. Bob Edwards was recently hired to cover the Ohio and West Virginia territory directly for the company since it is difficult to get qualified general reps for this market.

Manufacturer's representatives are paid on a commission basis. A 15 percent commission is paid on the basic machine and 10 percent to 15 percent is paid on added components for the basic machine. Advertising support is provided in trade magazines to get inquiries. Exhibit VI shows a typical advertisement that appeared in the June, 1984, issue of *Jobber Retailer*.

Products are built to order so no finished products are stocked. A substantial backlog of orders is considered desirable as an indicator of future sales and as an aid to scheduling production. Exhibit IV is a sales analysis for the 12 months ending in April, 1984. It shows the monthly billings and bookings by product line and the backlog.

Automotive Aftermarket

The automotive aftermarket for balancing has been primarily for high performance cars. It is believed to include the potential for 100 to 150 balancers per year. Hines HC-500 balancer for this market sells for about $16,500. The market potential has improved since the EPA and OSHA have backed off interfering with racing.

The automotive aftermarket has two other competitors: Winona Van Norman, which is now a foreign-made copy of Hines equipment, and Stewart Warner, who is now engaging in "puffing" to overcome Hines' advantage. To aid the marketing by manufacturer's reps, who also handle other machinery for rebuilding engines, Joann Huff advertises in five trade journals for the performance and rebuilding industry: *Automotive Rebuilder, Specialty and Custom Dealer, Jobber Retailer, National Dragster*, and *Circle Track*. Six half-page, two-color advertisements were placed in 1983, costing between $1,200 to $2,000 depending upon the publication. She has increased advertising in 1984 to one per month including some full-page ads which are 1 1/2 times the cost of the half-page ads. She would like to increase advertising to two per month in the latter part of

1984. She gets opinions from respected users as to which journals are most effective and tries to time Hines ads with articles about balancing, editorials about balancing or issues preceding trade shows. Extra copies of the journals preceding trade shows are often distributed free at the shows. An example of an article about engine balancing is shown in Exhibit X.

Special mailings, using articles such as Exhibit X, and telephone campaigns are conducted to promote to the automotive aftermarket. Mailings typically range between 200 to 600 but have gone as high as 2,500. The membership lists of associations such as Automotive Engine Rebuilders Association, Automotive Service Industries Association and Specialty Engine Machine Association are used for the mailings.

The company attends at least six trade shows per year. A balancing machine is displayed and Joann Huff as well as area manufacturer's reps are in attendance. Brochures describing the various machines made by Hines are available for use at trade shows as well as for use by manufacturer's reps and company sales personnel. Gordon Hines also attended the important Las Vegas AERA show in June, 1984. Seven orders totaling $175,000 were obtained as a result of the show. Other shows of the associations previously mentioned are held in March and October, respectively. The National Dragster show is held in September, the Oval Track show in February and the Pacific Automotive Show in March. Other wholesaler shows in individual states are attended by manufacturer's reps and a balancer is sent.

Joann Huff sees her job as being an educational process -- first manufacturer's reps and then customers. She said, "The market is there but needs to be made. About half of the rebuilders always balance and the other half never balance." An engine will last 50 percent longer if balanced, which is an important cost factor since the initial cost of engines is causing more and more to be rebuilt rather than replaced.

Diesel engine rebuilding is a new market that the company will be emphasizing. It is estimated by Gordon Hines that 5 percent of all truck engines are rebuilt each year and that 20 plus million trucks are on the road. Joann plans to use the trade journal [Renews] for advertising, which costs $2,600 for a full page. A heavy-duty HC machine with extra bed length will be used for this market. Better drive line tooling has helped the servicing of this market.

Another market that has potential is rebuilding shops that also wish to do some industrial work such as repairing and rebuilding electric motor armatures, pump impellers, fans and blowers. A microprocessor can be added to the balancers for shops doing this kind of work. The machines are designed and built in a modular form. Therefore, by simply adding or changing certain components, it is possible to "culture whole new products" that can be assembled to satisfy customer requirements. New market segments could be entered in this same way.

The company has a table top version of the HC500 called the HC10TC for turbo charger balancing. The machine sells for $10,000. The only competitor is a company that curiously is called Heins. One trade show, Automotive Diesel Specialists, can be used.

Another market is the 100 firms making up the Production Engine Rebuilders Association (PERA). A typical firm rebuilds as high as 70 engines per day using used parts obtained from tearing down used engines. Their business is increasing since the smaller engines used in production cars do not last as long because of higher speeds used in the engines.

Still another market is the clutch rebuilder. An HVR balancer without all of the "bells and whistles" is used for this job and costs about $11,000 versus the normal HVR price of $20,000. The size of this market is not known but is more like the PERA described previously. The trade group, Automotive Parts Rebuilder Association, puts on one show each year. Hines has three competitors in this business segment.

Driveline Market

The Drive Line Balancer is used primarily to balance the drive shaft for trucks. They have to be replaced frequently because of the heavy weights involved and the many miles of use each year. The current DL balancer was redesigned from the original version to bring it into conformance with the other balancers Hines makes. It is similar to the crankshaft machine, HC series.

Gordon Hines, as he typically does, sold the original concept to Dana Corporation, which is now the exclusive sales agent for the Dana High Tech Drive Line Package. Gordon is intensively involved in the initial design and marketing of a new product for six months or so, often spending long hours at it, and, then, he "eases back so his whole body can come back up." Mike Myers, who sells about one DL balancer to other customers a month, also tries to handle the big Dana account but really needs some help. Mike has a BA degree from the University of Michigan, including 2 1/2 years of engineering, and worked at Bal Tec for 15 years in mechanical design, computer programming and sales before joining Hines in December, 1983. Mike is Hines' internal computer expert and often provides help for those using Hines' three computers. He also is somewhat involved in mechanical design although Gordon provides the major mechanical design concepts. Gordon Hines believes the Dana account has a potential for $2 million per year with another $500,00 of DL balancers sold to others.

In addition to the DL balancer, Hines makes two other products which are related to the balancer and sold as part of the package Dana buys for $60-75,000. These are a push-up press and a specialty lathe. This group of machines allows Dana to do eight specific jobs essential to rebuilding shafts -- weld cutoff, tube cut and chamfer, push up, pull out, straighten, weld, straighten, and balance. The package includes specialized tooling designed and built to Dana's specifications Dana, in turn, sells the unit to the ultimate customer.

Industrial Market

The industrial market includes sales of the HO, HVR and HVS products with several size models of each to industrial producers of original equipment (OEM) using impellers, fans, blowers, pulleys, etc. John Ramer heads this activity and he and Bob Edwards personally sell the products along with the three manufacturer's reps. John Ramer has a degree in business administration from the University of Michigan and is an artist. He joined Hines in 1982 as his first full-time job. It is believed that there is a great deal of business to be had within a 300 to 500 mile radius and, therefore, company sales personnel can be very effective.

Both John and Bob try to stay "off the road" and do most of their selling by telephone and sending out literature. They use lists of pump and blower manufacturers obtained from their trade association, as well as referrals, to make their calls. Thus they make only "hot calls." Gordon Hines believes the market is too narrow to advertise in publications like the *American Machinist* so he prefers the "rifle" approach instead of a "shotgun." He believes the HVR market is $4 million per year and, if the balancing could be done automatically, the market could be $20 million. HC balancers are also being sold for industrial use. Hines is being successful against established competitors.

Balancing Service

The company offers a balancing service for local customers who need relatively small quantities balanced. The idea behind this venture is to provide a service to smaller customers, gain experience with other items needing balancing and, hopefully, sell balancers to the service customers when they grow large enough to warrant their own machine. For instance, Hines is now balancing 2,000 specialized parts per week for a Ford Motor supplier. This activity is managed by Robin Hines, Gordon's daughter. This activity, will be housed in a third building, along with demo units, containing 3,200 square feet which will be available July 1. This move will free up some of the space in the main building.

MANUFACTURING

Leonard Salenbien, 40 years old, is the manager of production. Prior to joining Hines he served in the same position at Balance Technology. He worked at Bal Tec for eleven years starting as a check-out technician and progressing to head of the service department before he became production manager there.

Hines Industries rents two buildings located in the light industrial area north of the Ann Arbor Airport. The main facility consists of 9,600 square feet located on one floor plus 1,600 square feet located on the second floor. Exhibit VIII shows the floor plan of the main plant. The second building, which is located nearby, contains 3,200 square feet. It is used for painting machines, storage of large parts, lumber storage, fabrication of pallets for shipping machines and storage of concrete bases for machines. Both buildings are quite crowded and thought has been given to the need for additional space. Unfortunately, the present buildings that are available or being built in the area are not big enough to house all of Hines' activities in one area.

The production area uses general purpose machines for the fabrication work. Most of the machinery was purchased used at auctions at very favorable prices. Later these machines were reworked by Hines to bring them up to the standards required. Some have been converted to numerical control using the microprocessors that Hines produces. The production equipment includes four lathes, two horizontal milling machines, six vertical milling machines, one jig borer, one radial arm drilling machine, one cylindrical ID/OD grinder, one cylindrical ID grinder, one face grinder, a Burgemaster machining center that is being retrofit for numerical control (NC) and a lathe retrofit to CNC. Hines makes many of its own parts and does the mechanical and electrical assembly work. Electronics assembly including the building of microprocessors is done on the second floor of the main building, which also includes mechanical drafting.

One of the unique features of the machines produced by Hines is the use of a precision-formed concrete base to provide the mass needed to support and dampen the balancing machines. These concrete bases are purchased locally from a company that uses the forms which were designed and built by Hines. Delivery time on the bases is a week so that it is not necessary to have many of the bulky units in stock.

All machines are thoroughly tested at Hines, using customer parts before they are shipped. Len Salenbien is often involved in the testing if trouble is encountered. An automotive aftermarket type machine such as the HC takes about two days to assemble and test if all of the parts are available. Hines also trains the customer's maintenance men at the Hines plant so that few field repairs by Hines are required.

Purchasing of standard parts from vendors is the responsibility of Dave Freed, who has been with Hines since August, 1983. He worked as a refrigeration contractor until three years ago when he was injured while water skiing. He subsequently took training on computers at Washtenaw Community College before joining Hines.

Dave gets verbal or written lists of materials required from seven or eight people who keep track of their own stock and determine what they need. These people and their area of responsibility are as follows:

Fran Longnecker -- crankshaft machines
Willie Woods -- shop materials and supplies
Gary Kwiecinski -- industrial machines, skidding and shipping

Dave Bloom (part time) -- industrial machines
Keith Kwiecinski -- painting
Larry Ketola -- special tooling and special parts for each machine
Kay Lamay (Doug Case's employee) -- electronics

Dave orders all of his parts by telephone. No purchase orders are sent to vendors. Dave maintains a list of purchase orders by number on the computer including all of the pertinent data on each order. Orders are placed by description of the part. No part numbers have been assigned by Hines and vendor part numbers are not used. Although Engineering is beginning to assign part numbers to mechanical parts required for the company's products, it has not yet decided if company part numbers will be assigned to standard purchased parts. A Bill of Material is not generated for each machine although the company wants to do this. In fact, the company does not presently have a comprehensive part numbering system.

Dave does not know how many different parts are in the products but believes there are at least 1,000 purchased parts, not counting internally manufactured parts. Partial inventories may be taken every six months or so. Parts are not actually counted but the quantity is estimated. There is no definite stockroom used but rather a series of stock locations by product assembly area. Parts may be stocked in more than one area. Sometimes parts are ordered a second time if an item is on back order. No production schedule is available.

Most of the parts Dave orders are available within a short time. Motors require a week and IC chips (integrated circuits) usually require a month. However, ICs could require 4 to 6 months if not in stock. Dave orders from vendors with whom Hines is on good financial terms based upon price, first, and delivery, second. Quality is important on some items.

Dave believes the company is "moving away from chaos" but not fast enough. He describes the big upswing in business in December, 1983, (Dana) was like a "cobra trying to swallow a pig." Although everyone knows basically how they fit in, what their job is, and how they do it, they are not enough aware of the company's goals and objectives, Dave believes. Items seem to be ordered on an emergency basis half of the time.

The big upswing in business created some cash flow problems, although Gordon Hines believes the worst is over. Since May, Dave has been required to check the price before ordering and he may be required to get approval for cash reasons. Sometimes he has ordered smaller quantities at a higher price in order to conserve cash. Sometimes he has delayed orders or challenged the size of orders. Sometimes, if a vendor required COD, Dave has had to find a new vendor since Gordon has said no COD shipments will be accepted.

116

Gordon and Len sometimes disagree on product design and ordering. Dave feels caught in the middle. About half of the time Gordon discusses the issue directly with Dave, thus resolving it. Dave would like to see more formal planning. Purchase requisition forms, which presumably will be used for preapproval before Dave sees them, are on order. The forms will be two part -- one for accounting and one for purchasing. If the originator wants a copy, a Xerox copy will be made.

Dave gets a copy of the Sales Order Information Form--Partial Release but is not sure why he gets it since he cannot order even long-delivery items based on this information. The form is used primarily by Ken Cooper to order outside mechanical items, he says.

Ken Cooper, whose responsibility is Materials Control, joined Hines in March, 1984. He worked at Bal Tec for 13 years and was Purchasing Manager when he left. Prior to Bal Tec, he worked in the machine shop at Bendix for 20 years. Ken orders some material directly and gets his purchase order numbers from Dave Freed. He subcontracts some of the mechanical parts work to outside firms on a time and material basis.

Ken schedules the shop and is supposed to schedule electronics but Doug Case really does it. Ken keeps a cardex inventory system of common manufactured parts. Based upon this information, he initiates orders for parts through Machining or through outside suppliers. The lot size ordered is based on previous experience with input from Willie Woods and Fran Longnecker. An inventory may be taken on individual items. Ken is trying to set up inventories by production area. He decides whether to make or buy an item.

Ken's goal is to get things running smoothly. He is getting shop costs by using the average actual hours secured from job tickets times $25 per hour, which includes burden. The actual cost of labor is about $7 per hour. If an item has not been made before, he estimates the cost based upon his previous experience.

Ken is concerned that production seems to always be behind and is "playing catch-up." He believes the men are learning but are operators and not machinists in that they cannot do setups well. Only WIllie Woods and Bob Boyce can do setups. There is not a formal training program. The last thing that gets made is customer tooling, which is what often creates the delays. He also believes more space may be needed soon now that the second Dana order has been received. Under ideal conditions he estimates 2 to 3 Dana Machines, 3 HCs and 3 HVRs or HOs could be assembled simultaneously if parts were available (maybe requiring multiple shifts) and if moves were carefully checked.

Ken describes the delivery commitment process in this way. Len Salenbien makes a tentative commitment to a sales person who has a potential order. If and when the order is actually received, it may be different than originally described. Also, other orders may have been received subsequent to the tentative commitment and be loaded into the shop. Thus the delivery commitment is frequently a problem. On the average, it takes two weeks from the beginning of assembly until the product is shipped but shipment could be delayed 6 to 8 weeks because of production planning problems, inadequate pretesting of components and delays in securing information and samples of customer parts for tooling fabrication.

ELECTRONIC DESIGN

The Electronic Design activity is conducted by Ron Anderson, who is 49 years old. Ron Anderson, who also worked for Gordon at Bal Tec, began working for Hines on a part-time basis but now is full-time. He has known Gordon personally for many years and began his work at Bal Tec as a consultant. He has a degree in electrical engineering and has specialized in electronic design. He had ten years' previous experience at the University of Illinois as director of electronics for the Chemistry Department, which involved developing specialized instrumentation. Ron tries to use standard techniques and approaches in designing the electronics for the products so that common modules are used in the various models whenever possible. Ron is happiest when there is some new design to be developed and admits to being bored when things are too routine.

ACCOUNTING

Dean Purdy, who is 55 years old, was hired in late March, 1984, as Controller. Dean had previously worked for Fansteel for 17 years. His last position was Controller of their V. R. Wesson Division plant at Ferndale, Michigan, which made tungsten carbide cutting tools. The Ferndale plant had 125 employees and 50,000 square feet of floor area. He also had previous experience with Midwest Machine Company which was an OEM for the auto industry. Thus Dean's background in the machining business fits well with Hines.

During his three months with Hines, Dean has learned the product line and internal workings of the company. He believes he has made progress in stabilizing the cash flow from receivables to payables. His personal priority is "to establish systems to do things in an orderly fashion" including inventory and production control and cost control.

The company presently uses two Altos computers, one with a 10 megabyte hard disk and one with 1 megabyte dual 8" floppy disks. The latter unit together with a small 64K dual 4 1/2" floppy disk computer is used by Purchasing. Thought has been given to buying a Radio Shack 30 megabyte hard disk computer for additional applications including accounting. Such a computer would cost about $15,000 including software.

Because the equipment for the industrial market and Dana typically have a longer delivery cycle than other products, Hines offers these customers, after receiving their order, a 2-5 percent discount if the customer will make an initial 30 percent down payment and will pay the balance within ten days after delivery. Gordon Hines believes this policy gives the company a competitive advantage in addition to improving the cash flow.

MANAGEMENT

Gordon Hines began to draw a $40,000 per year salary in May, 1984. Prior to that he was living off his proceeds from selling his Bal Tec stock. When asked how he spends his time at the company, he estimated the following: sales - 20 percent, design - 20 percent, general business - 20 percent, production - 25 percent, and new business planning - 15 percent. Gordon expects Dean Purdy will pick up a major share of his general business activities, which will free up some of Gordon's time to move into sales/design activities of other products or to develop new large accounts.

Gordon has also contemplated the need for a mechanical engineer who could handle design activities and manufacturing engineering activities. Such a person would be difficult to find and could be quite expensive in salary and relocation expenses. However, such a move would free Gordon from mechanical design activities, which do require a substantial amount of his time.

Gordon also would like to see all of the company's activities in a common location. He would continue to rent since he does not want to put scarce cash into "bricks and mortar." The location would need to be near the present location for the convenience of employees. The airport location is also convenient since Gordon shares an airplane with two other businessmen. Fortunately, the business that occupied the 3,200 square feet immediately adjoining Hines Industries is relocating to another part of the industrial park in July and Hines will be able to rent this space and combine it with the main plant area.

Gordon sees a strong growth potential for the company over the next two years barring another prolonged recession. He thinks fiscal 1985 should see $4 plus million in sales with the following year increasing another 50 percent. His overall management priorities are to manage cash first and profits second. In his view the October through December, 1984, period will set the stage for the following year.

EXHIBIT I
Hines Industries, Inc.
Balance Sheet
Years Ending February 28

	1981	1982	1983	1984
CURRENT ASSETS				
Cash	$9,005	$5,027	$11,361	$26,707
Accounts Receivable	96,509	124,905	129,413	215,222
Inventories				
Materials	60,448	33,715	83,176	269,268
Work in Process	35,656	135,031	21,794	45,219
	96,104	168,746	104,970	314,487
Loan Receivable, officer				49,935
Prepaid Expenses				
TOTAL CURRENT ASSETS	201,618	298,678	245,744	606,351
INVESTMENTS & OTHER ASSETS				
Investment in Affiliated Company				
Cash Value of Life Insurance				
PROPERTY & EQUIPMENT				
Leasehold Improvements	7,386	7,386	7,386	7,386
Machinery & Equipment	21,894	38,871	52,358	96,188
Office Equipment	5,451	7,680	13,604	29,557
Transportation Equipment	0	19,933	30,247	58,768
Leasehold Interest in Communication Equipment	5,060	5,060	5,060	5,060
Construction in Progress				
	39,791	78,930	108,655	196,959
Less Depreciation	6,485	20,747	42,084	82,258
	33,306	58,183	66,571	114,701
INTANGIBLE ASSETS	108	81	596	27
TOTAL ASSETS	235,032	356,942	312,911	721,079

120

EXHIBIT I
(continued)
Hines Industries, Inc.
Balance Sheet
Years Ending February 28

	1981	1982	1983	1984
CURRENT LIABILITIES				
Notes Payable, Bank	40,000	0	69,300	170,000
Current Portion of Long -Term Debt	6,632	2,626	12,100	27,353
Accounts Payable	77,273	88,765	72,432	181,684
Accrued Expenses	13,896	28,150	29,630	49,047
Accrued Taxes	5,930	8,579	6,748	20,288
Customer Deposits	30,074	117,513	10,000	218,091
Customer Returns due to Warranty Parts				
TOTAL CURRENT LIABILITIES	173,805	245,633	200,210	666,463
LONG-TERM DEBT	6,051	67,131	25,178	24,641
STOCKHOLDER'S EQUITY				
Common Stock, $1 par Value, 100,000 shares, 70,000 issued	70,000	70,000	70,000	70,000
Retained Earnings	(14,824)	(25,822)	17,523	(40,025)
	55,176	44,178	87,523	29,975
TOTAL LIABILITIES & EQUITY	235,032	356,942	312,911	721,079

121

EXHIBIT II
Hines Industries, Inc.
Income Statement
Years Ending February 28

	1981	1982	1983	1984
NET SALES	$394,498	$634,767	$1,114,201	$1,434,912
COST OF SALES				
Material	158,364	269,957	373,713	381,268
Direct Labor	36,345	107,362	174,321	209,747
Subcontract	63,842	27,514	8,288	7,063
Drafting	3,716	7,335	11,078	43,322
Installation	0	2,900	3,567	18,100
Manufacturing Overhead	27,605	80,317	207,173	281,656
	289,872	495,385	778,140	941,156
GROSS PROFIT	104,626	139,382	336,061	493,756
OPERATING EXPENSES				
Research & Development	10,945	5,506	25,750	53,449
Selling Expenses	36,498	54,084	131,851	302,048
General & Adm. Expense	68,204	79,000	128,123	173,892
	115,647	138,590	285,724	529,389
OPERATING INCOME	(11,021)	792	50,337	(35,633)
NON OPERATING INCOME (EXP)				
Interest Income	0	0	0	790
Interest Expense	(4,473)	(11,790)	(6,992)	(22,705)
Miscellaneous	670	0	0	0
Loss on Investment				
	(3,803)	(11,790)	(6,992)	(21,915)
INCOME BEFORE TAXES	(14,824)	(10,998)	43,345	(57,548)
LESS INCOME TAX	0	0	0	0
NET INCOME	(14,824)	(10,998)	43,345	(57,548)

EXHIBIT III
Hines Industries, Inc.
Years Ending February 28

	1981	1982	1983	1984
Manufacturing Overhead				
Supervisory Labor	$0	$0	$47,103	$67,654
Indirect Labor	2,638	2,829	8,635	12,640
Payroll Taxes	2,995	8,827	22,476	43,585
Insurance	2,662	6,469	26,642	37,200
Depreciation	3,469	10,874	15,019	22,710
Freight	4,799	14,118	13,657	30,099
Utilities	2,169	5,288	7,438	9,453
Maintenance	79	272	789	2,117
Tools	1,150	2,414	5,408	12,398
Rent	13,172	36,252	41,404	44,929
Supplies	4,618	4,442	7,885	10,584
Overhead Variance	(10,146)	(11,468)	10,717	(11,713)
Total	27,605	80,317	207,173	281,656
Selling Expense				
Advertising	$0	$0	$0	$8,175
Commissions	13,509	33,150	75,082	202,979
Payroll	0	0	20,990	35,747
Sales Promotion	11,616	11,158	18,018	49,460
Payroll Taxes	0	0	2,101	4,382
Travel & Entertainment	11,373	9,776	15,660	19,405
Total	36,498	54,084	131,851	320,148

EXHIBIT III
(continued)
Hines Industries, Inc.
Years Ending February 28

	1981	1982	1983	1984
General & Administrative Expenses				
Auto Operation	$8,171	$6,275	$6,473	$2,439
Airplane	510	3,408	3,688	1,876
Bad Debts	0	0	15,616	4,255
Contributions	0	270	394	3,741
Depreciation	1,332	3,388	8,586	17,464
Dues & Subscriptions	32	128	253	434
Equipment Rental	0	647	5,053	6,459
Insurance	1,785	724	8,641	13,956
Professional Fees	3,111	4,990	3,764	12,468
Maintenance & Repairs	0	382	0	1,048
Miscellaneous	942	1,761	2,175	2,511
Office Supplies	3,127	4,047	7,455	7,110
Clerical Payroll	24,781	35,046	39,083	65,275
Payroll Taxes	4,473	4,628	4,509	7,746
Sales Tax	406	273	715	667
Michigan Single Business Tax	219	960	3,900	4,100
Other Taxes	220	185	2,246	1,586
Telephone	8,515	11,888	15,572	20,757
Officer Salary	10,580	0	0	0
Total	68,204	79,000	128,123	173,892

EXHIBIT IV
Hines Industries, Inc.
Sales Analysis
Month Ending
(In Thousands of Dollars)

	4/84	3/84	2/84	1/84	12/83	11/83	10/83	9/83	8/83	7/83	6/83	5/83	4/83	3/83
BILLINGS														
Automotive	74.5	120.1	191.1	68.4	128.6	112.6	42.3	59.2						
Industrial	112.8	117.7		0.3	162.7	52.6	47.1	105.5						
Driveline	125.6	124.8	55.6											
Parts & Serv.	2.4	1.2	2.4	1.3	1.2	1.3	2.2	1.3						
Total	315.3	363.8	249.1	70.0	292.5	166.5	91.6	166.0	111.3	87.0	94.5	10.8	41.2	99.6
BOOKINGS														
Automotive	96.4	21.0	109.9	(22.9)	280.1	188.8	79.0	87.6						
Industrial	31.8	29.7	132.1	83.5	85.2	114.7	129.6	54.3						
Driveline		4.3	33.7	26.9				600.0						
Parts & Serv.	2.4	1.2	2.4	1.3	1.2	1.3	2.2	1.3						
Total	130.6	56.2	278.1	88.8	366.5	304.8	210.8	743.2	165.5	114.8	142.3	35.8	182.7	39.4
BACKLOG	792.9	977.5	1,285.1	1,256.1	1,237.3	1,163.3	1,025.0	905.8	328.6	274.3	246.5	198.8	173.8	32.4

EXHIBIT V
Hines Industries, Inc.
Product Sheet

HARD BEARING BALANCING MACHINES

Standard features of Hines Balancers:

ELECTRONIC DIGITAL READOUT
PERMANENT CALIBRATION
DIRECT INDICATION OF ANGLE
AMOUNT IN OUNCES OR GRAMS
COMPLETE TOOLING PACKAGES

Hines Industries manufactures a variety of balancers for different applications, all of which are available with **Microprocessor Analyzers.**

HO

ADDITIONAL STANDARD FEATURES:

- Single and two plane correction
- On machine correction capacity
- Automatic cycle
- Total enclosure of mechanicals
- Handles small and large unbalances
- Dynamic braking

OPTIONS AVAILABLE:

- Microprocessor analyzer
- Segmenting
- Tolerance function

APPLICATION:

Specifically designed for overhung part balancing like:

- Pump Impellers
- Blowers
- Fans

and similar parts

CAPACITIES:

8 models available range from .25 to 2500 lbs. part capacities.

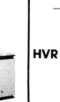

HVR

- Pure single plane balancing insensitive to couple unbalance
- On machine correction capacity
- Automatic cycle
- Low speed operation
- Dynamic braking

- Microprocessor analyzer
- Auto indexing
- Drill countdown
- Complete correction systems
- Tolerance function

Designed for single plane balancing of:

- Pulleys
- Clutches
- Impellers
- Flywheels

and similar parts

5 models available range from .1 to 200 lb. part capacities.

HVS

- Microprocessor based electronics
- Automatic electronic centering
- Outstanding sensitivity

- Segmenting
- Tolerance function
- Part lift off device
- Display hold

This nonrotating static balancer is for fast part checking and balancing of:

- Grinding Wheels
- Fans
- Brake Drums
- Wheels

and similar parts

7 models available range from .5 to 2000 lbs. part capacities.

HC

- Restraint/angle Indicator eliminates end stops
- On machine correction capacity
- Single and two plane balancing
- Simplified belt drive

- Microprocessor analyzer
- Segmenting
- Tolerance function
- Complete correction systems
- End drive

The HC Cradle Balancer will handle a variety of work pieces for job shop or production balancing, any part than can be run on 2 bearing surfaces or mounted on an arbor.

- Crankshafts
- Rolls
- Turbines
- Armatures

8 models available range from .2 to 15,000 lbs. part capacities.

DL

The DL driveline balancer is available in several models from 3-3000 lb. capacities.

- Digital readout
- Direct angle indication
- Heavy motorized spindles

FOR MORE INFORMATION ON THESE AND OTHER BALANCERS AVAILABLE CALL OR WRITE.

HINES INDUSTRIES Inc.
661 AIRPORT BOULEVARD, SUITE 2, ANN ARBOR, MICHIGAN 48104
PHONE: (313) 769-2300

EXHIBIT VI
Hines Industries, Inc.
Sample Advertisment

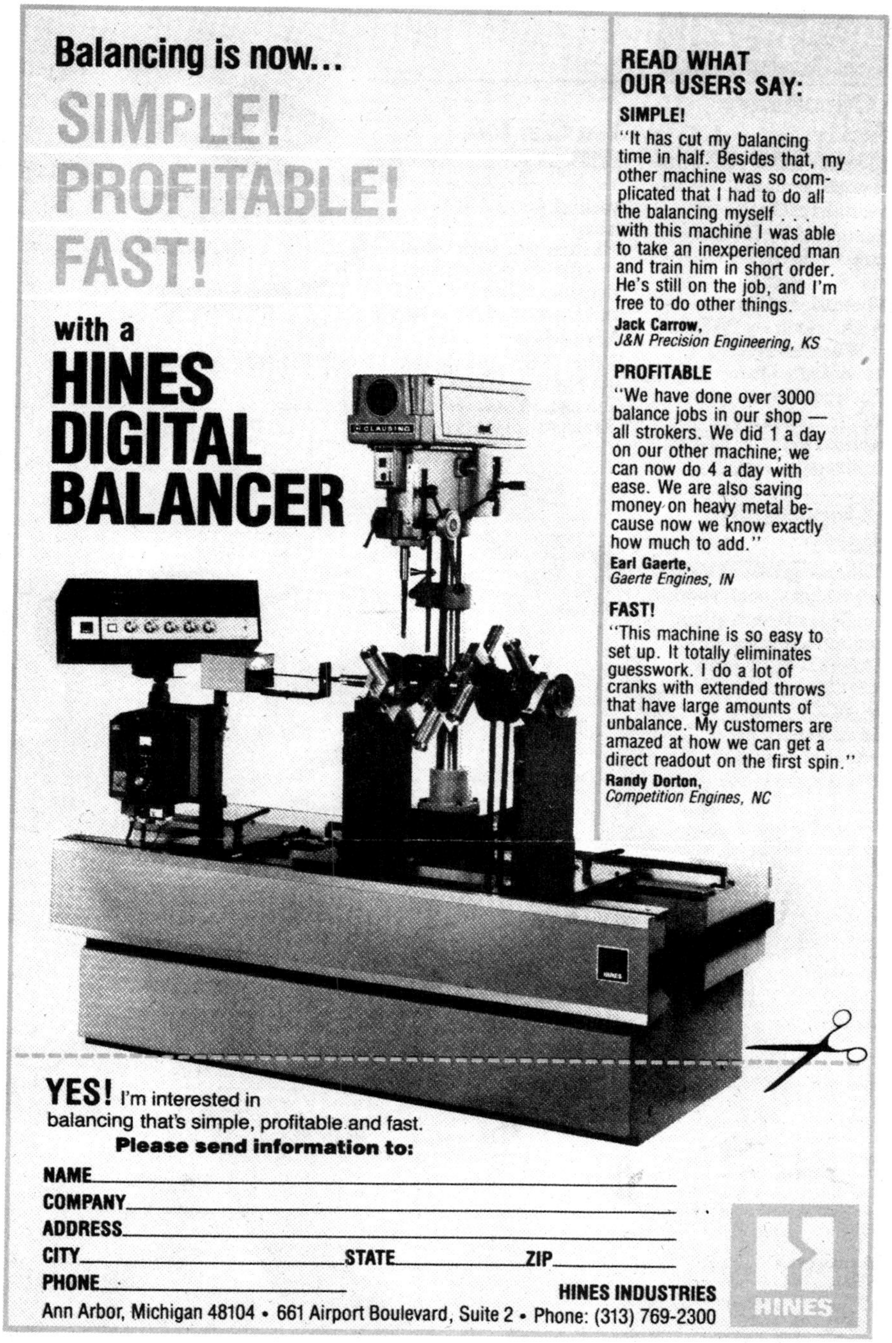

Circle No. 17 on Reader Service Card

EXHIBIT VII
Hines Industries, Inc.
Organization Chart

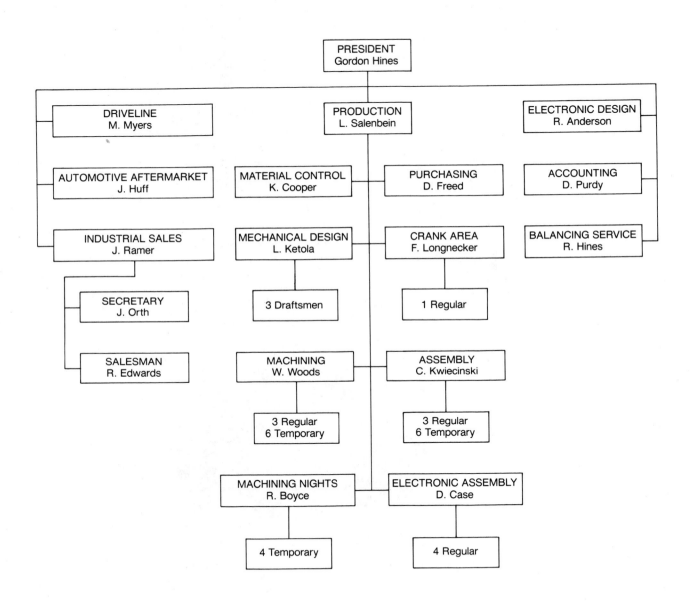

```
                              PRESIDENT
                              Gordon Hines

    DRIVELINE                 PRODUCTION              ELECTRONIC DESIGN
    M. Myers                  L. Salenbein            R. Anderson

    AUTOMOTIVE AFTERMARKET    MATERIAL CONTROL    PURCHASING    ACCOUNTING
    J. Huff                   K. Cooper           D. Freed      D. Purdy

    INDUSTRIAL SALES          MECHANICAL DESIGN   CRANK AREA    BALANCING SERVICE
    J. Ramer                  L. Ketola           F. Longnecker R. Hines

        SECRETARY                3 Draftsmen      1 Regular
        J. Orth

        SALESMAN              MACHINING           ASSEMBLY
        R. Edwards           W. Woods             C. Kwiecinski

                                3 Regular            3 Regular
                                6 Temporary          6 Temporary

                        MACHINING NIGHTS        ELECTRONIC ASSEMBLY
                        R. Boyce                D. Case

                                4 Temporary          4 Regular
```

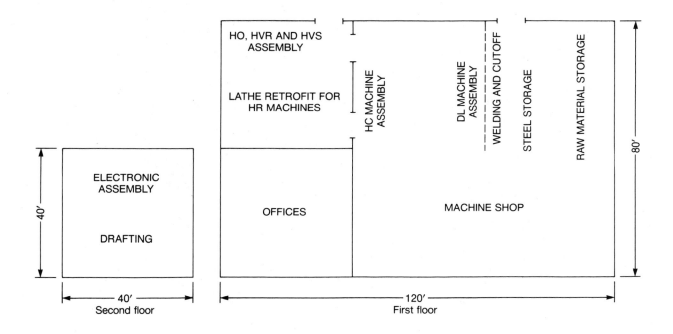

EXHIBIT VIII
Hines Industries, Inc.
Plant Layout

EXHIBIT IX
Hines Industries, Inc.
How Imbalance Is Measured

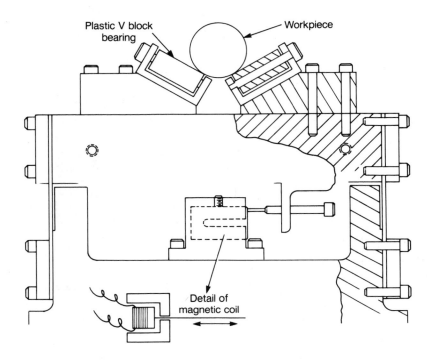

The workpiece is freely supported in the cradle on plastic V block bearings. It is driven by a belt and pulley. As the cradle moves due to an imbalance in the workpiece, the movement is registered in the magnetic field (N-S) and induces a current in the coil that is transmitted to an amplifier. The amplifier then shows the frequency and amplitude of the vibration in wave form and establishes where the center of mass is in relation to the geometric center,

EXHIBIT X
Hines Industries, Inc.
Engine Balancing Article

Engine balancing

by Mike Mavrigian

I t's high time that the bull stops concerning the area of engine balancing. When many machine shop owners/operators are asked to "balance" an engine, they automatically place the customer at hand into one category: racer/hot-rodder. For years, the only folks who offered balancing services out of their shop were regarded as "specialty speed shops," and out of the realm of the normal or "traditional" machine shop.

Wake up, folks. You cannot offer accurate and truly *complete* engine rebuilding services without including balancing as an integral part of your overall operation. It's called *doing the job right*.

That's right . . . we're suggesting that you go out and buy additional equipment if you don't already have it. That means increased operating bucks, right? Wrong. What it really means is additional profit opportunities.

An internal combustion engine features several moving parts, right? A crankshaft/damper-pulley/flywheel rotates within the engine block; and connecting rods/piston assemblies reciprocate up and down within their respective bores, while attached to the crankshaft. If there are unequal forces at work during engine operation, there is damaging stress being placed on engine bearings, and a loss of overall efficiency. Now, you know you can't dispute that fact, so why in the world are so many shops unwilling to look at balancing as the necessary service that it is?

Especially in these days of "downsized" powerplants that feature only six or four cylinders, balancing takes on a much more important role during engine rebuilding. Imbalance differences are proportionately more obvious and potentially damaging with the decrease in total number of cylinders. An imbalance condition in a V-8 engine that might go unnoticed has the potential to wreak havoc in a mill with only half the number of cylinders.

Let's take a look at a basic formula which illustrates how to determine the force that an unbalance condition produces. For a given unbalance condition, the force at the bearings is proportional to the speed of the engine *squared*. The relationship for force in pounds to due a given amount of unbalance in ounce inches is as follows: Force = 1.7738 x unbalance x Engine RPM. For example, for one ounce-inch of unbalance at 1000 RPM, the force is 1.7738 pounds. For 2 ounce-inches at 2000 RPM, the force is 14.2 pounds (formula courtesy Hines Industries, Inc.).

That's 14.2 *pounds* of force applied to the crank bearings *constantly* at 2000 RPM. With OE factory tolerances being what they are (speaking in generalities), it's not at all uncommon to experience this level of uneven balance in a majority of engines that come into your machine shop. We just can't take balancing procedures for granted as so-called "luxuries" anymore. Our purpose within this industry is to give the end-user the *best* and most reliable rebuild that we can possibly achieve. Anything less should not be acceptable.

Let's take a look at the specific items that are included under the broad heading of balancing: the *rotating mass* includes the crankshaft, damper, flywheel and clutch pressure plate (if any). The *reciprocating mass* includes connecting rods, pistons and pins.

Rotating mass

Internally-balanced engines (where the flywheel and or damper has no counterweights) offer you a choice: you can either balance the pieces installed on the crankshaft as an assembly, or you can individually balance off the crank.

Externally-balanced engines (flywheel and or damper features counterweights) require these units to be installed on the crankshaft prior to crankshaft balancing.

In-line engines (four cylinder, straight sizes) allow their crankshaft assemblies to be balanced on the crank balancer machine without the use of bobweights, while V-type engines require bobweights to be installed on the crank prior to balancing (to simulate rod/piston thrusts during crank balancing).

Reciprocating Mass

Here we want to balance piston/pin assemblies and connecting rod assemblies. What we are essentially after here is to make all piston/pin assemblies weigh the same; and for all connecting rod large-ends to weigh the same; and for all connecting rod small-ends to weigh the same. To do this, we basically find the lightest unit and remove metal from other similar units so that they all come down to the weight of the lightest. For example, in balancing pistons, we weigh each piston (clean and dry, with pins), finding the one that weighs less than all the others. We record that lightest weight. All other pistons are then ground carefully in their pin boss areas until they each weigh the same as

131

that lightest unit. Generally, your tolerance is thus: the piston/pin assemblies being lightened should weigh the same as the light assembly, within +.5 gram to .0 gram. Always constantly double-check your weights during and after all machining. Record the finished weight of each piston/pin assembly and mark each with cylinder number (if not already done).

The connecting rods are each weighed on a scale with the use of a special scale pan adapter. The rod ends (small and large) should be set up so that they are "square" with each other. Weigh each rod's large end and find your lightest end. Carefully grind material from all others to bring them down to this lightest rod-end's weight. The same procedure is followed for small ends. The tolerance to shoot for is +1 gram-.0 gram (for automotive engines). For heavy truck engines, the tolerance can be sometimes set at +2 grams to .0 gram. Most of the time, the very *end* surface of each rod end is the area from which material is ground. Be sure to record each rod's end weight as well as double-checking total rod weight. Identify them accordingly.

Record-keeping (on a bobweight card) is essential, not only for your immediate use, but for any future parts replacements that might be necessary. If you already know what weight a piston/pin assembly *must* be, you can choose an assembly for replacement that will maintain the balance job.

After rods and piston assemblies have been balanced, you can then set up the crank with the correct bobweights (if it's a V-block engine design).

Installation of bobweights, if needed, is critical from a centering standpoint. They must be accurately centered on the crank throws (spacing side-to-side across the bearing surface width). Orientation is not critical, so they do not need to be placed at right angles to each other. Bobweights, for those unfamiliar with this term, are the weights that are attached to the journals of

Weigh each piston to find the one which weighs the least. Then grind all other pistons to match that weight.

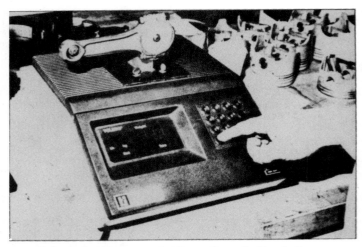

Rod ends should be set up so that they are "square" with each other when weighing.

the crankshaft of any V-type engine crank during balancing, on a dynamic crank balancer. They are adjustable, with flowable lead shot inside, and are there to cause the crank to respond to the balancer as if the rods and pistons were attached.

Determining needed bobweight

To determine bobweight needed, add up the figures on your bobweight card: add rod rotating weight (large rod end) plus rod bearing weight plus oil allowance (figure average 4 grams) plus piston/pin weight, plus locks (if any) plus piston rings plus the rod reciprocating weight. Add up all of these weight factors that a single rod throw of the crank has to handle, and you've got your total bobweight.

Again, keep in mind that straight-line engine crankshafts do not need the addition of bobweights in order to balance the crank.

Balancing, especially in today's marketplace, is a necessary service and not the grand luxury that some people deem it to be. Just imagine a clothes washer that has had an uneven load placed in it. The resulting vibration causes excessive wear in virtually every moving component in that machine, as well as eliminating the degree of efficiency that the machine is capable of. Translate that into engine operational terms. When a mechanical mass rotates, centrifugal force acts upon the entire mass. If the part is unbalanced, an *excess* of mass exists on one side. Everything is being pulled in the direction of the heavy side, or away from the mechanical axis of rotation. Definitely a no-win situation for main bearings, rod bearings, timing gear setup, transmission input shaft, etc.

Take full advantage of balancing

If your shop is content with simple repair and replacement methods, you are

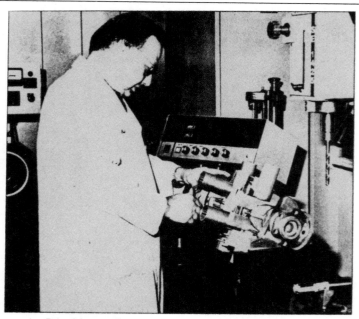

Bobweights must be accurately centered on the crank throws. They do not need to be placed at right angles to each other.

not taking full advantage of the capabilities that balancing equipment offers in terms of *correcting* faulty OE traits, many of which can be traced directly back to unbalance conditions. If you want your customers to be supplied with rebuilt engine assemblies that will perform to the *design* level of efficiency and horsepower *and* offer reliable, extended life service, you must investigate the excellent balancing equipment that is currently available on the market.

Increasing horsepower is not the all-encompassing goal that the traditional machine shop strives towards; rather, it is the *beneficial* byproduct of simply *doing it right*. So please, don't just regard balancing as an act performed by the speed-freak seals of the racing world. It should be an integral part of the efficient, quality-conscious machine shop that is concerned with producing the best possible product with currently-available methods.

We wish to thank the good folks at Hines Industries, Inc. (661 Airport Blvd., Suite #2, Ann Arbor, MI 48104, 331-769-2300) for their valued input for this article.

RESEARCH EQUIPMENT CORPORATION and the MONITOR.

It was nearing the end of the year, and Jerome Dumas needed to complete two major tasks before his new company, Research Equipment Corporation (REC), could become fully operational. He had to establish a nationwide distributor network for his company's only product, the MONITOR, and raise approximately $1.5 million. Once these two objectives have been accomplished, Jerry knew that his company would be able to manufacture and market the best fire protection system available. There was a real need for more advanced fire detection systems because standard smoke detectors were inadequate, only sounding an alarm after a fire had started.

More than 6000 people die by fire each year, and ten times that many are burn victims. Every ten seconds a fire starts somewhere in the United States and detectors now on the market have only limited alarm capabilities. They are dangerously insensitive to toxic fumes generated by burning synthetic materials and can only be installed in clean areas. In recent years, there have been considerable advances in building design and in the materials used in their construction. However, fire detection technology has failed to keep pace. Fire departments that must contend with growing traffic congestion and building heights are losing the critical battle of time.

Better fire detection could save lives and reduce the $6.7 billion of annual property loss significantly. According to Fire Journal, the journal of the National Fire Protection Association (N.F.P.A.), only 9.1 percent of fires in 1982 were reported by automatic detecting devices. During 1983, the percentage dropped to 6.1 and in 1984, only 5 percent of fires were reported by detecting devices. These low percentages of fires reported convinced Mr. Dumas that a pressing need and a potentially huge market for a sophisticated fire detection system existed.

COMPANY HISTORY

In the early 1980's, Jerome Dumas moved his product development company, Research Equipment Corporation, to Charleston, South Carolina, to develop the MONITOR, an early warning fire detection device. The company was originally located in a Control Data Corporation (CDC) business incubator. Since REC was operating on an extremely tight budget, the company benefited from the subsidized rent and shared services provided by the incubator. However, company expansion caused REC to leave the incubator and move to its present location in North Charleston.

Key Contacts and Board of Directors

To conserve his limited resources, Mr. Dumas utilized all the available free or relatively inexpensive services. He contracted with the engineering department at Clemson University and the physics department at the College of Charleston to develop and test parts of the MONITOR. He also assembled a seasoned board of directors and used the services of consultants whenever necessary. The following individuals agreed to be directors of the fledgling company: (see Exhibit 1 for additional information on the outside directors)

Andrew W. Ballentine
Marketing Executive, DuPont Company (retired)

Cornelius J. Duffy
Executive Vice President and Director, Eagle Star Insurance Co. of America

Jerome E. Dumas
Chairman and President, Research Equipment Corporation

W. Lorin Fortier
Vice President, Research Equipment Corporation

J. Addison Ingle, Jr.
Vice President, Heffron, Ingle, McDowell & Cooper Insurance

Joseph R. McPhee, Jr., Esq.,
Patent Attorney

Douglas C. Plate
Vice Admiral, U.S.N. (retired)

Henry B. Smythe, Sr., Esq.,
Partner, Buist, Moore, Smythe & McGee, Attorneys

Thomas E. Thornhill
Commercial Real Estate

The directors all brought needed skills to the new company, and they would be vital to the company's growth and profitability. In addition to advice and counsel, the directors also provided Research Equipment Corporation with its initial capital. The company was incorporated as an S corporation, and each director bought company stock. Mr. Dumas knew that once his company completed its product-development phase, it would have to become a C corporation so it could have more than 35 stockholders.

136

Development Phase

Research Equipment Corporation's agreement with Clemson University called for its engineering faculty to produce, in accordance with the company's design and specifications,

1) prototype models of the cloud chamber
2) the electrical/electronic circuitry
3) the DC Power Train
4) engineering drawings

The College of Charleston physics faculty were to assist in the testing of the cloud chamber assembly, relating to light sources and liquids used as part of the humidification process.

Developing the MONITOR required the following ten steps (the first nine steps have been completed or are nearly completed): (see Exhibit 2)

1. Cloud Chamber - Produce and test prototypes of the company's new cloud chamber (Clemson).

2. Circuitry - Develop circuitries (designed by Research Equipment Corporation) for the cloud chamber (Clemson).

3. DC Power Train - Design electronic systems, 12 colt DC supply, and stand-by power (Clemson).

4. Air Handling - Develop the best method for transporting air samples from zones to the monitoring unit, and design for the air intake heads (REC).

5. Engineering Drawings - Prepare documents for design assembly, installation, service and catalog piece numbering as work progresses (Clemson and the company).

6. Prototype Assembly - Determine the final configuration and layout within the MONITOR cabinet and assemble components to test the product (Clemson and the company).

7. Testing - Test and calibrate the system in simulated incipient fire conditions using the N.F.P.A. test procedures (the company and consultants).

8. Final Design - Set final design characteristics for units to be submitted to testing laboratories (the company).

9. <u>Units Assembled for Underwriters' Laboratories and Factory Mutual</u> - Prepare MONITOR units, specifications, and performance criteria for delivery to testing laboratories (the company and consultant).

10. <u>Testing by Underwriters' Laboratories and Factory Mutual</u> - Coordinate with test teams. Four months allocated for testing and listing.

Development Phase Funding

Much of the product development has been completed and the company has used much of the approximately $200,000 it needed during the development phase (see Exhibit 3). Startup and development capital was raised from the following sources: Sale of common stock to directors and other investors; a convertible debenture from Control Data Corporation (Research Equipment Corporation agreed that CDC would be its sole original equipment manufacturer for computers and applications); and a repayable non-interest bearing bond. Mr. Dumas was able to raise approximately $185,000 from these sources; however, more money would be needed as development began in earnest.

Additional funding proposals had been submitted to the U.S. Air Force for $48,000 and to the Federal Aviation Agency for $50,000. A development contract for $25,000 was submitted to the U.S. Navy, and the company expected to receive funds from the government through its Small Business Innovative Research Program. Funds were also solicited from the insurance, tobacco, and aircraft industries. Most funding solicitations were unproductive, but enough money was available to develop the MONITOR which is now being evaluated by Underwriters' Laboratories and Factory Mutual.

THE MONITOR

The technology employed by the MONITOR (see Exhibits 4 & 5) is based on continuous measurement of the population density of submicron-size particles in air that, under normal conditions, contains thousands of particles in each cubic centimeter. As material in a protected space (zone) is heated, it reaches the temperature at which thermal excitation causes molecules on its surface to gasify, leave the surface and unite into clumps of energetic submicron-size airborne particles. The process, called "thermal particulation," produce enormous numbers of submicron particles, even if the total mass of the particulated material is measure in micrograms. When this happens, the particle population density increases dramatically, is recognized by the MONITOR, and an alarm is activated at some point before combustion starts. That point could be as early as several minutes, or as long as a week; however, it should provide enough time for preventive action to take place after an alarm is given by the monitor.

Installation

Installation of the MONITOR and associated items (see Exhibit 6) requires the following:

Selection of appropriate zones having the same basic function, e.g., computer rooms, offices, etc.

Design (layout) installation of tubing with heads (see Exhibit 7).

Installation of the MONITOR is a secure area(s), e.g., closets.

Recording ambient conditions over a period of time, e.g., one week.

Selection of alarm levels (completed automatically by the computer).

Activation of the system.

A cloud chamber is used to measure the number of submicron particles per cubic centimeter (SMP/CC). A pressure drop in the cloud chamber causes water vapor to condense on the submicron particles in the air sample. The SMP/CC count measures the density of the vapor cloud, which depends on the _number_ of particles, _not_ on their _size_. Thus, the MONITOR system can be reliably used in "dirty" atmospheres where ionization or smoke detectors are useless.

Operation

Thin-wall tubing is installed to transport air samples (see Exhibit 8) from the zones being protected to the MONITOR for evaluation. The system is operated for a period of time so that ambient (normal) levels of SMP/CC for each zones can be determined and proper alarm levels can be established automatically by the computer. As the MONITOR counts particles, rather than merely detecting their presence or absence, various alarm levels can be established: WARNING-ALERT-ALARM. The WARNING level would ALERT the user to start looking for a "hot spot" within the zone. The ALARM level would be sent directly to the fire department. One MONITOR unit can be used to evaluate zones with different ambient/alarm levels, for example, a computer room and a laboratory. To eliminate possible confusion, the MONITOR unit's computer will report all zone levels on a scale of one to ten, regardless of the zones SMP/CC alarm level (see Exhibit 6).

Detection Sequence

At the MONITOR, a fraction of the air stream is drawn through the humidification chamber into the cloud chamber. A sudden adiabatic pressure drop causes a cloud to form in the chamber and the photoelectric circuit measures the cloud density. The output sample is digitized into SMP/CC and put into a computer memory for trend analysis. The sample is swept away and another sample takes its place. This cycle takes one second and, after fifteen separate samples are measured in succession from one zone, a valve operated to allow fifteen samples from the next zone to be measured. Cycling between each zone at 15-second intervals goes on continuously and generates a warning signal only after ten successive counts above the preset zone WARNING level have been registered.

The system operates on 12-volt direct current through a trickle charger to provide stand-by battery power, allowing the MONITOR to continue to provide temporary fire protection if power to the MONITOR fails. Loss of power triggers a trouble signal.

Production

MONITORS are produced at the company's facility in North Charleston. Most of the 250 parts used in the construction of the MONITOR are "off-the-shelf" type items that are produced by other manufacturers and assembled by one Research Equipment Corporation employee. REC should be able to produce 100 MONITORS a month within the next two years using 4 employees to complete the units. The computer used in the MONITOR was designed by the company, and a company engineer created the language used by the computer.

Patents

The company has filed registered letters with J. R. McPhee, Jr., Esquire, patent attorney, for protection of three basic items. Application to the patent office will be filed at the appropriate time.

1.   An INTEGRATED CIRCUIT with digital output to provide three fire condition stages (warming, alert, alarm) and circuitry which will continually interrogate the performance of the MONITOR.

2.   AIR FLOW measuring device of air being drawn into the system. Variance either above or below the designed CFM will generate a print out indicating which zone within the MONITOR system is experiencing difficulty.

3.   HUMIDIFICATION/CLOUD CHAMBER assembly designed by the company. The company will update data filed with Mr. McPhee as segments of the MONITOR advance in design and prototype testing.

MARKETING

MONITOR customers would be those companies, agencies, or organizations that need a sophisticated, computer-controlled system that employs proven technology, is not subject to false alarms, can protect an entire building (clean or dirty, wet or dry, hazardous or sterile), and is low in maintenance. The system would have to be economical to install and must alarm during the early stage of a fire. Mr. Dumas believes that any company with large facilities is a potential customer.

Target Market

The present market is divided into three sections--governmental, industrial, and residential--and generates approximately $3 billion in annual sales. Estimates are that less than ten percent of any commercial building is protected by a fire detection system, and the majority of buildings have NO protection at all. The commercial/industrial market for MONITORS is huge. At present, the residential market is not as attractive as the others because of the cost of the MONITOR system; however, the company plans to enter that market by the beginning or the third year of sales. People who are willing to pay $200,000 or more for a home will be able to afford a MONITOR system to protect their valuables, and bankers have indicated a willingness to include the MONITOR system in a mortgage package.

The government is potentially a major buyer of MONITOR systems. During the formative stage of the company, Mr. Dumas worked with federal representatives, members of the armed forces, and NASA officials to convince them that ships, aircraft, missile silos, and satellites should be protected by MONITOR systems. The MONITOR would also be useful to people who had to protect high-value equipment such as mainframe computers, telephone equipment, and radio-TV communications equipment. Finally, owners of high value storage areas for such commodities as grain and tobacco were potential buyers of MONITOR systems.

Competition

There are two types of fire detectors--smoke and heat. REC's competition is primarily the smoke type, of which there are two--ionization and photoelectric. Both have been successfully marketed and are well suited for restricted installation in homes, small offices, and computer rooms. Their major shortcomings are false alarms, installation limited to "clean" environments (free from dust, wind, high humidity, or vibrations), and frequent maintenance. These detectors can protect only a portion of the building and sound an alarm after a fire has started. There are approximately 25 producers of shelf-item type fire detecting products that are sold directly to dealers or wholesalers, such as ADEMCO. Pytronics, a division of Baker Industries, is one of the largest manufacturers of ionization units and BRK Electronics, Inc. is a major producer of photoelectric devices.

While REC recognizes manufacturers of shelf-item type fire detectors as potential competitors, it is mainly concerned with two major competitors,--Fenwal and Environment One. Fenwal has exclusive rights to market an Australian detection system,--the VESDA. Mr. Dumas contends that MONITOR is superior to VESDA because that system detects fires only when there is smoke and it is not computer-controlled. Environment One's Model Two operates on the same principle as the MONITOR, but it is not as well engineered as the MONITOR, and it is too cumbersome. The Model Two is also not computer-controlled.

Competitors have provided REC with one beneficial service. Companies such as Fenwal have aggressively marketed their systems to many of the same customers as REC has targeted; therefore, MONITOR dealers will not have to "educate" potential customers. Rather than trying to explain multi-zone fire detection systems to customers, MONITOR dealers will be able to concentrate on the factors that make their systems better than those offered by the competition.

Distribution

After much study and analysis, Mr. Dumas decided that the most efficient way to sell or lease MONITOR systems to end users was through a network of dealers. Selecting the best dealers would be vital to the future success of Research Equipment Corporation; therefore, the company established dealership selection criteria. Each dealership must:

* be in the fire detection and suppression industry,

* have qualified personnel to sell, design, install, and service systems,

* be financially capable of meeting minimum quarterly sales quotas,

* purchase a demonstration unit for a fee of $5,000,

* meet quarterly sales quotas.

* Once dealerships have been selected, the company will provide each dealer with:

* sales training on a continuous basis,

* instructions in installation, maintenance, and repair of the MONITOR,

* national advertising in publications such as Security World, Fireman's Journal, Fire Journal, and other relevant publications,

* company display at the National Fire Protection Associations. annual meeting, and

participation, on a joint basis, with dealers in regional fire prevention conventions and shows.

During the first two years of sales, REC expects to establish seven district offices under the direction of the corporate regional office in Charleston. The company expects to have selected 63 dealerships by that time. A corporate regional office, with three district offices, will be opened in San Francisco, and the company plans to have established 96 dealerships by the end of year two.

Dealers will be the primary distribution channel for MONITORS; however, the company does retain the right to sell directly to some customers. The company will sell directly to, but not limited to, the United States Navy, Coast Guard, commercial ships, and aircraft manufacturers (commercial and military).

Advertising

Advertising would initially be limited to providing dealers with sales brochures, catalogs, and other relevant promotional material that would facilitate MONITOR sales. As sales begin to increase, the company plans to place advertisements in national journals such as Fire Journal. Early advertisements (see Exhibit 9) will be generic and informative; however, future advertisements will target computer manufacturers and users, telephone companies, and high-rise building developers.

Pricing

The initial price of each MONITOR system was set at $3,000. This figure was essentially a "guesstimate" because management had no way of determining exactly what customers would pay for the system. However, as competitors like Fenwal and Environment One introduced their products, Mr. Dumas realized that the MONITOR was underpriced. The price to the dealer for each MONITOR system would be between $4,000 and $5,000 depending on the number purchased. Installation costs were estimated to be between $3,000 to $5,000, making the total installed price to the customer approximately $10,000 per system. Since each system could monitor a maximum of ten zones, some large customers would need to purchase multiple systems.

Customers who do not want to purchase the MONITOR would be able to lease a system. In fact, the MONITOR may be the only fire detection system leasable through firms such as U.S. Leasing. Customers will be able to treat leasing costs as a direct business expense and will not need much "up front" capital.

FINANCE

Limited equity financing, small grants, and several relatively small loans had brought the company from startup to the present. Now, however, REC needed major funding to allow it to begin manufacturing and marketing its MONITOR systems. Mr. Dumas believes that the company needs approximately $1.5 million to tide it over until sales revenues cover operating costs. Knowing that he would have to approach several sources for funding, Jerry created pro forma operating statements that he believes reflect the reality of his company and the industry.

To create pro forma operating statements, it is necessary to make the following assumptions:

1. First-year sales are based on dealers' sales and do not include systems sold directly to governmental agencies.

2. Second and third-year dealer networks will be in place in timely fashion.

3. Dealers will meet their quarterly sales quotas.

4. The market for fire detection devices will continue to grow at a steady rate.

5. Inventory will be kept at a minimum as units will be produced to meet dealers' quotas.

6. The company will have 35 employees by the end of its second year, including executives, office, manufacturing, assembly and testing personnel, regional sales managers and support staff in district offices.

7. Capital required for manufacturing and marketing will be obtainable from sale of company stock, banking arrangements, and/or personal guarantee loans.

Operating Statements

With prototype MONITOR units being evaluated by Underwriters' Laboratories and Factory Mutual, the development phase is nearly over and year two is about to begin. The pro forma operating statement for year two (see Exhibit 11) reveals that general and administrative expenses will amount to $477,600, and sales expenses will be $592,000. Total expenses, including depreciation, are expected to be $1,097,200. To repay existing debts and be prepared to cover expenses in the event predicted sales do not materialize, Mr. Dumas wants to raise $1.5 million from outside sources.

Income Statements

Relying on the previously articulated assumptions, Mr. Dumas has created income statements (see Exhibit 12) for the next four years. As with the operating statement, the development phase is nearly over and year two is the next year. Income is projected to increase from $1,244,000 next year to $7,520,000 at the end of year four. Year three is the first year the company is expecting to be profitable. Exhibit 13 provides summary income and expense data by month for years two, three, and four.

Funding

Mr. Dumas has brought his company from startup to the product-testing phase with financial support from himself and others. He now needs to utilize his projected income and sales figures to induce other people or institutions to provide $1.5 million to see the company through the next year. Mr. Dumas will solicit funds from one or a combination of the following sources: commercial banks and savings and loans; Small Business Investment Corporations (SBIC's); private investors; venture capitalists; the Small Business Administration; large private corporations; insurance companies; or any other interested investors or lenders. Mr. Dumas is not sure how he will acquire the necessary capital, but he is convinced that the product and the promise of substantial revenue will help him raise the funds from some source or sources.

EXHIBIT 1
RESEARCH EQUIPMENT CORPORATION
OFFICERS AND DIRECTORS

A.W. BALLENTINE

Retired Division Director, Communications Department of the E.I. Du Pont Company. Mr. Ballentine is a distinguished lecturer -- marketing, College of Business Administration at the University of South Carolina with additional work with the College of Charleston School of Business and Economics. His marketing and financial experience is of great value to the Corporation. Mr. Ballentine also serves as Secretary to the Corporation.

CORNELIUS J. DUFFY

President of Eagle Star Insurance Companies of America, New York. He also serves as Director, Pension Committee, Universal Maritime Services Corporation of New York.

J. ADDISON INGLE, JR.

Has been a senior executive in the insurance industry since 1950. He is Vice President and Secretary of Heffron, Ingle, McDowell and Cooper, Insurance, Charleston.

JOSEPH R. McPHEE, ESQ.

Has been legal and patent attorney for Mr. Dumas for eleven years, particularly as related to the fire detection instrumentation. Mr. McPhee is admitted to the bar of the State of New York, to many Federal Courts and to the Supreme Court of the United States.

DOUGLAS C. PLATE

A graduate from the United States Naval Academy in 1941, Vice Admiral Plate retired from active service in 1975. He was a member of the Citadel staff for six years and since has worked with a private consultant mostly to companies with maritime interests. His knowledge of fire hazards on ships is of great importance to the company in its marketing approach to the maritime industry.

H.B. SYMTHE, SR., ESQ

A senior partner of Buist, Moore, Symthe and McGee, Charleston, and has served as legal advisor to the Corporation for the past three years.

THOMAS E. THORNHILL

Served as Vice President and Treasurer of Charleston Oil Company, a distributor of petroleum products. He is a past president of the Clemson University Alumni Association and served on the board of visitors of the University. Mr. Thornhill is presently a commercial realtor in the Charleston area.

146

EXHIBIT 2
RESEARCH EQUIPMENT CORPORATION

Development Phase Flow Chart

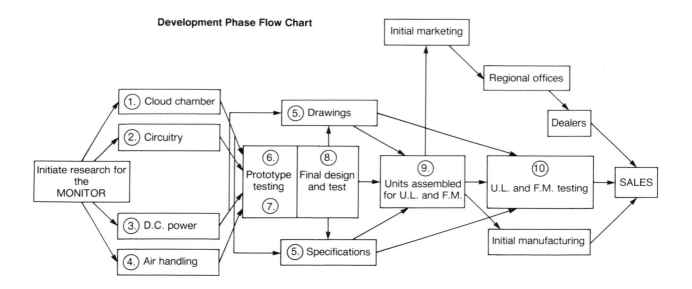

EXHIBIT 3
RESEARCH EQUIPMENT CORPORATION

R & D Phase Budget

	Apr	May	Jun	Jul	Aug	Sep	TOTAL
YEAR ONE							
GENERAL EXPENSES							
Wages and Salaries	5,000	5,000	5,000	5,000	5,000	5,000	$30,000
Tax	850	850	850	850	850	850	$5,100
Rent	500	500	500	500	500	500	$3,000
Tel & Tel	500	500	500	500	500	500	$3,000
Legal	0	1,000	0	0	0	0	$1,000
Audit	0	500	500	0	500	500	$2,000
Travel	1,500	1,000	2,000	2,500	3,000	2,000	$12,000
Auto Expense	200	200	500	500	500	300	$2,200
Insurance	800	800	1,000	1,000	1,000	1,000	$5,600
Miscellaneous	300	300	300	500	500	500	$2,400
Total	9,650	10,650	11,150	11,350	12,350	11,150	$66,300
Office Expenses							
Word Processing	500	500	700	700	700	700	$3,800
Misc. Office Exp.	200	400	400	500	500	500	$2,500
Total	700	900	1,100	1,200	1,200	1,200	$6,300
Consultants							
Cotty	0	700	700	700	700	700	$3,500
Fortier	0	2,600	2,600	2,600	2,600	2,600	$13,000
Gaddis	0	1,000	1,000	1,000	1,000	1,000	$5,000
Kane	0	0	3,000	0	3,000	0	$6,000
Total	0	4,300	7,300	4,300	7,300	4,300	$27,500
Purchase Parts							
CC/HC Mold	0	0	2,000	1,000	0	0	$3,000
Electronics	0	0	0	500	500	0	$1,000
Misc. Allowance	1,000	1,000	1,000	1,000	1,000	1,000	$6,000
Total	1,000	1,000	3,000	2,500	1,500	1,000	$10,000
Special Items							
Debt Service	0	2,000	0	2,000	0	0	$4,000
Clemson University	0	0	10,000	10,000	10,000	10,000	$40,000
F.M. & U.L. Units	0	0	0	2,000	4,000	4,000	$10,000
F.M. & U.L. Tests	0	0	0	0	20,000	20,000	$40,000
Total	0	2,000	10,000	14,000	34,000	34,000	$94,000
GRAND TOTAL	$11,350	$18,850	$32,550	$33,350	$56,350	$51,650	$204,100

148

EXHIBIT 4
RESEARCH EQUIPMENT CORPORATION

Control Cabinet Component Location

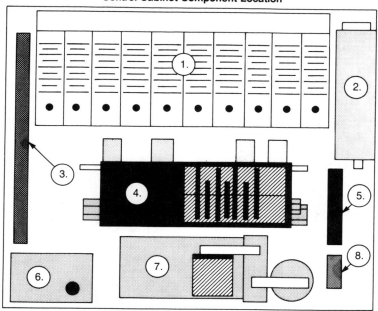

1. Air flow meters and air manifold assembly. (Paragraph 4.3.3)
2. Water supply. (Paragraph 5.2)
3. Microcontroller printed circuit board.
4. Manifold block assembly. (Paragraph 5.3)
5. Terminal block 2 (remote and malfunction alarm signal). (Paragraph 4.2.4)
6. Power supply. (Paragraph 5.5)
7. Vacuum pump/motor.
8. Terminal block 1 (electrical power). (Paragraph 4.2.3)

EXHIBIT 5
RESEARCH EQUIPMENT CORPORATION
SPECIFICATIONS OF MONITOR

FIRE SIGNATURE DETECTED: Invisible and visible products of
                                        combustion.

AREA PROTECTED: Up to 10,000 sq. ft.

AIR INTAKE PORTS: Six to ten,
                                        plastic 2-1/2" high x 2" diameter

MAXIMUM TUBE LENGTH FROM
CABINET TO AIR INTAKE PORT: 100 ft.

MINIMUM TUBE LENGTH: 25 ft.

ALARM CONTACTS RATING: 0.5 amps at 120 VAC (N.O.)
                                        1.5 amps at 30 VDC

TROUBLE CONTRACTS RATING: 0.5 amps at 120 VAC (N.O. or N.C.)
                                        1.5 amps at 30 VDC

POWER REQUIREMENTS:
   Voltage   115v A.C.
   Frequency   60 Hz
   Power   50 watts

WATER REQUIREMENTS:
   Quantity   One quart/three months
   Quality   Distilled

CONTROL CABINET:
   Size   17" x 16" x 8"
   Weight   42 lb.
   Position   Vertical $\pm$ 5 degrees
   Ambient temperature   32-104°F

TUBING: 1/4" O.D. aluminum alloy

SENSITIVITY: Independently set for each installation for
                                        warning, alert and alarm levels.

EXHIBIT 6
RESEARCH EQUIPMENT CORPORATION
INSTALLATION REQUIREMENTS

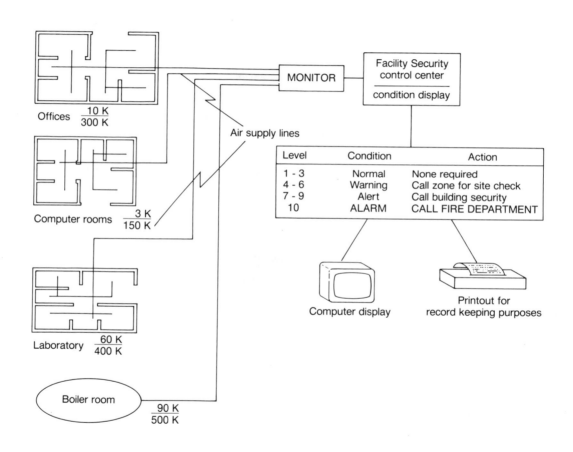

EXHIBIT 7
RESEARCH EQUIPMENT CORPORATION

Air Intake Port Assembly

1/4″ Tube x
1/4″ NPT fitting

1″

Flat washer

Lock nut

Ceiling panel

2 1/2″

Air filter

1/8″

2″

Air sample

Air sample

EXHIBIT 8
RESEARCH EQUIPMENT CORPORATION

Air Transport System Diagram

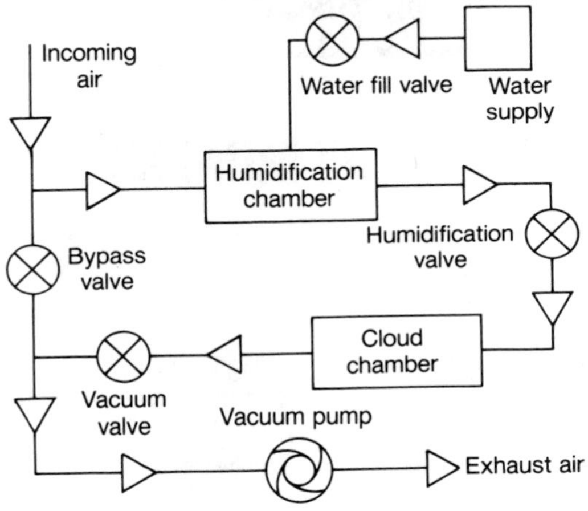

Incoming air

Water fill valve   Water supply

Humidification chamber

Bypass valve

Humidification valve

Cloud chamber

Vacuum valve

Vacuum pump

Exhaust air

EXHIBIT 9
RESEARCH EQUIPMENT CORPORATION
EARLY ADVERTISEMENT

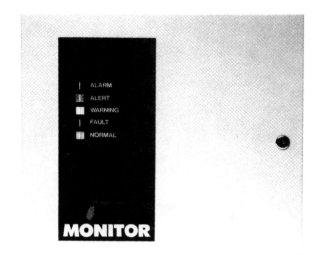

WHY MONITOR?

The Monitor can sense a fire before it starts. The Monitor continuously measures the density of submicron-sized particles of combustion in the air which are released whenever a combustible material is heated. The number of particles released increases as the heat increases.

The Monitor virtually eliminates false alarms. Because it ignores larger particles such as dust and cigarette smoke, The Monitor can be used in environments which cause other types of detectors to sound false alarms including warehouses, mines and manufacturing facilities. Airborne dust precludes the use of ordinary detectors. The Monitor provides warning, alert and alarms consistent with the progress of the hazard.

The Monitor's level of sensitivity can be adjusted. The Monitor's on board computer is programmed to ignore normal levels of particle density in the cafeteria, where smoking is likely to occur, or to respond to a much lower level in "clean" rooms. Thus it can protect an entire building by compensating for ambient conditions. For example, the alarm level setting in a computer room would have a lower particle density than an alarm level in a conference room.

The Monitor is easy to install, easy to maintain. No complex wiring or delicate sensors are needed. What's more, The Monitor's computer provides self-diagnostic functions for easy maintenance.

μ MONITOR

Research Equipment Corporation • 3125 Ashley Phosphate Road • North Charleston, SC 29418 (803) 760-1900 • FAX (803) 767-4952
Boston • Atlanta • Austin

EXHIBIT 10
RESEARCH EQUIPMENT CORPORATION
FUTURE ADVERTISEMENT

EXHIBIT 11

RESEARCH EQUIPMENT CORPORATION
PRO FORMA OPERATING STATEMENT

MONTH	1	2	3	4	5	6	7	8	9	10	11	12	TOTAL	%
GENERAL & ADMINISTRATIVE														
Wages and Salaries & Tax*	18,854	24,191	24,676	24,676	24,676	27,518	27,518	30,638	30,638	30,638	30,638	30,638	$325,300	29.65%
Rent	1,000	1,000	1,500	1,500	1,500	2,000	2,000	2,000	2,000	2,000	2,000	2,000	$20,500	1.87%
Tel & Tel	1,000	1,000	1,000	1,500	1,500	1,500	1,500	1,500	1,500	1,500	1,500	1,500	$16,500	1.50%
Legal	1,000	1,000	1,000	0	0	1,000	1,000	0	0	0	0	1,000	$6,000	0.55%
Audit	1,000	1,000	1,000	0	0	1,000	1,000	0	0	1,000	0	1,000	$7,000	0.64%
Office	2,000	2,000	2,000	2,000	2,000	2,000	2,000	2,000	2,000	2,000	2,000	2,000	$24,000	2.19%
Travel	2,000	2,000	2,000	3,000	3,000	3,000	4,000	4,000	4,000	4,000	4,000	4,000	$39,000	3.55%
Auto Expense	500	500	700	700	1,000	1,000	1,000	1,000	1,000	1,000	1,000	1,000	$10,400	0.95%
Insurance	700	700	1,000	1,000	1,000	1,500	1,500	1,500	2,000	2,000	2,000	2,000	$16,900	1.54%
Debt Service	1,000	1,000	1,000	1,000	1,000	1,000	1,000	1,000	1,000	1,000	1,000	1,000	$12,000	1.09%
Total	29,054	34,391	35,876	35,376	35,676	41,518	42,518	43,638	44,138	45,138	44,138	46,138	$477,600	43.53%
SALES EXPENSE														
District Office*	6,000	8,000	8,000	10,000	12,000	12,000	12,000	15,000	15,000	20,000	20,000	20,000	$158,000	14.40%
Regional Office	6,000	12,000	12,000	18,000	24,000	24,000	24,000	30,000	30,000	36,000	42,000	42,000	$300,000	27.34%
Dealer Training	2,000	3,000	2,000	3,000	5,000	4,000	4,000	7,000	7,000	8,000	10,000	8,000	$63,000	5.74%
Advertising	2,000	3,000	3,000	2,000	2,000	2,000	2,000	2,000	2,000	2,000	2,000	2,000	$26,000	2.37%
Trade Show Annual (1)	0	0	0	0	0	24,000	0	0	0	0	0	0	$24,000	2.19%
Housing Expense (2)	5,500	500	500	500	500	5,500	500	500	500	5,500	500	500	$21,000	1.91%
Total	21,500	26,500	25,500	33,500	43,500	71,500	42,500	54,500	54,500	71,500	74,500	72,500	$592,000	53.96%
DEPRECIATION EXPENSE														
Fixtures & Equipment	2,300	2,300	2,300	2,300	2,300	2,300	2,300	2,300	2,300	2,300	2,300	2,300	$27,600	2.52%
GRAND TOTAL	$52,854	$63,191	$63,676	$71,176	$81,476	$115,318	$87,318	$100,438	$100,938	$118,938	$120,938	$120,938	$1,097,200	100.00%

Notes:
(1) Annual N.F.P.A. Convention
(2) Local Housing for Trainees & Executives, Relocation

EXHIBIT 12

RESEARCH EQUIPMENT CORPORATION
PROFORMA INCOME STATEMENT

($,000 omitted)

	YEAR 1•	YEAR 2••	YEAR 3	YEAR 4
INCOME				
SALES	$0	$1,244	$4,180	$7,520
(-) *MANUFACTURING COST*	$0	$339	$970	$1.551
GROSS INCOME SALES	$0	$905	$3,210	$5,969
OTHER INCOME	$0	$315	$165	$120
TOTAL GROSS INCOME	$0	$1,220	$3,375	$6,089
EXPENSES				
OPERATING COST	$204	$477	$659	$873
DISTRICT SALES OFFICES	$0	$158	$205	$510
REGIONAL SALES OFFICES	$0	$300	$645	$915
SALES EXPENSES	$0	$113	$101	$215
HOUSING EXPENSE	$0	$21	$16	$26
TOTAL OPERATING EXPENSES	$204	$1,069	$1,626	$2,539
DEPRECIATION EXPENSE	$0	$27	$30	$78
TOTAL EXPENSES	$204	$1,096	$1,656	$2,617
NET PROFIT (LOSS)	($204)	$124	$1.719	$3,472
ACCUMULATIVE PROFIT (LOSS)	($204)	($80)	$1,639	$5,111
MONITORS SOLD (UNITS)	0	311	1,045	1,880

• *Year one is devoted to product development and submission of the MONITOR to Underwriter Laboratories and Factory Mutual*
•• *Sales of the MONITOR begin in year two.*

EXHIBIT 13

RESEARCH EQUIPMENT CORPORATION
INCOME STATEMENT

YEAR TWO

	1	2	3	4	5	6	7	8	9	10	11	12	TOTAL
DEALERSHIPS	2	3	2	3	5	4	4	7	7	8	10	8	63
DEALER ACCUMULATIVE	2	5	7	10	15	19	23	30	37	45	55	63	63
UNITS SOLD	2	5	7	10	15	19	23	30	37	45	55	63	311
INCOME													
SALES @ $4,000	8,000	20,000	28,000	40,000	60,000	76,000	92,000	120,000	148,000	180,000	220,000	252,000	$1,244,000
EXPENSES													
COST OF MANUFACTURING	2,400	6,000	8,400	12,000	18,000	22,800	27,600	31,500	38,850	47,250	57,750	66,150	$338,700
NET INCOME FROM SALES	5,600	14,000	19,600	28,000	42,000	53,200	64,400	88,500	109,150	132,750	162,250	185,850	$905,300
OTHER INCOME													
DEALER FEES	10,000	15,000	15,000	15,000	25,000	20,000	20,000	35,000	35,000	40,000	50,000	40,000	$315,000
TOTAL INCOME FROM OPERATION	15,600	29,000	29,600	43,000	67,000	73,200	84,400	123,500	144,150	172,750	212,250	225,850	$1,220,300

YEAR THREE

	1	2	3	4	5	6	7	8	9	10	11	12	TOTAL
DEALERSHIPS	5	8	2	5	4	2	1	3	2	1	1	0	33
DEALER ACCUMULATIVE	5	13	15	20	24	26	27	30	31	32	33	33	63
UNITS SOLD	68	76	78	83	87	89	90	93	94	95	96	96	1,045
INCOME													
SALES @ $4,000	272,000	304,000	312,000	332,000	348,000	356,000	360,000	372,000	376,000	380,000	384,000	384,000	$4,180,000
EXPENSES													
COST OF MANUFACTURING	71,400	79,800	81,900	87,150	91,350	93,450	74,250	76,725	77,550	78,375	79,200	79,200	$970,350
NET INCOME FROM SALES	200,600	224,200	230,100	244,850	256,650	262,550	285,750	295,275	298,450	301,625	304,800	304,800	$3,209,650
OTHER INCOME													
DEALER FEES	25,000	40,000	10,000	25,000	20,000	10,000	5,000	15,000	5,000	5,000	5,000	0	$165,000
TOTAL INCOME FROM OPERATION	225,600	264,200	240,100	269,850	276,650	272,550	290,750	310,275	303,450	306,625	309,800	304,800	$3,374,650

YEAR FOUR

	1	2	3	4	5	6	7	8	9	10	11	12	TOTAL
DEALERSHIPS	2	2	2	2	2	2	2	2	2	2	2	2	24
DEALER ACCUMULATIVE	2	4	6	8	10	12	14	16	18	20	22	24	63
UNITS SOLD	98	102	108	116	126	138	152	168	186	206	228	252	1,880
INCOME													
SALES @ $4,000	392,000	408,000	432,000	464,000	504,000	552,000	608,000	672,000	744,000	824,000	912,000	1,008,000	$7,520,000
EXPENSES													
COST OF MANUFACTURING	80,850	84,150	89,100	95,700	103,950	113,850	125,400	138,600	153,450	169,950	188,100	207,900	$1,551,000
NET INCOME FROM SALES	311,150	323,850	342,900	368,300	400,050	438,150	482,600	533,400	590,550	654,050	723,900	800,100	$5,969,000
OTHER INCOME													
DEALER FEES	10,000	10,000	10,000	10,000	10,000	10,000	10,000	10,000	10,000	10,000	10,000	10,000	$120,000
TOTAL INCOME FROM OPERATION	321,150	333,850	352,900	378,300	410,050	448,150	492,600	543,400	600,550	664,050	733,900	810,100	$6,089,000

FOWLER TOOL & DIE, INC.

"Another shipment back from Saginaw, Boss. Same thing." They had just received 25,000 washers rejected by a customer. It was not the first time it had happened.

"How the ---- can they reject parts when their own receiving inspection report shows no defects?" queried Mr. Hanson.

THE COMPANY

Fowler Tool began life in 1939 as a small supplier of tools and fixtures to the automotive industry in Detroit. For the first ten years of its existence the company remained a six-person shop in a small town outside Detroit. In 1949 the company was bought by its current owner, a war surplus industrial machinery salesman. Using contacts built within the industry, he transformed the company into a high-volume metal stamping components supplier to the automotive industry.

The company was organized as a closely held family corporation, with Mr. Hanson holding the majority of shares and the rest distributed among his immediate family. The company slowly grew and prospered, gaining its first million dollar gross sales year in 1963. Indeed, slow growth was the rule for Fowler Tool as Mr. Hanson saw rapid expansion as dangerous in a cyclical industry, and also as a threat to his ability to personally control the firm. The firm was very much a one-man operation, and Mr. Hanson ran it as a feudal fiefdom. An industrial engineer by training, he immersed himself in every detail of operations. One of his favorite homilies was, "I've noticed that it's when people think for themselves that we get into trouble around here."

Nevertheless, he was able to recognize talent (if not acknowledge it) and build a small core of able staff, and by paying them more than their educational background required in this industry segment would seem to warrant was able to command their loyalty.

The shop superintendent (father of eight children) was married at an early age. He became a milk route salesman after completing high school, and wasn't able to make a go of it. Starting at Fowler as a press operator in the mid-fifties when the shop had fewer than ten employees, he quickly rose to superintendent as number two person after Mr. Hanson. Among his duties were coordinating production and shipping.

He was also the buffer between labor and Mr. Hanson. Much of his time was spent responding to customer inquiries as to expediting the blanket orders, as well as integrating the secondary operations such as heat treat, plating, grinding and sorting (outside labor).

The foreman joined Fowler after completing 16 years as an engineer's mate in the submarine service. His responsibility was to keep presses running, assigning workers to various jobs, and knowing what to do when a press malfunctioned or a product defect was apparent. He soon learned with the help of the superintendent when and when not to bother Mr. Hanson about a shop-related problem.

FINANCE

Financial Statements are provided in Exhibits I through V. They include the Balance Sheet, Income Statement, cost of goods manufactured, selling expense, and administrative expense for the years 1983 through 1985. Exhibit VI is the source and use funds for 1984 and 1985.

Never one to be beholden to creditors, Fowler Tool eschewed any form of debt except trade debt, because it was usually free. Since Mr. Hanson was the sole signatory authority for the company, trade creditors were usually paid after repeated phone calls, when Mr. Hanson could spare time from details of operations. After all, "Someone has to keep this place running so they can be paid at all." Nevertheless, suppliers continued to supply because they were usually paid, eventually. (If there was a discount to be had, however, he would take it.) Payment delays were rationalized by, "We'll pay them when our customers pay us," "Prove to me that these were all good supplies," and "Watch the nickels and dimes and the dollars will take care of themselves."

The place continued to slowly grow, additional capacity being added on to the original plant as money from operations became available. By the 1970's Fowler Tool was grossing over $3 million annually with about 50 employees. Over 95 percent of its sales were to the big three automotive companies and over half of that to Chrysler.

MARKETING

Fowler Tool was little different than hundreds of other small suppliers to the automotive industry. In the past, marketing consisted largely of personal contacts developed among buyers and engineers and maintained by a manufacturer's representative who was paid a two percent commission on sales he originated. In the past two years, increasing amounts of sales were generated from direct inquiries to Fowler rather than through the representative. These contacts resulted in a request to bid, and Fowler's price was competitive. The representative, a former buyer himself, knew that frequent visits, social and otherwise, and prompt follow-through on any problems were important in keeping buyers satisfied. More recently purchasing agents from the big three automakers have been making tours of supplier operations and basing buying decisions on more quantitative criteria such as lead time required, number of problem parts and percentage of rejected parts.

OPERATIONS

Fowler Tool made small metal parts destined for use in automobiles, ranging from washers to much more complex shapes, such as wing nuts to hold down spare tires. Punch presses, exerting pressures from one thousand pounds to 75 tons per square inch, contained dies that shaped the metal as they punched it out of flat metal strip. Parts were ejected from the die into cardboard boxes and the resultant metal scrap likewise ejected into large hoppers. The smaller parts were put through a deburring process before being counted and placed in shipping cartons.

The metal was typically steel of various metallurgical grades, but sometimes non-ferrous metals such as brass or copper were used. It came in strips ranging from half an inch to six inches wide and in thicknesses of 0.004" to nearly one quarter of an inch, depending on the part being made. Strip were rolled into large coils weighing from fifty pounds to several thousand pounds each. They were put individually onto reels and were fed into the presses so that every downstroke of the press made one part, sometimes two. The process ran at speeds of one to two strokes per second and ten or more strokes per minute on larger parts.

After a coil was loaded onto the reel a machine operator was expected to start feeding the coil into the press, start the machine, spot check finished parts for critical specifications as it ran, stop the machine when a coil was expended, and generally be alert for any misfeed or machine malfunction to prevent damage to the machine. A coil would yield 700 to 7,000 parts. Sometimes one operator ran two machines, depending on the complexity of the parts being made. The operator was central to the successful operation of the company.

THE INDUSTRY

The early 1980's were a time of turmoil for the domestic U.S. auto industry. Emerging from the worst recession since the Great Depression and the near bankruptcy of Chrysler Corp., the industry was also staggering from continued worldwide market share loss to foreign competition. Besides their pricing disadvantage linked to the then high riding U.S. dollar, the automakers came to the belated recognition that product quality was of central concern to the buyer. Survey after survey showed that American cars ranked lower than their imported cousins on nearly every score: quality perception, consumer complaints, frequency or repair, size of repair bills and so on.

Industry response was a wide-ranging and interrelated program to streamline operations and simultaneously attack the quality problem (not just the perception of

161

quality).   Automobile production is primarily an assembly operation, relying on components from a vast network of suppliers, some wholly owned and many more being independent operations.

Exhibit VII shows the domestic automobile production from 1972 through 1984.

JUST IN TIME (JIT)

The idea was reduce the number of suppliers to one - or perhaps two - suppliers for each component, whereas before they had preferred to keep a stable of vendors in order to have an ongoing competitive network of suppliers. With fewer suppliers they would then negotiate guaranteed long-term contracts with them, in terms of years rather than by the job as before. In return for this commitment suppliers could concentrate on streamlining their operations. This streamlining included the capability to deliver parts to the assembly line as they were needed. In effect, the carmakers were shifting their warehousing burdens to their vendors.

Using parts in a steady stream as they are received from suppliers, besides eliminating the warehousing function, also does away with receiving inspection, and this in a time when product quality is of paramount concern. The solution was to certify suppliers as having the capability to produce the necessary quality. In eliminating receiving quality inspection of components, the carmakers were instead inspecting the supplier of those components for quality. A supplier could sneak in a substandard shipment, but only once.

SQC AND SPC

In specifics this meant the capability of suppliers to practice statistical quality control (SQC) and statistical process control (SPC). Where previously quality control meant taking a random sample of product and ensuring that the sample was within specification, SQC meant taking a sample and ensuring that plus or minus three standard deviations from the mean of the sample (i.e., 99.75 percent of the population) fell within specifications. Thus a shipment could be rejected despite having no defects, because SQC "predicted" that some parts would be outside the range of specification. More detail is given in Exhibit VIII.

This capability was generally within the domain of many if not most quality departments, where product is checked by quality control when it is finished. When product is being checked for parameters critical to its performance as it is being made, the aim is to rectify a production process before defects are produced. The goal of SPC is to ensure that defects are never made. Continuous sampling (with the associated three standard deviations) has to spot trends in process before they become "out of control."

THE FUTURE

SPC presented special problems in a workforce in which high educational achievement is not a requirement, nor was an appreciation of statistical theory. Before, it was relatively simple to have a machine operator occasionally take measurements and stop a machine if a bad part was detected. How were they to be told to take a sample of critical dimensions, calculate the mean, determine the standard deviation, and see if plus or minus three standard deviations of the mean fell within specifications, all when parts were being produced by tens to hundreds per minute?

Fowler Tool has already received rejected shipments that had no defective parts but in which the dispersion of the critical parameter around the mean was simply too great as determined by the buyer's Quality Control Department. Mr. Hanson had received his technical education in the 1930's and had no training in statistical theory. He was consequently spending more of his time on the phone arguing with customers that they had to accept parts that were within specification, even while the parts were on truck en route back to their place of manufacture.

Not just competitiveness but survival was at stake. If the industry was going to reduce the number of its suppliers by half, it was critical that Fowler Tool not just adopt but embrace the new capabilities demanded by its customers. There were systems based on pencil and clipboard, though they had no one who understood them, and there were computer systems that monitored parts as they were being made. There were also consultants everywhere waiting to take money.

Mr. Hanson wondered what options he faced, and how would each affect the "bottom line." He could resign and let the Board of Directors replace him, or he could ask the Board to agree to sell the firm to someone more familiar with the new Quality Control technology.

But Mr. Hanson just wasn't up to quitting just yet. Should he find a "right hand person" with this statistical knowledge and compatible with the rest of the team, so he could come in to the office a few days a week and go over the books as he had enjoyed doing so many years? He really couldn't see himself changing but was there a way he could find or create a buffer between himself and the customer? He was sure there were other ways of solving his problems, but it was time to go home.

EXHIBIT I
FOWLER TOOL & DIE, INC.
Balance Sheet
(In Dollars)

	1985	1984	1983
CURRENT ASSETS			
Cash	420,674	350,625	44,252
Accounts Receivable	755,297	739,185	700,025
Inventory	553,440	660,582	721,086
Prepaid Expenses	69,731	106,725	14,093
Total	1,799,142	1,857,117	1,479,456
FIXED ASSETS			
Land	28,425	13,599	13,599
Building	157,971	157,971	157,971
Machinery & Equipment	347,111	395,327	459,480
Total	533,507	566,897	631,050
Less Depreciation	475,461	493,880	569,349
Total Net	58,046	73,017	61,701
OTHER ASSETS			
Loan Receivable – Officer			60,182
Unamortized Organ. Costs	10,281	23,330	36,378
Other	6,425		17,250
Total	16,706	23,330	113,810
TOTAL ASSETS	1,873,894	1,953,464	1,654,967
CURRENT LIABILITIES			
Accounts Payable	627,828	823,073	496,343
Short Term Debt	4,707	10,701	23,942
Accrued Expenses	118,296	97,908	181,625
Total	750,831	931,682	701,910
LONG-TERM DEBT			
Deferred Compensation			37,500
Unfunded Pension	90,096	90,096	90,096
Total	90,096	90,096	127,596
TOTAL LIABILITIES	840,927	1,021,778	829,506
EQUITY			
Common Stock	30,002	30,002	30,002
Paid-in Capital	504,786	504,786	504,786
Retained Earnings	498,177	396,899	290,673
Total	1,032,965	931,687	825,461
TOTAL LIABILITIES & EQUITY	1,873,892	1,953,465	1,654,967

EXHIBIT II
FOWLER TOOL & DIE, INC.
Statement of Income
(In Dollars)

	1985	1984	1983
SALES	5,807,178	5,625,122	5,402,777
COST OF GOODS SOLD	5,265,486	5,125,290	4,808,910
GROSS INCOME	541,692	499,832	593,867
OPERATING EXPENSES			
Selling Expense	76,286	88,871	112,455
Administrative Expense	398,117	359,433	291,884
Total	474,403	448,304	404,339
OPERATING INCOME	67,289	51,528	189,528
OTHER INCOME (EXPENSE)			
Sale of Scrap	113,913	140,249	124,709
Interest Income	31,464	15,318	6,476
Depreciation	(19,272)	(21,680)	(23,769)
Total	126,105	133,887	107,416
Income Before Tax	193,394	185,415	296,944
Income Tax	92,115	79,190	105,791
NET INCOME	101,279	106,225	191,153

EXHIBIT III
FOWLER TOOL & DIE, INC.
Cost of Goods Sold
(In Dollars)

	1985	1984	1983
Beginning Inventory	660,582	721,086	677,813
Purchases - Materials	2,376,842	2,330,691	2,374,105
Freight & Cartage	56,070	67,310	54,438
Total	3,093,494	3,119,087	3,106,356
Less Ending Inventory	553,440	660,582	721,086
COST OF MATERIALS	2,540,054	2,458,505	2,385,270
OUTSIDE LABOR	920,457	816,951	660,185
DIRECT LABOR	712,398	738,654	658,938
MANUFACTURING EXPENSE			
Officer's Salary	120,279	117,722	116,804
Deferred Compensation			37,500
Supervision - Other	280,022	260,675	296,927
Shop Supplies	212,455	224,707	121,358
Repair & Maintenance	52,880	64,437	162,101
Heat, Light & Power	58,310	65,898	51,459
Taxes	135,275	140,874	126,254
Insurance	163,250	165,983	127,419
Pension & ESOP	70,106	70,884	64,695
Total	1,092,577	1,111,180	1,104,517
COST OF GOODS SOLD	5,265,486	5,125,290	4,808,910

EXHIBIT IV
FOWLER TOOL & DIE, INC.
Selling Expense
(In Dollars)

	1985	1984	1983
Advertising	167	742	87
Commissions	65,687	71,855	93,516
Travel & Entertainment	10,433	16,274	18,852
TOTAL SELLING EXPENSE	76,287	88,871	112,455

EXHIBIT V
FOWLER TOOL & DIE, INC.
Administrative Expense
(In Dollars)

	1985	1984	1983
Outside Consulting	58,901	23,250	
Office Salaries	84,596	73,701	55,509
Officer Life Insurance	71,454	17,819	2,267
Telephone	23,043	24,668	18,263
Office Expense	33,245	34,851	67,715
Legal & Accounting	79,104	112,313	142,691
Misc. Expense	47,774	72,831	5,439
TOTAL ADMINISTRATIVE EXPENSE	398,117	359,433	291,884

EXHIBIT VI
FOWLER TOOL & DIE, INC.
Sources & Uses of Funds
(In Dollars)

	1985	1984
Income from Operations	101,279	106,226
Depreciation	13,203	11,406
Funds from Operations	114,482	117,632
Accounts Receivable	(16,112)	(39,160)
Accounts Payable	(195,245)	326,729
Inventories	107,142	60,504
Other Current Liabilities	36,995	(92,633)
Current Liabilities less Debt	20,388	(83,717)
Property, Plant & Equipment	1,769	(22,722)
Other Assets	6,624	90,480
Total	(38,439)	239,481
Funds Excess (need)	76,043	357,113
Financed By		
Cash	(70,049)	(306,372)
Short-Term Debt	(5,994)	(13,241)
Long-Term Debt		(37,500)
Total	(76,043)	(357,113)

EXHIBIT VII
U.S. AUTOMOBILE PRODUCTION

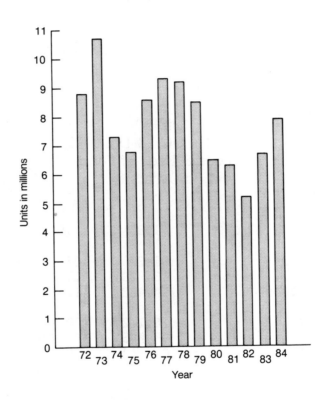

Exhibit VIII
FOWLER TOOL & DIE, INC.
More on Statistical Quality Control

The goal of "zero defects" was important for two reasons other than bragging about quality. Safety considerations on critical parts often mandated parts to be within specification to preclude failure as a part wore. The other reason was the increased use of automated assembly procedures. A single bad part in a steady stream could jam an assembly machine, causing expensive down time. In either case, a shipment of 10,000 parts that is 99.99% defect free could pose serious problems.

SQC calls for a normal bell curve inclusive of three standard deviations superimposed over the allowable range of specifications to have no part of the curve exceeding the specification.

In one particular instance, a washer called for an inside diameter of 1.729 inches to 1.732 inches. In the production process a washer blank is placed in a die and a punch going through a striper ring punches out the center. As production progresses, the stripper ring gradually wears minimally, producing a larger inside diameter. To get more use from the stripper ring, the dimensions are set to the lower end of the specification, 1.729 inches. Thus a production run was composed of a large number of washers with an inside diameter of 1.729 inches and others with an inside diameter of 1.730 inches. A 30 piece sample yielded no pieces at 1.729 and 10 at 1.730, for a mean of 1.729 and plus or minus three deviations yielded a range of 1.728 to 1.731 if a normal distribution is assumed, and it was. In effect, SQC predicted that 23.6% of the parts would be below the lower limit of the specification. The diagram below shows the plot of the curves.

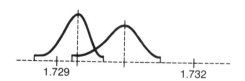

1.729   1.732

In this case the parts were sent back to the customer when it could be shown that the distribution was not normal (it was highly skewed). But it was resolved when a consultant could speak the language of statistics to the customer. But Mr. Hanson still could not understand why they were rejected in the first place.

WAVERLY PHARMACY, INC.

Five years ago Edward Kelly bought half interest in Waverly Drug Store in Waverly, Ohio, which is 54 miles south of Columbus, from Wayne Schmidt who had been the sole owner. The business operated as a partnership and included the drug store, which rented the first floor and basement of the building on the corner of Main Street and Washington Street, which was owned equally by Edward Kelly and Wayne Schmidt, and the Waverly Card and Gift Shop also located on Main Street. Mr. Schmidt had decided to sell his business because he was 58 and experiencing some health problems.

Edward Kelly began working at Waverly Drug Store 27 years ago at the age of 13 while attending school. His experience working at the store stimulated his interest in pharmacy so he studied it at Ohio State and graduated in 1959. He then returned to full-time employment at the drug store as a pharmacist. He also worked part-time as the pharmacist at Oakvale, a psychiatric hospital located in nearby Chillicothe.

The Waverly Card and Gift Shop was originally purchased by Mr. Schmidt when it was the competing drug store and the owner wished to retire. It was then changed to a patent medicine discount store by Mr. Schmidt and operated as such for a number of years. Finally, it was converted to the present card and gift shop as an outlet for Hallmark cards. Mrs. Mary Williams manages the store, which employs the equivalent of another full-time clerk. The store, which is leased, contains 1200 square feet of floor space. It breaks even at a sales volume of about $8,500 per month.

The Next Five Years

Within a year of Edward Kelly's entering the business, the nature of pharmacy began to change. The Methodist Retirement Home of Waverly asked Waverly Pharmacy to supply its drug requirements. Business at the store increased as well and Ed found he had insufficient time to spend at Oakvale so he resigned.

By July, 1975, the other older chief pharmacist at Oakvale decided to retire so the hospital asked Ed to return. He agreed to provide a pharmacist service through the company to Oakvale for a monthly fee. Since Ed did not have enough personal time, he provided the service by hiring other pharmacists on a part-time basis.

Because of continuing time pressures, Ed decided he needed additional management help. By chance William Bremer, who was District Manager of the Value X Drug Stores in Ohio at the time, contacted Ed regarding employment.

Bill and Ed had gone through pharmacy school together at Ohio State and were good friends. Bill had gone to work for Value X, a division of a large grocery chain, as a store manager upon graduation. After three years he was promoted to District Manager responsible for 14 stores in Ohio. After a year in this job Bill had become dissatisfied because he did not have the flexibility he desired to make decisions and he disliked the traveling required.

After further discussions Ed and Wayne decided to restructure the business. On July 1, 1974, the business was incorporated and Bill Bremer entered the business by buying 80 percent of Wayne Schmidt's interest. Thus the final ownership became Ed Kelly - 50 percent, Bill Bremer - 40 percent and Wayne Schmidt - 10 percent. A buy-out arrangement was also made for Ed and Bill to each buy half of Wayne's share when he dies or wishes to sell.

Waverly Drug Store

The first thing Ed did to the drug store upon taking over management of it was to get rid of the soda fountain, which had not been profitable and took up a valuable part of the 2000 square feet of floor space. The store was rearranged and the liquor section put in place of the soda fountain. The store is a Rexall outlet. It sells health and beauty aids, greeting cards by American Greeting Card, tobacco products, magazines, liquor, special sale items such as electric broilers, etc., and over-the-counter and prescription drugs.

The "front" part of the store is run by Audrey Vale, who is 62 years old and has worked at the store for many years. She supervises the equivalent of 4 clerks who are young women, high school age or somewhat older working on a part-time basis.

The prescription counter does 55 percent of the dollar volume of the store, which is higher than the normal 30 percent. The equivalent of 5 full time pharmacists is utilized behind the counter, including the two active owners. Part of the explanation for this high volume may be the services provided to customers.

A patient profile is maintained on regular prescription customers as shown in Exhibit I. Exhibit II is the instruction sheet given the customer before he fills out the profile form.

The patient usage of hypertensive drugs is monitored and a reminder card sent out if a prescription is not renewed as required by the prescribed dosage. If there is no response within five days, the patient is called as an additional reminder. The store uses pharmacy interns from Ohio State to operate this monitoring system. The store also has a series of descriptive instruction sheets for patients describing how to administer medications such as eye drops and ointments, nose drops and ear drops.

The store is open from 8 a.m. to 9 p.m. six days a week and from 9 a.m. to 1 p.m. on Sunday. Pharmacy interns are used for weekend work.

Contract Pharmacists Service

The company provides a pharmacist service to Oakvale Hospital for 62 hours per week, up from the original 40 hours. Oakvale buys their drugs directly but the pharmacist supervises the preparation of the dosage amounts prepared by technicians and checks the drug trays after they are prepared. The pharmacist delivers the drug trays to the individual nursing stations. This involvement of the pharmacist with the nurses is unusual but helps smooth out problems and cements relations between the nurses and the pharmacist.

The company has been supplying drugs to the Waverly Medical Center. However, the Medical Center is going to establish an in-house pharmacy and the company will provide the pharmaceutical service to the Medical Center. The equivalent of two full-time pharmacists will be provided with duties similar to those provided at Oakvale, except the pharmacists will also mix intravenous solutions for administration to patients. Once a hospital exceeds 75 beds it is considered economical to purchase drugs directly. However, it is not convenient to employ pharmacists in many cases because of the hours to be covered.

Unit Dose System

As mentioned earlier the company began providing a drug service for the Methodist Retirement Home four years ago. Soon after, the same service was begun for a 54-bed nursing home in Lucasville, which is 18 miles south of Waverly. The Lucasville Nursing Home was added because Waverly Pharmacy, Inc., would use the unit dose system.

The unit dose system, which was conceived and is marketed by Uniscript of Fort Wayne, Indiana, consists of providing individually pre-packaged dosages for each patient for each time the drug is taken in a day. The drugs are packaged in a sealed, disposable bubble packet individually marked with patient's name, the name, lot number, expiration date and strength of the drug and the dispensing pharmacy. Uniscript provides the packaging supplies, trays and delivery carts for hospital use. The unit dose system has the advantages of less chance for a mismatch between patient and drugs required, minimizing nurses' time in disbursing drugs and not requiring a resident pharmacist. Exhibit III shows the individual packets, nurse's tray and standard nursing station. Exhibit IV describes the system.

Once Waverly Pharmacy began the unit dose system it proved popular with nursing homes and hospitals. Three more nursing homes were added in Circleville, Ohio, which is about 33 miles northeast of Waverly toward Columbus. These homes contacted the company requesting the service, having heard about it from nurses from other facilities using it. Oakville Hospital and Waverly Medical Center also use the unit dose system as the result of Waverly Pharmacy.

Waverly Pharmacy does all of the preparation of the unit doses in a remodeled former apartment in half of the second floor over the drug store. The balance of that floor is another apartment. A dumbwaiter was installed to transport the material up and down to the store.

The unit dose operation is supervised by Beverly Cole, who is 25 years old. She had worked at the drug store as a clerk while in high school. She attended Ohio State for one year taking general business courses. Although she made A grades, she was dissatisfied and dropped out of school to return to work at the store. She also prepares the accounts receivable data for Medicaid patients, which are forwarded to a computer service for subsequent billing. Sue White, one of the clerks, prepares the accounts receivable data for Blue Cross patients.

There are the equivalent of 8 full-time technicians including Beverly, who prepare the unit doses. A reproducing typewriter is used to prepare the labels. A sealing machine prepares the bubble packs. Drugs are stored in individually labeled compartments in cupboards or refrigerators.

As the unit doses are prepared, they are placed in individually labeled compartments of trays for each nursing station for each time period. These trays are then checked by a pharmacist and placed into locked carrying cases for subsequent delivery.

The company employs two drivers, one of whom acts as the supervisor. Deliveries are made every day between 2 and 8 p.m., since only a day's supply is prepared because dosage and drugs used for a patient may vary day to day. Changes in the drugs prescribed can be made up to 2 p.m. and still be delivered the same day. A company-owned van is used for delivery as well as a leased station wagon and four-wheel drive vehicle. The wagon and four-wheel drive vehicle are used by Ed and Bill when deliveries are not being made. The company has never failed to make a delivery even during severe winter weather.

Waverly Pharmacy will have 1000 beds on the unit dose system with the addition of two more nursing homes within the next two months. Ed believes the 1000 square feet used for preparing the doses will limit future business. He estimates 2000 beds would be required to justify a second facility.

Obtaining additional unit dose business appears to be easy since all business thus far has been unsolicited and received as the result of favorable comments by nurses who had moved to another nursing home and had spread the word. There is no competition in the area for this kind of service. In fact, Ed had to turn down a request from a chain of three nursing homes, containing 1000 beds located in Portsmouth, 29 miles to the south because of space limitations. He believes he could obtain this account in the future if conditions change.

Purchasing

Purchasing activities are dispersed. One of the pharmacists purchases the prescription drugs. The driver supervisor orders the over-the-counter drugs. Cosmetics, tobacco, etc., are ordered by Audrey Vale who supervises the "front" end of the store. All drugs are ordered through a distributor and the company gets the maximum discount because of its high volume.

Employee Relations

Waverly Pharmacy employs 35 people in all of its operations. Many of them are working part time while they attend school or by choice. Turnover is very low. Ed does not believe in asking anyone to do something he would not do himself and has demonstrated his interest by instituting a number of benefits since assuming the management.

The benefits provided include company-paid life insurance and full Blue Cross medical coverage for all full-time employees. Vacations are provided: 1 week for up to 3 years service, 2 weeks for 3 to 5 years service, 3 weeks for 5 to 10 years service and 4 weeks after 10 years service. Sick leave is given selectively but full time employees are always paid for time lost due to illness.

A Christmas bonus up to $1000 is paid to employees. The amount each employee shall receive is decided jointly by Ed and Bill. Each make up a listing and then the lists are compared and differences worked out. Few differences have been noted since each is closely involved with all employees and knows what was paid the previous year.

The company does not have a pension plan for the employees. Both Ed and Bill participate in a Keogh retirement plan for themselves.

The company provides a birthday party for each employee and semi-annual store parties in July and December. These store parties are held in a restaurant or an employee's home. Occasionally other social events are held like a skiing weekend to Petoskey, Michigan. All expenses were paid by the company with the group staying at a former employee's home there.

Clerks are started at $2.30 per hour and technicians at $2.75 per hour. Performance is evaluated every six months and an increase of $.25 per hour given if the evaluation is satisfactory. All employees including the owners are paid on an hourly basis for the time they work. Three full-time pharmacists are employed in addition to the owners. They are paid between $8.50 to $10 per hour depending upon their experience. Part time pharmacists are paid $8 to $10 per hour.

175

Finance

Waverly Pharmacy has an accounting firm prepare a monthly income statement. Exhibit V shows the balance sheets for the years 1972-76 and Exhibit VI shows the income statement for the same years. Bill maintains and prepares the financial data the accounting service uses.

The drug store extends credit to its customers. The customer must make a credit application, which is then checked with the Chillicothe Credit Bureau before credit is extended. Interest is charged at the rate of 1-1/2 percent per month after 30 days. If the account is not paid after 60 days a notice is sent requesting payment within ten days or the account will be turned over to a collection agency. Accounts are turned over to a collection agency after 90 days.

Accounts receivable are also incurred in the unit dose part of the business. One of the nursing homes has patients billed individually. All state Medicaid patients, who are 80 percent of the patients, are billed individually. A computer billing service is used to make Medicare billings because of the volume involved and because it updates the prices of drugs automatically each week. These government programs and private insurance programs such as Blue Cross have a fee schedule which ranges from $2.19 to $2.45 per prescription plus the cost of one month's supply of the drug. The average patient has five medications so the prescription fee is about $11.50 per patient plus the drug cost.

When discussing the financial aspects of the company Ed noted that accounts receivable had increased from $6500 seven years ago to $26,400 presently. Medicaid payments from the state tend to be irregular and slow depending upon financial conditions of the state. For instance, last October payments were not received for six weeks.

Ed said, "I was surprised by the need for cash turnover when I took over the business." In addition to the receivables mentioned above, the biweekly payroll has risen from $2000 five years ago to $8200 now. The company has not had to borrow recently to handle cash flow but could without any problem because the receivables are solid and represent good security.

Management

Although the company does not have a formal organization chart, Exhibit VII shows how the organization of the company functions. Ed and Bill divided the management duties between themselves since Wayne is relatively inactive in the business. Bill is very interested in the financial aspects of the business and Ed in the personnel. Both actively work behind the prescription counter at the store part of the time. They meet informally each day to review the business and discuss any problems that have arisen.

176

Ed works an average of 50 hours per week. He spends about half of his time outside the store on the hospital and nursing home aspects of the business. Of the half of his time spent in the store, he spends about half of it behind the prescription counter. He likes meeting people and would miss not being behind the counter.

Ed says he is not particularly interested in making a lot of money. Rather he is interested in the employees and providing good steady employment for them. He believes in being active in local affairs and has been the township clerk for a number of years.

Bill works an average of 55 hours per week. He shares the liaison with Ed for the nursing homes, works behind the prescription counter and handles the financial aspects of the business. He says he is motivated by money and wants his family to have some of the things he could not afford when he was growing up. He also likes the people contact that goes with the behind the counter work. He noted that the newer pharmacists do not seem to desire this patient contact, instead wanting a closer relationship to the physician. A pharmacist can make about $10 per hour working in a hospital.

Bill believes that "What is good for the town is good for Waverly Drug." For instance, he thinks the Card and Gift Shop is needed by the town as a public convenience. He would like to see Waverly Drug undergo a reasonable expansion over time. He believes some day the town will be able to support a shopping mall. He is active on a the Parks and Recreation Board and the school improvement committee.

EXHIBIT I
PATIENT PROFILE

Name _____   Address _____

Date of Birth _____   I.D. _____

Childproof Top Exception

Pay Status
- ☐ Cash
- ☐ Charge
- ☐ Blue Cross
- ☐ Medicaid
- ☐ Mediment
- ☐ PCS
- ☐ Paid

Chronic Illness
- ☐ Heart Disease
- ☐ High Blood Pressure
- ☐ Diabetes
- ☐ _____
- ☐ _____
- ☐ _____

Allergies/Adverse Effects
- ☐ Penicillins → _____
- ☐ Sulfa → _____
- ☐ Aspirin → _____
- ☐ _____ → _____
- ☐ _____ → _____
- ☐ Foods _____ → _____
- ☐ _____ —
- ☐ Hay Fever/Sinus ← _____
- ☐ Asthma ← _____
- ☐ Insect Sting → _____
- ☐ No known allergies

1. Nausea
2. Vomiting
3. Drowsiness
4. Rash, Hives
5. Itching
6. Wheezing/ Choking
7. Swelling/ Edema
8. Passed out/ Syncope
9. _____

Notes

M.D. _____   Educational Aids

Sig	#	R	Rx No.	M.D.	$	1	2	3	4	5	6	7	8	9	10	11	12

EXHIBIT II
INSTRUCTION SHEET

PATIENT MEDICATION PROFILE

Dear Patient:

Please take a few minutes to provide us with some information which will assist our pharmacists in the safe guarding of your health.

<u>Purpose</u>   Your individual profile will be used for the following purposes:

1.   To keep a record of prescription and non-prescription medications (for example cough syrups) you may purchase.

2.   To evaluate the medication and to help make sure it will not influence other medications you may be taking.

3.   To evaluate the effect of the medication on any possible allergies or conditions you may have that we know about.

<u>Benefits to the patient</u>   Your individual profile is designed to make sure that the course of your medication goes smoothly, causes you no extra problems and acts as a reminder if you forget to take any of the medicines you should be on regularly. While problems do not occur frequently, this is added insurance that your medication will do what it is supposed to, return you to a better state of health.

<u>Confidentiality</u>   Information is kept under security and is confidential. No patient information will be divulged to any person or agency without prior written authorization from you, except to health professionals providing care to you.

If you have any questions regarding your profile, please ask your pharmacist.

EXHIBIT III
UNIT DOSE PACKAGING

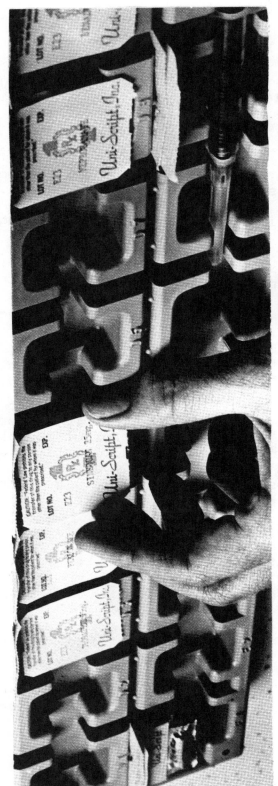

The Standard Nursing Station is of convenient size and wieght and is constructed such that everything is utilized into a med pass cart, thereby saving many steps.

Uni-Script provides a complete unit dose in-service training program for nursing home personnel with each new installation plus we offer a well balanced continuing education program.

180

EXHIBIT IV
UNIT DOSE SYSTEM

The Pharmacy Counter. Time saving techniques, simplified methods, and other innovations all combine to save time and thereby lower drug costs.

UNISCRIPT

unit dose as a concept

Unit dose, as a concept, is the prepackaging of one dose of a drug in a single, sealed, disposable container to be administered accordingly. The advantages of unit dose over the traditional prescription vial containing many doses, as employed in nursing homes and hospitals, include cleanliness, proper identification and labeling (even though upset or spilled), greater prescription accuracy (safety factor), time-saving convenience, elimination of waste, and providing the ultimate in drug control and prevention of theft and drug abuse. An emergency cabinet and a back-up cabinet are maintained at the facility by the pharmacy, and they contain hundreds of doses of medication. This means urgent medications are available immediately, instead of waiting for delivery.

daily delivery service

The Uni-Script unit dose system for nursing homes and hospitals provides for daily delivery of a 24-hour supply in a locked carrying cassette case from the pharmacy. When the medicine nurse unlocks the case, this means essentially that her set up work has already been performed for her at the pharmacy. Traditionally, the nurse located and opened a prescription bottle, took out a dose, put it in the patient's souffle cup, and replaced the Rx vial. For every 100 patients, she performs this operation 21,000 to 24,000 times per month, plus calling in refills. A true unit dose system eliminates this labor and saves 6 to 8 hours per day of nursing time per 100 beds. The nursing facility pays nothing for this service so that the savings may be utilized in terms of either time or money, depending on the facility in question (more and better nursing care and/or elimination of salary expense).

servicing the system

We have devised techniques and designed labels which save a substantial amount of the pharmacist's time in servicing the system under present procedures. Also, for the medium size and larger pharmacies, we have worked out a method whereby the pharmacist reduces his label typing time by at least 75%. This represents a very important savings in pharmacist's time and salary expense. The pharmacy storage tray will accept both dry and liquid unit dosage cups, and the same label may be employed interchangeably on either dosage form.

prescription costs

Uni-Script prescription costs to the patient population are approximately the same as traditional prescription procedures. Nursing homes like it because they can advertise that they are providing better nursing care and the professional advantages of unit dose at no extra cost to the patient. The Uni-Script unit dose system is superior to all others in several respects. Our "universal nurse's tray" (patent pending) will accommodate all forms of unit dose medications, such as all dry and liquid medications plus syringes, ampules, suppositories, etc., not just dry, oral forms. Uni-Script will accommodate various pharmaceutical manufacturer's designs of unit dose packaging, thereby further reducing drug costs. We also have devised a unique liquid unit dose cup (patent-pending) which will greatly reduce the cost of liquid unit dosages and provide much greater ease of administration to the patient. Our nurse's tray has "anti-bounce" features built into the design, and our carrying cassette case can be transported on the back seat of any compact car.

EXHIBIT V
BALANCE SHEET
Dollars

	Waverly Drug Store			Waverly Pharmacy	
	12/31/72	12/31/73	6/30/74	6/30/75	6/30/76
CURRENT ASSETS					
Cash	2,746	3,466	(1,428)	5,819	1,274
Accounts Receivable	6,517	14,110	7,552	28,553	26,370
Inventory					
Waverly Pharmacy	56,100	77,956	76,990	97,293	98,892
Card & Gift Shop	23,638	15,550	13,700	19,520	20,918
Total	79,738	93,506	90,690	116,813	119,810
Total Current Assets	89,001	111,082	96,814	151,185	147,454
FIXED ASSETS					
Leasehold Improvements				451	451
Furniture & Fixtures	58,964	60,461	61,808	70,783	72,924
Remodeling	9,677	9,677	9,677	9,677	9,677
Total	68,641	70,138	71,485	80,911	83,052
Less Depreciation	50,169	54,724	56,472	61,958	66,472
Net Fixed Assets	18,472	15,414	15,013	18,953	16,580
OTHER ASSETS					
Liquor License	15,000	15,000	15,000	15,000	15,000
Goodwill	25,000	25,000	25,000	25,000	25,000
Total Other Assets	40,000	40,000	40,000	40,000	40,000
TOTAL ASSETS	147,473	166,496	151,827	210,138	204,034

EXHIBIT V
(continued)
BALANCE SHEET
Dollars

	Waverly Drug Store			Waverly Pharmacy	
	12/31/72	12/31/73	6/30/74	6/30/75	6/30/76
CURRENT LIABILITIES					
Accounts Payable	44,843	55,869	46,346	55,868	42,086
Payroll Taxes Payable	1,169	1,971	1,911	2,554	2,504
Taxes Payable	3,844				
Total Cur. Liabilities	49,856	57,840	48,257	58,422	44,590
TERM LIABILITIES					
Waverly Bank	9,448	23,665	29,165	50,165	38,165
Other Loans	3,170	2,244			
Bremer				6,600	8,497
Kelly				9,460	16,629
Schmidt				7,400	6,782
Total Term Liabilities	12,618	25,909	29,165	73,625	70,073
TOTAL LIABILITIES	62,474	83,749	77,422	132,047	114,663
EQUITY					
Bremer	37,893	39,163	35,482		
Schmidt	47,106	43,584	38,923		
Common Stock				50,000	50,000
Retained Earnings				28,091	39,371
Total Equity	84,999	82,747	74,405	78,091	89,371
TOTAL LIABILITIES & EQUITY	147,473	166,496	151,827	210,138	204,034

EXHIBIT VI
INCOME STATEMENT
Dollars

	Waverly Drug Store			Waverly Pharmacy	
	Year	Year	6 Months	Year	Year
	12/31/72	12/31/73	6/30/74	6/30/75	6/30/76
SALES - Drug Store					
Prescriptions	194,035	259,645	153,607	391,869	495,042
Merchandise	138,782	180,530	90,636	207,751	215,417
Liquor	62,242	61,322	25,707	67,362	62,473
Candy	13,679	17,491	10,793	27,668	40,514
Magazines	21,488	23,160	11,448	24,682	24,850
Cigars	15,497	17,805	10,664	25,381	24,306
Sales Tax	6,250	7,803	4,270	9,516	9,455
Total Drug Store	451,973	567,756	307,125	754,229	872,057
Less COST OF GOODS SOLD	313,474	374,400	205,910	503,304	578,260
Gross Profit	138,499	193,356	101,215	250,925	293,797
SALES - Card & Gift Shop					
Merchandise	60,382	40,833	18,471	47,761	53,622
Cards	14,760	31,134	18,035	41,590	44,302
Records	3,736	6,402	2,551		
Sales Tax	3,216	3,213	1,574	3,558	3,851
Total Card & Gift	82,094	81,582	40,631	92,909	101,775
Less COST OF GOODS SOLD	56,003	57,155	28,753	65,644	71,838
Gross Profit	26,091	24,427	11,878	27,265	29,937
TOTAL GROSS PROFIT	164,590	217,783	113,093	278,190	323,734
OTHER INCOME					
Professional Serv. Sold					40,535 *
Purchase Discounts	4,783	2,531	1,184	8,993	7,221
	4,783	2,531	1,184	8,993	47,756
Profit Before Oper. Exp.	169,373	220,314	114,277	287,183	371,490

* Management estimates the total cost associated with this revenue to be $32,000.

EXHIBIT VI
(continued)
INCOME STATEMENT
Dollars

	Waverly Drug Store			Waverly Pharmacy,	
	Year	Year	6 Months	Year	Year
	12/31/72	12/31/73	6/30/74	6/30/75	6/30/76
Less COST OF OPERATIONS					
Salaries	56,446	76,774	44,964	104,019	146,679
Executive Salaries	33,161	34,610	16,545	45,000	64,266
Sales Tax	15,022	17,522	7,549	18,046	14,219
Employment Taxes	3,329	4,875	2,995	9,450	13,439
Insurance	5,727	6,376	4,822	9,572	10,248
Supplies	3,942	7,905	6,467	20,692	24,989
Rent	5,865	6,697	3,180	8,792	8,425
Utilities	3,044	3,837	1,819	5,233	6,789
Auto & Truck	1,262	1,700	626	1,127	6,250
Billing & Inv. Service				939	7,011
Property & Other Taxes	3,319	1,875		2,030	3,985
Advertising	411	487	316	2,191	3,463
Equipment Rental		293	668	6,465	3,883
Repair & Maintenance	577	875	532	2,023	1,948
Depreciation	5,697	4,555	1,747	5,528	4,513
Freight & Postage	563	899	813	1,656	2,380
Medical Expenses				1,026	2,623
Legal & Accounting	1,440	1,822	400	3,121	1,805
Interest	197	1,356	1,954	3,658	168
Bonuses		2,349		2,553	490
Travel & Bus. Entertain.	259	442	265	1,351	1,210
Licenses & Fees	266	538	351	932	816
Dues & Subscriptions	376	524	221	2,682	1,125
Bank Charges	232	183	150	339	650
Miscellaneous	1,353	96	456	667	745
Total	142,488	176,590	96,840	259,092	332,119
NET PROFIT	26,885	43,724	17,437	28,091	39,371

185

EXHIBIT VII
ORGANIZATION CHART

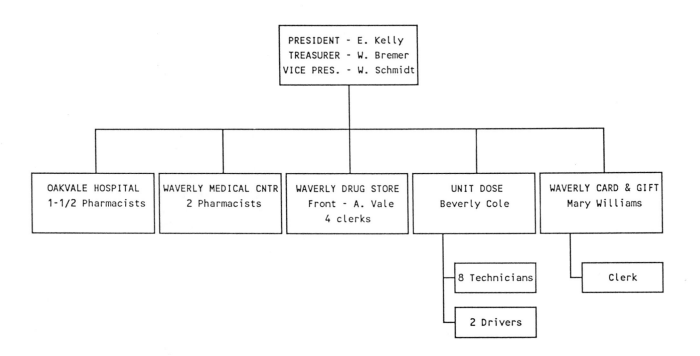

Balance Sheet Dollars

	Waverly Drug Store			Waverly Pharmacy	
	12/31/72	12/31/73	6/30/74	6/30/75	6/30/76
CURRENT ASSETS					
Cash	2,746	3,466	(1,428)	5,819	1,274
Accounts Receivable	6,517	14,110	7,552	28,553	26,370
Inventory					
Waverly Pharmacy	56,100	77,956	76,990	97,293	98,892
Car and Gift Shop	23,638	15,550	13,700	19,520	20,918
Total	79,738	93,506	90,690	116,813	119,810
Total Current Assets	89,001	111,082	96,814	151,185	147,454
FIXED ASSETS					
Leasehold Improvements				451	451
Furniture and Fixtures	58,964	60,461	61,808	70,783	72,924
Remodeling	9,677	9,677	9,677	9,677	9,677
Total	68,641	70,138	71,485	80,911	83,052
Less Depreciation	50,169	54,724	56,472	61,958	66,472
Net Fixed Assets	18,472	15,414	15,013	18,953	16,580
OTHER ASSETS					
Liquor License	15,000	15,000	15,000	15,000	15,000
Goodwill	25,000	25,000	25,000	25,000	25,000
Total Other Assets	40,000	40,000	40,000	40,000	40,000
TOTAL ASSETS	147,473	166,496	151,827	210,138	204,034

186

HEALTH & BEAUTY PRODUCTS COMPANY

As Bill Axelrod looked at the results of the first half of the 1986 fiscal year, he could not help being satisfied with his efforts and yet he knew luck had been with Health & Beauty Products Company (H & B) also. Bill, the President, owned and operated the company along with John Schroeder, Vice President of Finance, and Tom Smith, Vice President of Sales. H & B is a small over-the-counter (OTC) pharmaceutical company that markets products in the diet aid category. The numbers Bill enjoyed studying showed a net profit for the six months of $325,000 on net sales of $2,483,000, not bad considering net profit for the same period last year was $82,000.

Even more fantastic was the fact that the three owners had been able to pay off their large debt to the former parent company and buy out the fourth silent partner with $234,000 in cash, which has accumulated from operations within a short span of three months in 1985. In spite of all this good fortune and hard work, Bill confessed to being concerned about attaining the planned sales goal for fiscal year 1987 of $5,500,000, given the size of his company and the nature of competition.

Company History

In 1946 Richard Dumont founded Dumont Drug Specialties in Decatur, Illinois. Dumont, a returning veteran, decided to get into the marketing of OTC remedies to independent pharmacists. Among his products was an appetite suppressant with the chemical name of phenylpropanolamine hydrochloride (PPA). Dumont was moderately successful until the late 50's, when he stumbled upon the advertising concept, at the suggestion of one of his customers, that he provide her with money to run small classified ads in the local newspapers about his products. He tried her idea and that particular account grew rapidly so Dumont expanded the concept to other areas with the result that his business grew very fast. As his business grew, he began to use the telephone heavily in his marketing efforts and, in effect, was the forerunner of telemarketing. With all of his success he was unable to figure out how to get to the chain drugstores, who today control the business. His sales eventually reached $500,000 with substantial profits.

In late 1975 Dumont, who had become quite wealthy, decided to sell his company. Through a friend he became acquainted with an executive of a conglomerate who made him an offer for his company. He sold out and agreed to stay for a year until a new manager was located. After the sale the name of the company was changed to H & B in order to more descriptively reflect the nature of its products. In early 1976 Bill Axelrod, who had been working for a major regional drug wholesaler as Vice President of Sales, was hired to manage the company. When Bill started, the base of the business was small independent pharmacists. Bill's first moves were to expand the product line and repackage the products so that they could be favorably presented to drug wholesalers and chains. In effect, the company had been operating as a franchiser since one retailer in each town was picked to handle Dumont's products exclusively, ignoring the rest of the drugstores in the town. Having had extensive experience with a drug company that did franchise, Bill knew the risks of this strategy and wished to avoid them. The first two years under Bill's leadership were good with sales reaching $1.5 million and profits before taxes of $260,000.

In 1978 because of the faddish nature of the business Bill decided to get into two weight loss product lines, fiber concept and liquid protein. Both lines proved to be disastrous. The company, as did other companies in the business, took back all the liquid protein product when people died as a result of not eating regular meals even though the labeling called out the need to do so. In the OTC drug business, companies not only stand behind their products but a sale to a drugstore is really not considered final by the drugstore until the product is sold to the ultimate consumer. Thus drug companies may have to take back products that do not sell well and certainly those that are risky as the liquid protein product proved to be. Within a matter of months sales and profits had plummeted and H & B was for sale by the conglomerate.

Bill had specified in his original employment agreement that he was to have the first opportunity to buy the company should it be placed on the market. In early 1979, Bill Axelrod and three others, John Schroeder who is now Vice President of Finance, Tom Smith who is now Vice President of Sales and Don Black, who was then a consultant to the company on product development, all remortgaged their houses, etc., in order to raise $120,000 for operating capital and proceeded to buy the company on a leveraged buyout basis. Bill owned 40 percent of the company, John and Tom owned 17 1/2 percent each, and Don owned 25% percent. The buyout created a debt of $412,000 with monthly payments of $6,750 plus interest at 2 percent above the prime rate in Chicago. A sharing of the profits or a consulting fee if the company lost money was also required, which amounted to $1,500 minimum to $3,000 per month. These latter conditions subsequently were renegotiated to raise the profit sharing from 25 percent to 37.5 percent because the company was in arrears. As a further agreement among the four new owners, Don Black, who was to continue to act as a consultant, was to receive a "consulting fee" whether he consulted or not.

On March 1, 1979, the company was officially sold to the management. The conglomerate as one of their last acts terminated all of the employees so that the new management could hire back only those they wished to keep. Only about 20 previous employees were subsequently rehired.

In February, 1982, the FDA Monograph Committee on weight control products sent its preliminary findings to the Food & Drug Administration (FDA) stating that PPA had been found to be a safe and effective appetite suppressant. Although a preliminary finding has no force of law, the industry typically reacts quickly to such recommendations which happened in the case of PPA. Very quickly large companies such as Smith, Kline & French, American Home Products and Lee Pharmaceuticals joined Thompson Medical, who had dominated the market, in the appetite suppressant business. Within two years all of the big companies dropped out because they were unable to make significant inroads on Thompson's market share. H & B suffered greatly from all this competition and was near bankruptcy. In addition to the heavy competition, the company made some bad advertising decisions by trying to give the appearance of being a national company with national marketing clout without sufficient money to do the job. H & B was "grasping at straws to stay alive and grasped the wrong straw."

The strategy that brought the company out of this disastrous period was the 100 percent consumer rebate offer whereby the company offered to rebate the entire retail purchase price of the product. Although the company was terrified to make the offer, they found out what others had known for a long time -- that people are procrastinators and few ever get around to sending in the rebate request. As a result the company became marginally profitable in 1984 and went on to profitable years in 1985 and the first half of fiscal 1986. Exhibit III shows the income statements for the fiscal years 1980 through 1985. Exhibit IV shows the balance sheets for the same years. Exhibit V shows the income statements for the first half of fiscal 1985 and 1986.

The 100 percent rebate offer idea came from two sources, a manufacture's representative from Chicago whom Bill Axelrod was working with and a buyer from Revco, a large drug chain. The buyer, using another product's promotional material, showed Bill how the promotion could be done for appetite suppressant products, which had not been tried before. He told Bill that he was positive that the redemption rate on the 100 percent rebate offer was about 10 percent, which is high compared to coupon offers. The traffic and demand created in the stores was dramatic. Today Revco is H & B's biggest customer, accounting for over $800,000 worth of business.

The Industry and Competition

The OTC drug market represented 8.6 percent of total drugstore sales in 1984 or $4.5 billion. Exhibits I and II show drugstore sales statistics for 1982 through 1984 by various categories. The diet aid sales by drugstores in 1984 represented 38 percent of the total diet sales of $711 million. Drugstores were a much less significant channel of distribution for diet aids, which were popularly purchased from supermarkets and discount stores, than they were for other OTC items. Between 1983 and 1984, diet aid sales in total increased by a large 28 percent. Most of the diet aid sales increase came from outlets other than drugstores.

A significant industry development has been calcium supplements. Calcium supplements, continuing a trend begun in 1983, had an outstanding year due to the large advertising campaigns linking osteoporosis to a lack of calcium, particularly in the case of women. In 1985 researchers at the Oregon Health Sciences University at Portland, Oregon, announced preliminary findings that calcium lowered blood pressure. Private labeled calcium supplements sold the most of the combined units sold.

The diet aid category was dominated by synthetic sweeteners in 1984 as shown in Exhibit II. This segment in turn was dominated by G.D. Searle's NutraSweet. The next highest segment was appetite suppressants, which was dominated by Thompson Medical Company, which was thought to have about 80 percent of the market. Exhibit VI shows the financial statements for Thompson from 1981 through 1984.

Thompson is a master marketer but contracts out all purchasing, manufacturing, testing and warehousing of its products. In fact, the formulation of Thompson's products is contracted out as well. Thompson's products include Dexatrim, an appetite suppressant, and Slim Fast, a meal replacement product that was reformulated and reintroduced in late 1983 and accounts for about 90 percent of the meal replacement sub-category. Thompson markets its products primarily through "Appetite Control Centers," which are special display racks in drugstores, supermarkets, and mass merchandise chains such as K mart, which is its biggest customer. Thompson puts approximately 30 percent of its annual revenues into advertising. Acutrim, Ciba Geigy's appetite suppressant, has about a 10 percent market share with the remaining 10 percent being divided between Jeffery Martin's Aids, Allegheny's Permathene 12, Alva Amco's Thinz, O'Connor's Dex-A-Diet and H & B's Dexathin.

According to Ted Gladson in the August 5, 1985 issue of *Drug Topics*, "Meal replacement sales almost doubled last year, coming close to $200 million." He forecast moderate growth in 1984 although supermarkets had a 17 percent increase in unit sales. The typical space allocation to diet aid products in a drugstore is four to eight running feet according to Drug Topics. Gladson projected total sales of diet products in 1985 to be $782 million with drugstore sales of $375 million at a 35 percent to 49 percent gross margin.

In the August 19, 1985, issue of *Drug Topics* the role the pharmacist plays in recommending OTC products was discussed. As might be expected for products such as cold remedies the recommendations follow a seasonal pattern, but in the case of nutritional supplements the recommendations are quite constant. In the case of calcium supplements 80 percent of pharmacists made recommendations for a total of 218,000 recommendations weekly. The median number of recommendations per week was 3. In the case of weight loss products 74 percent of pharmacists made recommendations for a total of 147,000 recommendations weekly. The median number of recommendations per week was 2 and recommendations appeared to peak in the spring/summer periods. In April, 1985, when recommending weight loss products, 38 percent of the pharmacists suggested some form of Dexatrim, 26 percent Acutrim and 10 percent a store brand or generic. Acutrim appears to be gaining market share (from 16 percent) on Dexatrim which dropped from 47 percent in October, 1984, and store brands and generics may be gaining as well.

In the February 18, 1985, issue of *Drug Topics* the use and effect of cents-off coupons on drugstores was discussed. In 1983 according to data from Nielson 143 billion coupons were distributed and the projection for 1989 is 350-400 billion will be distributed. The largest distributor accounting for 49 percent is the free-standing sunday paper insert, which has a redemption rate of 2.8 percent. A 1982 study by Arthur Anderson indicated that "92.5 percent of all coupons are redeemed in supermarkets, only 5 percent in drugstores." A nationwide 1983 study done by Point-of-Purchase Advertising Institute of 20,000 drugstore purchases showed that 4.8 percent of all purchases involved newspaper ads (either manufacturers' or retailers') while only .8 percent involved coupons from direct mailing and .6 percent from magazines. Ad retailer coupons were used in 2.2 percent of the purchases. In another survey, double couponing was reported to be used by 15 percent of the druggists and 54 percent of the grocery stores. It attracts customers who want to save money. In its present form coupons are somewhat of a nuisance because of handling and recording problems. However, new developments such as electronic coupons using banks as a clearing house or video couponing could ameliorate this nuisance problem.

Marketing

Like most small companies in the diet aid business, H & B is primarily a marketing organization. The responsibility for the marketing activities including sales is shared by Bill Axelrod, President, and Tom Smith, vice President of Sales. The organization chart for the company is shown in Exhibit VII. Bill, who is 50 years old, is a graduate of the University of Illinois with a degree in commercial art. While attending school, he worked part time in a drugstore in Champaign where his father was the pharmacist. He received national recognition from a national wholesale drug firm from his door-to-door sales of vitamin products and subsequently went to work for them directly upon graduation He worked in most of the marketing areas of the company and rose to the level of Vice President before leaving to take over the management of H & B.

The company's products include the major category of diet aids, which includes appetite suppressants containing PPA, appetite suppressants combined with vitamin C, a meal replacement powder and the new fiber concept diet plan. The company markets its products through 18 manufacturer's representatives who in turn use about 50 salespeople to call on drugstores, drug chains, supermarket chains and discount houses.

The manufacturer's reps are compensated by commissions that range from 5 percent to 10% averaging about 7 1/2% based upon the product lines and their margin. The reps were selected based upon two characteristics, their entree to good accounts and their follow-up. The company has about 10,000 accounts of which about 8,000 are small drugstores. The 25 large drug chains, 15 major discount chains such as K mart and the major supermarket chains make up 80% of the company's sales following

Pareto's Law. Bill believes that manufacturer's reps are the only economical way to sell his products because a sales level of $200 million is needed to support an inside sales force. No in-house accounts are maintained.

In addition to his general management responsibilities, Bill spends about one day per week calling on top key accounts with manufacturer's reps. He also works on new product development with outside consultants and develops sales promotions and marketing sheets. The company uses a small Chicago advertising agency for whom H & B is the largest account. Package design under Bill's direction is done by a design firm in a Chicago suburb.

In 1985 the company spent about $196,000 on all forms of advertising. Although TV advertising is thought to be the most effective, it is also the most expensive. Since the company has limited funds, it limits its TV advertising to spot markets selected by analyzing the various markets the company is engaged in. Radio advertising has not been found to be effective. The bulk of the company's advertising in the past has been devoted to cooperative advertising in omnibus newspaper ads, flyers or coupon books. The company will reimburse retailers 100 percent of the actual advertising cost up to a maximum of 5% of the retailer's purchases. Various requirements are made for proof of expenditure, the use of the H & B brand names in the ad and the type of media used.

The beginning of 1985 saw a shift in the advertising for the company. Because of the emphasis being put on the importance of fiber in the diet by physicians and the general public, the company resurrected on old product from 1978 that had "bombed" at that time. It uses the fiber concept for controlling weight: the fiber swells in the stomach making the user feel full so less food is eaten. Fiber products typically do not contain an appetite suppressant. Sales skyrocketed as a result of this product in the first six months of calendar 1985. The company spent about $450,000 on television advertising during the first six months of fiscal 1986 on this product.

Tom Smith, who is 42 years old, has been with Dumont and its successor, H & B, for his whole professional career since he completed two years of community college. He has handled all of the jobs within sales at one time or another. He visualized the company as a promotional, house which is similar or superior to a national brand house. In addition to the rebate strategy, he sees the company's strategy as offering a price to the retailer which is 25% below the leader in the product. The company projects a national brand quality image with a superior product packaged in a creative way. The company tries to tune into what the customer wants.

Tom notes that although the product leaders, such as Thompson in the case of appetite suppressants, will retaliate against H & B with rebates, the rebates are usually smaller but media expenditures are greater. The company has also used trial size packages effectively since operations can package them efficiently with its packaging equipment. These trial-size packages of a three-day count are typically priced at $.39 to

$.49 with a coupon worth $.50 cash upon the purchase of a full-size package. Often the consumer will buy two samples for a six-day trial so the price point is critical.

Sales for H & B are quite seasonal. Diet aids have a strong peak in the January through May period with a minor pickup again in the Fall. This seasonal pattern makes it difficult to judge how well a new product is doing depending what the season is.

Pricing followed the typical pattern outlined below.

```
- Retail Price          $4.29
- Warehouse Price       $2.29
- Distributor Price     $2.06
- Company Price         $ .41
```

Tom sees the company's strengths to be its recently found financial strength, its building brand loyalty, the knowledge of its market niche and good contacts that could be transferred to other drugstore items. In turn, he is concerned about the tough competition, the limited working capital to support advertising and the inadequate activity of some of the company's reps. He describes Bill as "demanding but fun." Tom notes that the company is strongest in the Midwest and Southeast. The Southwest is reasonably strong and there are pockets of strength in the West. The Central section is relatively weak and the Northwest seems to be declining.

Operations

The Operations Department is managed by Jim Fast, Plant Manager. He is 35 years old and has been with the company since completing three years of college. In addition to managing the packaging operations, he is responsible for purchasing of all items needed for packaging including the bulk product. Bulk tablets and capsules account for about 65 percent to 70 percent of the cost of Goods Sold. They are purchased from six different formulators located in the Midwest and on the eastern coast. Quality for all of these suppliers is consistently good so price and delivery is the determining factor on vendor selection. A perpetual inventory is maintained of the bulk stock, which has a lead time of 10 to 12 weeks.

Other items purchased include printed folding boxes with a 4-to-6 week lead time, which are supplied by two vendors as well as inserts, labels, bottles, caps and clear wrapping film. There are about 120 inventory items in all of which 50 to 75 are active and 30 are very active. A physical inventory is taken once a month. Jim knows the monthly usage of boxes from experience. He uses two times the lead time as a rule of thumb in establishing inventory levels on all items.

The building is leased with three years remaining on the lease and contains about 15,000 square feet and is 15 feet high. Office space takes up 2,800 square feet, excess storage space on a balcony over the office consumes 2,800 square feet, four production rooms utilize 1,800 square feet and the balance of the building is used for storage of raw materials and finished goods. There is sufficient space for rent in the area should the company need to expand.

The plant operates on one shift and employs six women permanently for packaging operations at $4.50 to $6.50 per hour plus fringe benefits, which amount to about 30 percent of the labor costs. A maintenance man who has worked for the company for ten years and is a backup for Jim fast handles all maintenance and janitorial work as well as working part time in Shipping and Receiving helping the other full-time employee there. Other labor is hired on a temporary basis from Kelly at $5.00 per hour and no fringe benefits, of course. Two temporary women are employed on the average except during the summer months. Up to ten temporary women may be employed during the busy season from January through May. The company provides free cokes and coffee to all employees as well as a Christmas party and birthday parties. The company is not unionized.

The company has sufficient equipment for its needs, in fact the machines run only half of the time as a general rule. There are two strip sealers for packaging 250,000 capsules or tablets per shift each, a bottle filling line, a bagger, a cartoner, which prints the lot number and a shrink tunnel used primarily for bottles packed in trays. A new automatic blister pack machine was considered for purchase recently. It would cost $300,000 and had a three year payback period based on utilizing three people in place of the 15 people now used to do the same job. The machine had a one-year lead time so it was not ordered, because Bill and Jim were not that certain of the demand for its use although it would improve the package by providing a higher quality, more attractive appearance.

The Quality Control function is run by Emily Smart, who reports to Bill Axelrod in this capacity. She also does packaging work in her free time. All incoming materials go immediately into a quarantine area until the certified assay is received from the manufacturer. The company does stability testing on all products using elevated temperature for the two-year stability study. All products are shipped by lot number to facilitate recall should a problem be encountered. The FDA makes an annual inspection, which has become routine because of the use of quality control manuals which were set up originally by Don Black.

Jim sees his ability to react quickly to packaging needs and to ship orders quickly as company strengths. He tries to ship orders the same day they are received. He believes the packaging needs to be improved, however, and would like to see the product line expanded.

Finance

John Schroeder, who is 40 years old, graduated from DePaul University with a degree in Accounting. He worked for the drug division of a supermarket chain before joining H & B in 1978. John is responsible for all data processing, accounting and personnel benefits for the company.

Data processing is done on an IBM System 36 computer with five terminals and two printers. In addition John has a stand alone IBM PC which is tied into the System 36 for data accessibility. Software for the computer is provided by an outside firm. All accounting is done on the computer including billing, accounts receivable, inventory, payroll, accounts payable, general ledger, sales analysis and sales performance. Auditing is done by a local outside CPA firm.

John believes the company has a strong receivables program. Terms are 2 percent/10, net 30. Statements are issued monthly and receivables are aged. Those past due over 60 days are called and then turned over to an outside agency if payment is not forthcoming. Most customers pay on receipt of their statement and 90 percent pay within the credit terms. There is an unwritten rule in the OTC business that returns will be taken back for full credit.

Recently an outside consulting firm was retained to completely review and reorganize the filing system, which was accomplished with excellent results in eliminating costly duplication of records. John believes some work need to be done to improve inventory control. The present system does not match the inventory to minimums or maximums. Finished goods inventory is tightly controlled by packaging to order, except for major products, with a one-to two-day turnaround.

John is involved in developing strategy and makes up the company's budget one year in advance based upon the forecasted volume of sales. Performance against budget is shown and variances calculated. During the first half of fiscal 1986 everyone was agreeably surprised by the fact that 50 percent of the volume was supplied by the recycled fiber diet product. John does formal cash planning using spreadsheet programs on his PC. Buying decisions are made at a monthly meeting with the principle used being conservative but still able to supply product to customers as needed.

John sees the company's strengths as being Bill's and Tom's relationship with strong manufacturer's reps, strong telemarketing and a strong lawyer for FDA work. As potential problems he sees competition, the FDA, the risk of the fiber product concept, the distribution chain is high and the pipeline is changing. He sees supermarket and discount chains increasing in importance, and they are not the company's strong marketing channel.

When thinking about goals for the company, he talks about growing at 25 percent to 50 percent per year while maintaining the present good profit margins. Diversification into health and beauty aids is mentioned by buying existing products that are being poorly marketed. Alternatively, he can see going public or even selling the company if the price were right. In any event, decisions are made by consensus and then everyone pulls together.

Presidential Musings About The Last Year

As he thought about the last twelve months Bill Axelrod continued to be amazed. The takeoff of the fiber product brought in an unexpectedly large amount of cash that allowed H & B's management to pay off its debt to the conglomerate of $178,000 and buy out Don Black for $56,250. The cash had accumulated after the year-end statements so that the conglomerate was unaware of it and was so pleased to escape from what it considered a risky situation that it forgave the rest of the fees and profit sharing that were still owing. Fortunately, Don Black did not probe either because of the risk he perceived.

But with those pleasant events behind, what about the future? Would the faddish fiber product prove to be enduring and profitable, particularly since others already were copying it? Diversifying seemed to make sense but good categories were hard to find and even harder to launch with big dollar expenditures required -- more than the company had. He thought of buying some existing brand and even visited a broker in Chicago. Bill came away wondering if his situation was not good enough to sell instead of trying to buy. And yet the company could now breakeven at $1,500,000 in sales but it was vulnerable because of its size, product categories and the strong competition. Finally, this was a family business. In fact, his daughter noted that it looked like nepotism was the policy. Bill's wife, John's wife, and Jim's brother as well as two other employees who were related all worked for the company.

Then there was the latest news about another new product that could be solid or yet another fad. A small competitor had come out with a grapefruit appetite suppressant diet plan that was producing rapid sales. This competitor had piggy-backed onto the interest created by a direct response company's advertising in newspapers. And what about the interest in calcium supplements, a segment the company had not entered? At least there was never a dull moment or a time to relax.

EXHIBIT I
TOTAL DRUGSTORE SALES
(in Millions of $)

	1982	1983	1984
Prescription Drugs	13,795.2	16,706.0	17,541.9
Over-the-Counter Drugs	3,270.9	4,250.9	4,510.0
Other Merchandise	25,673.2	27,219.2	30,401.4
TOTAL SALES	42,739.3	48,176.1	52,453.3

Source: Drug Topics

EXHIBIT II
SALES OF DIET AIDS
(in Millions of $)

	Drugstores			All Outlets		
	1982	1983	1984	1982	1983	1984
DIET AIDS						
Appetite Suppressants	137.4	151.4	166.5	228.1	240.2	264.3
Metered Caloric Products	13.1	20.8	28.0	62.3	90.3	121.9
Synthetic Sweeteners	24.7	39.0	58.5	130.7	195.0	292.5
Dietary Supplements	13.0	13.7	15.1	28.8	29.7	32.1
Total Diet Aids Sales	188.2	224.9	268.1	449.9	555.2	710.8

Source: Drug Topics

197

EXHIBIT III
HEALTH & BEAUTY PRODUCTS COMPANY
INCOME STATEMENT
For years ending February 28
(in Thousands of $)

	1980	1981	1982	1983	1984	1985
Sales	1,811.3	2,541.3	2,094.5	1,430.3	1,941.0	2,806.8
Less Returns	138.2	124.4	219.4	146.3	169.3	145.5
Less Discounts	60.0	58.1	37.1	35.0	41.6	64.5
NET SALES	1,613.1	2,358.8	1,838.0	1,249.0	1,730.1	2,596.8
COST OF GOODS						
Material	489.8	675.9	583.3	523.4	701.0	1,038.3
Labor & Overhead	156.7	226.2	187.7	47.1	37.2	63.9
Total	646.5	902.1	771.0	570.5	738.2	1,102.2
GROSS PROFIT	966.6	1,456.7	1,067.0	678.5	991.9	1,494.6
LESS EXPENSES						
Shipping	10.7	17.0	15.0	4.3	5.6	35.0
Marketing	459.4	1,150.4	779.5	351.6	518.0	717.8
General & Adm.	374.6	409.2	371.4	285.6	358.4	461.3
Interest	64.7	84.0	113.3	73.3	78.3	63.3
Management Fee	18.9	18.8	18.8	27.5	31.9	105.4
Total	928.3	1,679.4	1,298.0	742.3	992.2	1,382.8
PLUS OTHER INCOME	2.2	2.0	3.6	2.9	2.0	(6.0)
NET OPERATING INCOME	40.5	(220.7)	(227.4)	(60.9)	1.7	105.8
Extraordinary Items	16.1					
Federal Income Tax	(0.8)	(0.8)				
Forgiveness				127.3	7.3		50.0
NET INCOME	55.8	(221.5)	(100.1)	(53.6)	1.7	155.8

EXHIBIT IV
HEALTH & BEAUTY PRODUCTS COMPANY
BALANCE SHEET
For Years Ending February 28
(in Thousands of $)

	1980	1981	1982	1983	1984	1985
CURRENT ASSETS						
Cash	63.3	7.5	5.4	(10.9)	21.4	78.2
Accounts Receivable	264.5	393.1	265.1	112.7	200.7	460.9
Less Allowances	(75.2)	(99.1)	(134.3)	(143.8)	(26.1)	(43.3)
Net Receivables	189.3	294.0	130.8	(31.1)	174.6	417.6
Inventories						
Bulk Drugs	107.6	175.7	137.6	153.4	130.8	76.4
Packaging Supplies	97.9	111.2	116.3	113.6	113.8	95.6
Finished Goods	95.8	75.0	30.1	35.6	73.7	113.0
Returned Goods	12.9	12.8	12.6	12.6	19.4	20.8
Total	314.2	374.7	296.6	315.2	337.7	305.8
Prepaid Expenses	45.2	79.7	8.0	13.0	4.8	8.3
Investments	0.8	0.8				
Total	612.8	756.7	440.8	286.2	538.5	809.9
FIXED ASSETS						
Equipment	109.7	112.5	114.1	107.2	107.2	107.2
Furniture & Fixtures	13.8	15.0	12.5	12.5	12.5	12.5
Office Equipment	62.3	81.1	89.3	90.7	93.3	98.9
Leasehold Improvement	13.7	20.2	20.9	20.9	20.9	20.9
Total	199.5	228.8	236.8	231.3	233.9	239.5
Less Depreciation	(43.1)	(73.7)	(103.4)	(132.1)	(164.0)	(192.2)
Net Fixed Assets	156.4	155.1	133.4	99.2	69.9	47.3
OTHER ASSETS	38.7	26.0	33.1	17.0	9.5	8.3
TOTAL ASSETS	807.9	937.8	607.3	402.4	617.9	865.5
CURRENT LIABILITIES						
Note - Bank	6.8	150.0	112.5		25.2	
Accounts Payable	109.7	397.5	240.0	200.6	165.6	247.1
Accruals	131.0	132.0	70.3	128.1	257.9	324.9
Current Portion of						
Long-Term Debt	75.2	82.2	32.6	87.7	221.0	228.8
Total	322.7	761.7	455.4	416.4	669.7	800.8
LONG-TERM DEBT	368.2	279.0	354.9	242.3	202.8	163.6
TOTAL LIABILITIES	690.9	1,040.7	810.3	658.7	872.5	964.4
EQUITY						
Capital Stock	37.5	37.5	37.5	37.5	37.5	37.5
Less Treasury Stock	(2.3)	(2.3)	(2.3)	(2.1)	(2.1)	(2.1)
Total	35.2	35.2	35.2	35.4	35.4	35.4
Retained Earnings	81.8	(138.1)	(238.2)	(291.7)	(290.0)	(134.3)
Total Equity	117.0	(102.9)	(203.0)	(256.3)	(254.6)	(98.9)
TOTAL LIAB. & EQUITY	807.9	937.8	607.3	402.4	617.9	865.5

EXHIBIT V
HEALTH & BEAUTY PRODUCTS COMPANY
INCOME STATEMENT
For Six Months Ending August 31
(in Thousands of dollars)

	1985	1986
GROSS SALES	1,521.9	2,820.4
Less Deductions		
Freight	58.0	61.4
Returns & Allow.	112.7	211.2
Discounts	30.2	64.8
Total	200.9	337.4
NET SALES	1,321.0	2,483.0
COST OF GOODS SOLD		
Direct Material	506.6	607.1
Disposed of Goods	1.0	24.3
Direct Labor	26.4	28.6
Temporary Labor		30.8
Total	534.0	690.8
MANUFACTURING OVERHEAD		
Salary	17.5	21.7
Bonus	1.8	2.5
Maintenance	0.1	0.7
General Plant Expense	4.0	3.9
Quality Control	0.4	1.4
Rent	1.4	1.8
Utilities	0.6	0.6
Depreciation	7.1	7.0
Payroll Taxes	6.6	6.6
Group Insurance	1.9	3.4
Auto Expense	1.2	1.4
Total	42.6	51.0
SHIPPING DEPARTMENT		
Labor	2.8	8.1
Supplies	3.2	3.6
Payroll Taxes		0.5
Total	6.0	12.2
SALES DEPARTMENT		
Inside Sales Salaries	6.9	3.9
Field Sales Salaries	18.7	21.4
Phone Sales Com.	2.9	2.3
Broker Agencies Com.	68.8	166.1
Bad Debt Expense	6.7	12.9
Telephone	10.3	7.6

	1985	1986
Travel & Lodging	7.9	8.0
Auto Expense	1.9	0.4
Misc. Selling Expense	4.7	3.4
Advert. Bill Backs	45.6	87.9
Sales Promo. Samples	3.5	4.0
Sales Meetings	1.4	2.5
Payroll Taxes	3.0	3.7
Group Insurance	1.6	1.5
Coupon Redemption	0.1	0.2
Total	184.0	325.8

MARKETING DEPARTMENT

	1985	1986
Media Expense	21.8	572.5
Classified	6.9	0.4
Production Costs	21.8	13.0
Full Manuf. Rebate	175.0	64.6
Total	225.5	650.5

GENERAL & ADM. EXPENSE

	1985	1986
Adm. Salaries	17.2	24.7
Supervisory Salaries	18.7	20.7
Office Wages	28.4	28.2
Administrative Bonus		74.2
Payroll Taxes	7.8	9.0
Employee Benefits	5.1	8.0
Group Insurance	3.8	2.7
Medical Reimburse.	1.8	3.0
Officers' Life Ins.	2.3	9.8
Credit & Collections	1.2	0.7
Employee IRA	4.6	5.1
Telephone	3.2	2.3
Travel & Lodging	6.6	9.1
Dues & Subscriptions	1.9	1.9
Building Maintenance	2.5	3.7
Office Maintenance	1.2	1.6
Equipment Rental	0.6	0.6
Auto Rent	3.6	3.1
Miscellaneous Expense	0.5	0.5
Property Taxes	4.9	4.9
State Taxes	7.0	15.6
Office Supplies	6.0	6.8
Postage	11.7	5.9
Insurance	11.7	29.4
Professional Fees	49.7	45.0
Building Rent	12.9	15.9
Utilities	5.1	5.7
Depreciation	6.7	7.1
Amortization	1.2	
Computer Costs	6.4	8.2
Total	234.3	353.4

201

	1985	1986
OTHER EXPENSE & INCOME		
Interest Income	(1.5)	(8.1)
Interest Expense	32.5	5.4
Discount on Purchases	(0.4)	(6.3)
Miscellaneous Income	(0.7)	(0.9)
Miscellaneous Expense	7.5	
Outside Consult. Fees	0.0	
Forgiveness of Debt	(41.0)	(164.7)
Total	(3.6)	(174.6)
NET INCOME BEFORE TAXES	98.2	573.9
INCOME TAXES		249.1
NET PROFIT	98.2	324.8

EXHIBIT VI
THOMPSON MEDICAL COMPANY, INC.
For Years Ending November 30
(in Thousands of $)

INCOME STATEMENT

	1981	1982	1983	1984
Net Sales	83,879	90,984	149,442	197,245
Less Cost of Sales	22,951	25,106	47,875	66,320
Gross Profit	60,928	65,878	101,567	130,925
Less Selling & Adm. Expense	41,021	45,963	71,925	91,097
Plus Interest Income	1,208	2,508	2,592	2,642
Net Operating Income	21,115	22,423	32,234	42,470
Federal Income Taxes	10,781	10,805	15,717	21,262
Net Income	10,334	11,618	16,517	21,208

EXHIBIT VI
(continued)
THOMPSON MEDICAL COMPANY, INC.
BALANCE SHEET
For Years Ending November 30
(in Thousands of $)

	1982	1983	1984
ASSETS			
Cash & Investments	25,685	36,495	29,344
Accounts Receivable	11,435	21,025	20,005
Inventories	11,273	16,308	26,823
Due from Officers		175	
Income Tax Refund Receivable	474		
Prepaid Expenses	601	698	1,165
Total Current Assets	49,468	74,701	77,337
Net Property & Equip.	803	1,282	1,769
Formulas & Trademarks	3,241	2,745	2,183
Net Cash Value of Insurance	761	798	846
Other Assets	2,074	2,455	3,153
Total Assets	56,347	81,981	85,288
LIABILITIES			
Accounts Payable	5,323	10,155	4,948
Income Taxes	845	5,010	3,819
Accruals	4,846	8,366	9,359
Total Current Liabilities	11,014	23,531	18,126
EQUITY			
Common Stock ($.10)	500	1,000	1,000
Paid-in Capital	302	302	302
Retained Earnings	44,531	57,148	75,496
Less Treasury Stock			(9,636)
Total Equity	45,333	58,450	67,162

Source: Moody's Industrial Manual

EXHIBIT VII
HEALTH & BEAUTY PRODUCTS COMPANY
ORGANIZATION CHART

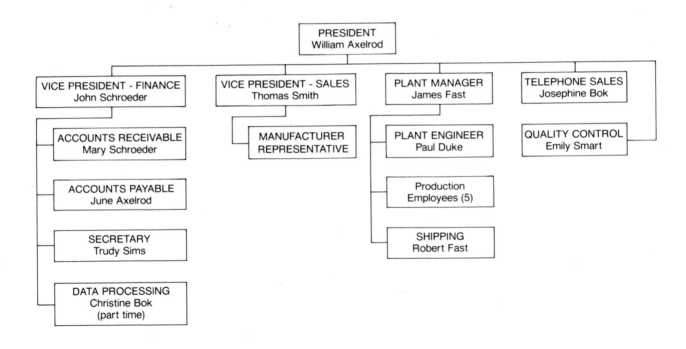

MILLER STAMPING & DIE, INC.

Peter had worked for Miller Stamping in the summer of 1972, prior to his last year in graduate school, so he had a degree of familiarity with the company and its way of doing business. Besides, it helped that Mr. Miller, the owner and General Manager, had long been close to his family, but he didn't know what to do with information about a favored employee.

THE COMPANY

Miller Stamping began life in 1939 as a small supplier of tools and fixtures to the automotive industry in Detroit. For the first ten years of its existence the company remained a six-person shop in a small town outside Detroit. In 1949 the company was bought by its current owner, then a war surplus industrial machinery salesman. Using contacts built within the industry, he transformed the company into a high-volume metal stamping components supplier to the automotive industry.

The company was organized as a closely held family corporation with Mr. Miller and his wife holding half the shares and the rest distributed among his immediate family. The company prospered, gaining its first million dollar gross sales year in 1963. Slow growth was the rule for Miller Stamping, as anything more could threaten Mr. Miller's control of it. The firm was a one-man operation.

Never one to be beholden to creditors, Miller Stamping eschewed any form of debt except trade debt, because it was usually free.

Since Mr. Miller was the sole signatory authority for the company (he collected embezzlement stories from the newspaper to prove "You can't trust anyone"), trade creditors were usually paid after repeated phone calls when Mr. Miller could spare time from details of operations. After all, "Someone has to keep this place running so they can be paid at all." Nevertheless, suppliers continued to supply because they were usually paid eventually.

This case was prepared by Eric Fuchs, consultant, in conjunction with Professor Charles F. Hoitash, Management Department, Eastern Michigan University and is intended to be used as a basis for class discussion rather than to illustrate either effective or ineffective handling of the situation. The names of the firm and individuals have been disguised to preserve the firm's desire for anonymity.

The company added to its physical plant as money from operations became available. By the 1970's Miller Stamping was grossing over $2 million annually with about 40 employees. Over 95 percent of its sales were to the big three automotive companies and over half of that to Chrysler.

THE OFFICE

In the summer of 1973, Peter was hired to bring the company into the age of computers. An economist by training, he had gathered knowledge of computers and their capabilities, utilizing them in various research projects as a student and through several programming projects. The automotive industry was beginning to utilize computers extensively for their data processing needs and most of their suppliers were following suit. After negotiating the purchase of what was then a sophisticated small computer (7K of operating RAM, dual cassettes for bulk storage), Peter settled himself into programming company operations for application on the new technological marvel.

The office he came into was comprised of a cadre of five people besides Mr. Miller. The shop superintendent translated Miller's sometimes combative manner into operational directives for the shop. It was this man in combination with Mr. Miller who was responsible more than any other single factor for the success of Miller Stamping. The others were a production control clerk, an invoicing clerk, a purchasing agent and a bookkeeper, all long-time employees. They were a tight-knit group that worked well together, perhaps partly in reaction to Mr. Miller's operating style. Peter experienced no problem in working with them.

The company's bookkeeping operations were soon running on the computer. Inventory and production control were more difficult because of Mr. Miller's habit of making small changes in production and steel orders and not informing anyone. Nevertheless, a job reporting and raw material inventory control system Peter introduced succeeded in reducing inventory levels by over 25 percent, without affecting operations adversely.

Because it was a small company, Peter often found himself doing many other jobs for the company other than simply data processing and programming. Sometimes he would be driving a truck with a shipment of stampings to a customer at eight o'clock at night, because the customer was in danger of running out of parts or shutting down an assembly line. When supplier relations people from the customers visited, he spent the day showing them the plant and explaining operations. When OSHA inspectors came around, he was expected to show them the plant and then to ensure compliance in follow-up. He also became the company's first-aid person (the metal-working industry has one of the highest accident rates). Every time a steel shipment came in (nearly daily) he was at the dock with receiving inspection to ensure that the numbers going into the computer were true. A big part of the job was ensuring the veracity of numbers on paper.

After ten years it was still a varied job with always something different to do.

A NEW FACE

In January, 1983, Mr. Miller hired a new secretary to be a "Girl Friday" for the office. In the first week she missed two days followed by all of the next week. She explained that she had friends coming from Britain that she had to entertain, and then a window was broken in her apartment, so she had to stay to let in the repairman, who didn't show up.

In auditing that week's payroll, Peter noticed that along with her regular salaried check she was paid for eight hours overtime on Saturday. The overtime was confirmed by Mr. Miller.

In the months that followed a pattern developed. Three days seemed to be a normal work week, paid at salary for five plus Saturday (sometimes Sunday) overtime. The reason for not coming in one time was that a friend had told her about a daytime television show she couldn't miss. By way of remedy Mr. Miller bought a portable television for her desk. He explained to the office that she was smart enough to do both her work and watch television simultaneously, and people should be prepared to make allowances for the eccentricities of genius.

It had become apparent by now that there was a special relationship between Mr. Miller and his new secretary. It was shortly after this that Peter was saddened to learn that Mr. Miller's wife of 38 years separated from him and filed for divorce. Needless to say, office morale sagged considerably. Three months later, the secretary moved into Mr. Miller's home.

Then late that summer when the company bookkeeper -- an eight year veteran employee -- returned from her vacation she was told she was to be dismissed because of a heretofore unstated company policy against having both husband and wife employed by the company (she has been married to a fellow employee for over six years). She was to be replaced by Mr. Miller's "secretary" and the bookkeeper was invited to stay on two weeks to train her replacement. She replied that she would be happy to stay on to consult as necessary, at fifty dollars an hour. She was summarily fired, but her unemployment was later contested on grounds that she quit.

Peter was called in and told that he had to show the new bookkeeper how to use the computer to do the bookkeeping job. During ensuing tutorials he found his new student sometimes gazing absentmindedly at flashing lights on the computer, sometimes seemingly lost in the glow of her cigarette tip, other times alternately dozing off or hyperactively yelling at him for showing her too much too fast. Her first attempts at payroll were disastrous, requiring two weeks to correct, while the accounts receivable became a quagmire of mispostings.

209

For a month little changed from this new norm at the office: three day work weeks, inattention to detail, mistakes compounding mistakes. Payroll problems snowballed and it became impossible to determine any given customer's account status. Again Peter was called in and asked to try to show more sensitivity to someone who was admittedly "eccentric" but given the chance would be a tremendous asset to the company. He tried to tell Mr. Miller that the problem was a seeming inability or unwillingness to learn, perhaps compounded by a personality clash. In reply he was told that if he could not show some common civility he would join the former bookkeeper in the unemployment line.

Two weeks later after an absence of three consecutive days without calling in, she came to work and explained that she had been sick, and that subsequently bats had invaded her room. She had captured one in a box and it was in her car. She offered to show it to everyone to prove it. The box was empty.

Peter had seen the effects of drug abuse while a student, and something in her story clicked with him. That evening he stopped in the local library to get an old William S. Burroughs book he had once read for an English class. The "Girl Friday's" story coincided almost exactly with Burroughs' description of heroin withdrawal. Further research revealed all the corresponding symptoms. Another book described bad hallucinations as common in withdrawal.

While pondering what to do with this information, another employee at the plant confidentially said that the lady in question had an extensive police record of arrests for drug possession, prostitution, forgery and other offenses, but because of the source Peter could do nothing with the information.

Peter took three vacation days, first visiting an old school friend who was a lawyer, finding out the difference between private and public information and how to search the system of court records. The next two days were spent in the courthouse of the neighboring county, where he gradually put together a story safe from libel or slander charges and fully documented. It told of a young college student who had her first serious trouble with the law in a drug deal gone bad, followed by a fake bank checking account scheme and then by forging stolen checks. With each conviction she was sentenced to probation with drug treatment. She violated probation by going first to Boston and then to Atlanta, Georgia. She was arrested in both places for drug possession, prostitution and other charges but never tried. Returning to Michigan, she was arrested for theft and this time spend a year in prison. It was shortly after her release that she began working at Miller Stamping.

Now that Peter knew her background he was at a loss as to what to do. Risks to the company and to Mr. Miller were apparent. Peter didn't know if Mr. Miller knew about her past but knew he had the right to know. Peter wondered what he should do.

THOMPSON DISTRIBUTING COMPANY

The beginning of what was to become the Thompson Distributing Company occurred about 1964 when William Thompson, Jr., the entrepreneur, emerged. Bill continued to drive a wholesale beer route but began to utilize his spare time to service dog food and pet racks in retail stores in the Toledo, Ohio, area. He bought from manufacturers and sold to retailers thus performing the wholesaler function. Additionally, he became the owner and manager of a retail pet store in Maumee, Ohio. A husband and wife proposed managing a retail pet store that was available at a very low rent if Bill would put up the money. He agreed, and the store was rented, but the couple withdrew and Bill became the manager.

Utilizing the basement of the pet store in Maumee as the base of operations for his wholesale business, Bill continued to expand the business. In 1972 he rented a former automobile dealer's garage in Toledo because he had outgrown the capacity of the basement with sales of $197,000. By fall 1974, with sales of $779,000, the need for more space caused Bill to buy a warehouse building of approximately 22,000 square feet in a small industrial park on the outskirts of Maumee. Bill discontinued his beer truck route in 1969 in order to devote more time to the wholesale pet supply business and the retail store. The pet supply business was incorporated in October, 1975, but it was wholly owned by Bill Thompson and continues to be operated as a family business.

THE WHOLESALE BUSINESS

The Thompson Distributing Company sells wholesale pet supplies to retail stores in the northwestern Ohio and southeastern Michigan area. Most business is done within a 150-mile radius because transportation costs become prohibitive beyond that distance. Bill believes there is plenty of business in his own backyard. Many retailers order weekly from the five salesmen employed by the company. These orders are delivered two days later by drivers who follow a self-designed route.

There are six wholesale competitors in the same market area so competition is intense and is based upon price and service. Fast delivery is stressed, and items out of stock with one wholesaler are quickly purchased from a competitor. The most recent competitor "bought" a share of the market three years ago and has been slowly raising his prices ever since.

A strong wholesale pet supply distributor will do $7,000,000 a year in business. In the fiscal year ending July, 1977, Thompson Distributing Company did $1,219,000 in business. Most of the competitors are in the $3 -- $6,000,000 range and are, therefore, larger than Thompson.

MARKETING

Most of Thompson's customers are small retail stores whose average order is $100 to $150. Although there are about 400 customers on the customer list, there are only 150 to 200 active customers. There is a rapid turnover of customers. While there is no trouble getting new customers, others are leaving at the same time. Thompson has found its computer useful in determining which customers are not ordering.

Many of the customers are in borderline financial condition and bankruptcy is common. Thus, Thompson must watch its receivables closely. However, customers may use credit extension as a reason for changing wholesalers.

Sales are made by customers coming to the warehouse and picking up their order or by salesmen taking orders on their rounds with these orders being subsequently delivered by truck. Thompson employs five salesmen, three full-time and two part-time. Two of the salesmen also deliver part-time. All salesmen, except one, are paid on a straight 7 percent commission on what their customers buy even though they did not personally take the order. Each salesmen pays his own traveling expenses.

The business done by the warehouse, which is not attributable to a salesman, is 40 percent of the dollar sales volume. About 10 percent of the dollar sales volume is picked up by the customer rather than delivered by company truck. A 10 percent discount is given on all orders over $100 which are picked up by the customer except for dog food. If merchandise is delivered, the following schedule applies to all orders based on volume:

$ 50 - $ 399 --   2%
400 -   699 --   5%
700 -   1200 --   7%
over -   1200 -- 10%

Bill Thompson estimates the average discount is 5 percent.

Out-of-stock items are a problem since no back orders are carried. Recently, out-of-stock items have been running 10 to 12 percent of the weekly orders. These items are out-of-stock because of late shipments from manufacturers and, more frequently, because of working capital limitations, i.e., the previous account payable must be paid before another shipment will be made.

The company has about 3,000 items for sale in its catalog. The number of items is limited by the size of the computer disk since the catalog is printed by the computer. The single best selling item is Science Diet Maintenance dog food, which is a premium food used by owners of show dogs, etc. Sometimes an item that is sold in multiple colors or sizes has only one product number in the computer in order to conserve memory space.

Pricing is accomplished by multiplying the freight prepaid manufacturer's cost by 1.43 and the non-prepaid freight cost by 1.67. Special items are placed on sale each week. These items are selected by Tom Collins, the Warehouse Manager, based upon slow-moving inventory items or items that were purchased at a particularly advantageous price. A sheet listing the specials is printed by the computer and given to the salesmen for subsequent distribution to customers as the salesmen may desire. Some salesmen see the sale price as reducing their commission and do not publicize it.

An example of another form of sales special is shown in Exhibit I. These items were purchased at the special price, which is shown below the exhibit together with the normal cost to illustrate the kind of savings passed on to the customer. The company also has special lower prices on some products if case quantities are purchased.

The company does virtually no advertising but relies on word-of-mouth referrals from satisfied customers. No specific territories have been assigned to salesmen. Each is free to seek additional business wherever he wishes, which results in some overlapping.

A new discount has recently been added by Thompson. For those customers who write their own order, which must average over $500 per week, an added 4 percent discount is given. The salesman does not receive a commission on these orders. Although this new discount was intended to attract the bigger potential customers with whom Thompson was not presently doing business, few customers have taken advantage of it. Perhaps this is true because the policy has not really been made known to non-customers and is somewhat resented by the salesmen.

Bill Thompson expressed some concern for the need for professional sales management. He believes the salesmen need motivation and direction. A sales forecast is needed also, he believes, to help the purchasing function get out of its reacting mode. He wonders if he needs to set up detailed sales policies and procedures.

Beginning in October, 1977, Thompson Distributing began selling supplies to a wholesaler of tropical fish in Toledo, who wanted to sell fish supplies as well as fish. Bill Thompson reasoned that, even though he was a competitor, if Thompson did not sell to him someone else would so Thompson might as well get the added volume. Thompson sells to this wholesaler at 2 1/2 percent above cost and collects cash on delivery so that the 2 percent discount on the account payable can be taken. The wholesaler pays the freight, and the order is supposed to be shipped separately by truck and unloaded directly into the wholesaler's truck. In practice, it does not work this smoothly since shipments are often combined with Thompson's and require sorting when unloading.

This wholesaler does not have to sell at Thompson's prices and has done some price cutting. Thompson's salesmen are not pleased with the arrangement since they receive no commission and the wholesaler is a competitor. He has purchased significant quantities -- up to $6,000 per week -- while he is building inventory.

Thompson Distributing also sells to two customers who operate a catalog mail order pet supply business. These customers pay the normal prices.

MANAGEMENT

Bill Thompson is the President of the company and is the Chief Executive Officer. Although the company does not have a formal organization chart, the working relationships are depicted in Exhibit II. Bill spends Saturday through Monday working at the company and the balance of his time at his home near Port Sanilac on Lake Huron. He is normally in daily telephone contact with his daughter, Alice Smith, who runs the office.

A number of family members are employed in the business as noted below along with their relationships to Bill:

William Thompson, Sr. - father
Alice Smith - daughter
Barbara Jones - daughter
Dave Thompson - son
Keith Smith - son-in-law
Joe Paterno - brother-in-law
Helen Southward - sister-in-law
Kenneth Jones, CPA - son-in-law

Bill Thompson, who is 47 years old, took about six courses in business at Toledo University in the middle 1950's while he was driving a beer truck and long before he started his wholesale business. When the pet store was started, he dropped the beer route and devoted most of his time to the retail store business. The retail store was and still is the best customer of Thompson Distributing. It now accounts for 8 percent of the dollar sales volume.

About the middle of 1976, he sold a 5 percent interest in the retail pet store to the manager and began to spend less time at the store. The manager subsequently purchased another 5 percent interest and will buy another 10 percent on July 1, 1978. A land contract will then be drawn up for the manager to purchase the balance of the retail pet store over a 12- to 14-year period. In recent years, Bill drew a salary of $500 per week from the retail store. Beginning January 1, 1978, he will no longer draw a salary but will charge a management fee. He is spending relatively little time with the store operation now.

Bill spends his time on weekends running and studying various computer reports about the business and determining which accounts payable to pay. He reviews the inventory dollar position as well as the accounts receivable and weekly sales data. His rough measure of the "net worth" of the company, which he uses as a control device, is to add inventory, receivables, and cash on hand, and subtract payables. He does this manually each month and records the figure on a control sheet.

For three years, beginning in 1973, Bill Smiley, who is now a salesman, was General Manager of the company. Bill Thompson describes him as from the "old school" as far as management style -- that is, he is a perfectionist and expected everyone to do exactly as he said. During this time, all salesmen were on straight salary since Bill Smiley does not "believe in commissions." His previous experience included managing a grocery store. Bill also did the purchasing.

About two years ago, Otto "Bud" Von Weiss was brought into the company to set up the computer operations. He did this and subsequently became Sales Manager. Bill Smiley saw Bud as a threat and resisted the coming of the computer. Their personalities seemed to be incompatible; Bill is slow and plodding, and Bud is fast-acting and intellectually bright.

Within a six-month period, Bill Thompson moved Bill Smiley to a salesman's job on straight salary and resumed full control of the business himself. The purchasing was divided among three people, one of whom was Bud. Unfortunately, the company was unable to pay Bud a large enough salary so he left the company to teach computer courses at the University of Toledo. He still does computer consulting work for Thompson Distributing when requested.

When Bill Thompson is not at the company, no one person is left in charge. All do their own job as they understand it. In fact, Bill Thompson's management philosophy is to "work through people" and to "give them their head." He has not set up a rigid organizational structure.

Tom Collins, the Warehouse Manager, comes the closest to being in charge of operations. He and Joe Miller split the purchasing and the order picking duties. Joe keeps track of the drivers. Tom handles customer telephone orders and is particularly good at telephone selling. Tom also supervises the packers who are both part-time employees.

Tom, who is 47 years old, attended Ohio State University for two years and took a specialized agriculture course. He began working for Bill Thompson in 1970 as a pet-rack serviceman and salesman and continued in that capacity for 20 months. Because of his son's ill health, he left Thompson to move to Florida and later Utah for the next four years. During this time, he worked as an industrial salesman of abrasives and a foreman in a plant making abrasives. He also has had retail sales experience in selling building supplies and farm and garden supplies. He returned to Thompson in his present capacity in October, 1975.

Joe Miller, who is 28 years old, began working for Thompson Distributing Company in June, 1976. Previously, he had worked for Bill Thompson in the retail pet store in Maumee for 2 1/2 years. He also attended Ohio State University for 2 1/2 years majoring in biology before he was drafted into the army for 18 months. He served as a clerk in the army.

In addition to purchasing and picking orders, Joe supervises the delivery drivers and fills in as necessary for drivers and salesmen when they are absent. He sets up the delivery sequence for routes into Toledo and Detroit which account for 8 of the 13 route days. A route in the city usually has about 15 customers per day. The remaining 5 route days are to out-of-state areas along the major expressways. The driver decides on the delivery sequence for these out-of-state routes.

Keith Smith, who is 23 years old, will become the Sales Manager in January 1978. He has been a salesman for nine months after beginning work at Thompson as a delivery-truck driver. He attended Kent State University, majoring in music. He dropped out of college and worked as a carpenter and in a machine shop before joining Thompson Distributing. Although Keith has not had much experience in sales, his father is a sales manager, and Bill hopes he has inherited some talent in this area.

Alice Smith, Bill's 24-year old daughter, attended Kent State for a year majoring in special education before she married Keith. After marrying, she worked in the retail pet store in Maumee until 1972 when she joined Thompson Distributing.

Barbara Jones, Bill's 26-year old daughter, attended Dennison University for a year majoring in commercial art. After leaving school she worked in the pet store and then opened her own gift shop in the basement of the store when Thompson Distributing moved to the rented building in 1972. She operated the gift store for a couple of years and then worked in a clothing store in the Southgate Shopping Center near Maumee for awhile. She joined Thompson Distributing in 1976 and learned to work with the computer.

OPERATIONS

The basic operations of Thompson Distributing Company are purchasing, warehousing, order picking, packing, invoicing and delivery. Office and record-keeping activities are substantially handled by a computer the company owns.

PURCHASING

Purchases are made from approximately 130 vendors. Purchasing is divided between Tom Collins and Joe Miller. Bill Thompson has established a total inventory limit

216

of $120,000 because of the company's financial constraints. Actually the inventory has generally been around $125,000 and has exceeded that number five of the last eighteen months. In fact, inventory has been as high as $160,000 during the middle of a month. The vendors are divided by Tom and Joe so that Tom handles those who generate about two-thirds of the inventory and Joe handles the remainder.

As an aid for ordering a computer report called an Order Posted Report is printed for each vendor on request by either buyer and contains the following data:

Item Number
Description
Vendor Number
Master Pack Size
Sales - Current Quarter
Sales - Previous 3 Quarters by Quarter
Sales - Previous 4 Quarters
Date Last Ordered
Cost of Each

Quantity on Hand
Quantity on Order
Quantity Sold - Past Quarter
Quantity Not Sold - Past Quarter
Total Quantity Demanded
Average Weekly Sales - Last Fiscal Year
Weeks in Stock
Weeks in Order
Cost of One Week's Sales

The report is used as a worksheet by Tom and Joe to place orders and then the report is rerun in order to show the current quantities on order. Most of the data shown on the report is not actually used by the buyers because they find the on-hand and on-order figures are not necessarily accurate.

The receiving reports, which are run on the computer at a convenient time, show the following data:

Item Number
Description
Vendor Number
Quantity on Hand Before
Quantity Received

Quantity on Hand After
Quantity on Order Before
Quantity on Order After
Total Quantities Received

Each buyer tries to make the best deal possible with each vendor. Sometimes they are able to make special buys at reduced prices. These items then often become the basis for special sales offers by Thompson.

In order to find inventory errors, which are evident on the Order Posted Report, Tom Collins checks through the Inventory Value Report at home in the evening about once a week using his memory of what was on the shelves to spot errors. He informs Bill Thompson of these errors who in turn makes a physical count on the next weekend and corrects the computer record. A complete physical inventory has not been taken since the computer records were initiated eighteen months ago.

Bill Thompson notes that when he first began checking inventory items that appeared incorrect, he found more large items in that category. Now he is finding smaller items are incorrect. When Bud Von Weiss was at Thompson, an inventory of a given category on a rotating basis was made using warehouse employees to count. These employees seemed to make many errors so the program was discontinued. Theft could be a possibility since Bill has been liberal with the keys to the building. In fact, he says, "Feedback from the family is that I should be tougher in general." He does note less traffic in and out on weekends now that he is regularly in the building on weekends.

The Inventory Value Report is run about twice a month and contains the following data:

Item Number	Quantity on Hand
Description	Extended Value
Vendor Number	Sub Total by Vendor
Unit Cost	Grand Total

The report is a typical example of Pareto's Law in action. Of the inventory on hand from 131 vendors on the October 16, 1977, report totaling $130,941, twenty-five of the vendors supplied inventory exceeding $100, which accounted for 78 percent of the total inventory. In fact, inventory from seven vendors accounted for 50 percent of the total inventory.

WAREHOUSING

The warehouse is arranged in rows of pallet racks three tiers high. Items are stocked and subsequently picked using three-digit location numbers. The first digit indicates the aisle number, the second digit the pallet section number, and the third digit which of three shelves the item is placed upon. All stocking and order picking is done by Tom and Joe. Items are usually stocked at the end of the day they are received. They are stocked in the containers received and only one box is opened at a time.

Orders are picked by using a computer-generated picking form that shows the location number of each item. The order information is entered by Barbara Jones from another computer-generated order form on which the salesman or customer has indicated the items desired. Orders can also be noted on three other forms: a blank form, an add-on-to form, and a special order form. Orders for a few items taken on the telephone or by salesman often are recorded on the more compact blank form. Locations are not shown on these last three forms.

The person picking the order uses an enlarged and strengthened supermarket shopping cart. The cart is pushed down the indicated aisles and items on the order are placed in the cart as a supermarket shopper would do. As shipping cartons are emptied, they are thrown on the floor to be cleaned up at the end of the day. For large orders, more than one cart will be used. The picker indicates the quantity picked on the picking sheet. Items not in stock are recorded as zero since items are not back ordered.

Once the order has been completely picked, the cart or carts are moved to the packing area located adjacent to the truck loading area. Part-time employees pack the individual items on the order into large boxes that are obtained from incoming shipments. The packer does whatever wrapping or padding he feels is necessary to prevent damage in delivery. The packer also verifies the quantity being shipped.

The shipping cartons are subsequently loaded into the two trucks or one van by the truck drivers for delivery to the customer the following day. Customers' orders are loaded on to the truck in reverse order of delivery to facilitate unloading. Orders taken on Monday, for instance, are picked on Tuesday and delivered on Wednesday.

INVOICING

The preparation of the invoice is done by the computer using the form shown in Exhibit III. Input data for the invoice is entered into the computer by Barbara Jones using a keyboard input device with a CRT display. She enters the picked quantity, description, etc., from the picking form. The invoice is taken along with the merchandise for delivery, and cash is collected at the time of delivery unless credit has been extended.

The prices applied by the computer to the order are established using the mark-ups previously mentioned. This information is put into the computer, including any changes, by Bill Thompson on weekends using manufacturers' price list for the cost figure. The computer applies the appropriate discounts by order size. The discount for picking up the order is entered by Barbara.

A Daily Invoice Register is printed by the computer which shows the following data:

Customer Number	Cost
Customer Name	Discount Amount
Invoice Number	Percent
Amount	Salesmen

Total for columns above

Summary at the end of the report:
Total Sales by Salesman
Profit After Expenses
Items Not Shipped
Description
Number Out Quantity

Dollars by Category
Total Dollars in Adjustments
Total Dollars in Out-of-Stock
Total Dollars in No Charges

The profit after expenses figure is calculated by the computer by subtracting the estimated daily expense figure, supplied by Kenneth Jones, from the net margin figure. Bill uses the total dollars in out-of-stock as a rough measure of the adequacy of inventory.

OFFICE ACTIVITIES

Cash receipts are turned in by the drivers at the end of each day along with the invoice papers. Alice Smith is responsible for verifying the cash count against the invoice and depositing the money. Bill Thompson believes it is particularly important to have a member of the family handle this key job. Alice and Barbara also handle credit memos, walk-in business (although the customer picks his own order) and checking of accounts receivable.

FINANCE

The accounting for Thompson Distributing Company is handled by Kenneth Jones, an independent CPA, who is Bill's son-in-law. Ken graduated from Toledo University. While attending college, he worked for Bill in the retail pet store, in Maumee. He worked for the accounting firm that handled Bill's records through the 1977 fiscal year, so he is quite familiar with the business.

Ken prepares monthly income statements and balance sheets as well as general ledger and journal entries on his firm's computer. The Thompson Distributing Company was incorporated in October, 1975, but the fiscal year was changed to July-June in 1976. Exhibit IV shows income statements for the period October, 1975 through December, 1977, by quarter. During the period from October, 1975, through June, 1976, the company's financial records were maintained by another accountant. As a result, the expense reporting is on a less-detailed basis. Exhibit V shows balance sheets for the company during the same time interval. The financial results of the pet store in Maumee have been excluded from all of the figures shown in the exhibits since it has been operated independently since incorporation.

In the liabilities portion of the balance sheet, the Note Payable, under Current Liabilities, is payable to a Toledo bank. Under Long-Term Debt, the installment loans are payable to Ford Motor Company and General Motors Acceptance Corporation for trucks. The note payable is payable to a computer leasing firm. The stockholder and officer's loans are payable to Bill Thompson. The mortgage payable on the warehouse building is payable to a Toledo bank.

The company has elected to be taxed as a proprietorship under subchapter S of the Internal Revenue Code so no income taxes are shown on the income statement. The company is on a cash basis for accounting purposes.

The cost-of-goods sold entry on the income statement, according to Kenneth Jones, is obtained by adding the items purchased to the beginning inventory plus the change in accounts payable and then subtracting the ending inventory. However, Bill Thompson understands the figure to be the purchases actually paid for during the time period of the income statement. The accounts payable figure is supplied to Ken by Bill Thompson. Between the time that a purchase order is placed and the bill is received, there is no record of the amount owed. Any variations in the accounts payable figure, as reported and as finally determined, is debited or credited to the "over and short" account on the income statement.

The Management Fee account is the draw that Bill Thompson takes from the business each month to cover his management work. He will begin drawing a regular salary of $800 per week in January, 1978.

Kenneth Jones noted that he believes a cash receipts journal should be instituted. The internal control which is now exercised is carried out by Bill's two daughters. Without the presence of the daughters, he believes there could be control problems since the computer does not tie everything together at the present time.

Bill Thompson has been trying to improve the company's image as far as the paying of bills. The company has been unable to take advantage of a rebate program by the manufacturer of one of Thompson's major product lines because the manufacturer required the customer's bills to be paid up currently. Thompson is now able to get the rebate and is actually taking advantage of the 2 percent/10 days terms from that particular manufacturer.

Thompson Distributing occupies about 65 percent of the building. The remaining 7,000 square feet are rented to two other firms. Exhibit VI shows the sales and gross margin by month for the past eighteen months. Exhibit VII shows the 28 highest selling product lines which account for 80 percent of Thompson's sales indicating the average weekly sales, the cost of the items sold, the markup-on-cost factor, the inventory of the product line as of January 3, 1978, and the number of weeks of inventory in stock.

Blue Cross hospitalization insurance is provided for Tom Collins, Joe Miller, Alice Smith and Barbara Jones. Vacation time is also provided for these employees.

An Accounts Receivable report is prepared on the computer once a week. It contains the following information:

Customer Number   Current Amount
Customer Name   Over 30 days Amount
Telephone Number   Over 60 days Amount
Salesman Code   Over 90 days Amount
Invoice Number   Sub Total by Customer
Type of Invoice or Payment   Summary Grand Total
Date   Amount

A card is maintained in the office for each customer stating their status for credit purchases. Comments like "checks consistently ok" or "credit ok --pay in 30 days" are put on the cards. Bill Thompson finds it hard to make firm policies regarding credit extension because he is concerned about losing good customers.

THE FUTURE

Bill Thompson is quite optimistic that the business is finally moving into profitable territory after many months of unexpected losses or poor profits. He knows the business is there to be had but is still plagued by the uncertainty of profits.

Bill has planned a month-long midwinter vacation in Hawaii to rest and gather a fresh perspective on his company. The December loss of $4,300 on a high sales volume made him wonder if he should cancel his reservations after all.

EXHIBIT I
THOMPSON DISTRIBUTING COMPANY
EXAMPLE OF SALES SPECIAL

Dear Thompson Friend:

It's our very real pleasure to bring you these Thompson coupon selections for 1977...ideas developed especially with you in mind, our good friends, for the Holiday season.

Bringing you this wide selection of saving coupons from many of the companies that Thompson distributes for --- at substantial savings --- is our way of saying a sincere "Thank You"...

...you see, last year, many more sales than ever before were the direct result of referrals, and kind words on the part of our customers.

You are helping us grow! That's why we owe you our sincerest thanks thanks....and why we looked for some way we could express those thanks to you.

You'll find many wonderful money-saving coupon ideas attached. Books from Westers Publishing, air stones from Hagen, corner filters from Geisler, BJ's 40 count chew stix to mention a few. All at special savings!

Although all these special coupons are in effect until December 16th, we do strongly suggest that you order right away...the earlier the better, so you can have the merchandise for the Holiday season.

With the very best Holiday wishes from all of us here at Thompson Distributing to you and your family....

                                        Sincerely,

                                        William Thompson, Jr.

P.S. I'm also enclosing my personal gift to you -- a special certificate that brings you a little extra "Thank You" if you help us beat the rush by ordering and redeeming your coupons before December 1st

                    THOMPSON DISTRIBUTING COMPANY

650 Illinois Avenue   Maumee, Ohio

                    Tel: 419 - 429-5000

223

WESTERN PUBLISHING	SUBURBAN	HAGEN 1″ Air Stones
Golden Guide Books **98¢** ea. with coupon	CD-1 Dish **35¢** ea. Limit 3 dozen with coupon	Coupon good for one 4 dozen package **10½¢** ea. with coupon

MARINELAND
Maxi-Flo
Power Filters

$7⁹⁹ ea.
with coupon

Coupon good for 1 case (6)

		GEISLER #311 Corner Filters
While They Last! Limited Supply **LAMBERT-KAY** Gallons only Medi-Clean Wheat Germ Shampoo **$10⁰⁰** ea.	**HAUGEN** **Kitty Pottie** Yellow Brown Avocado Beige Blue No limit **$9⁰⁰** ea. with coupon	**35¢** ea. Limit 3 dozen with coupon
BJ's 40 CT Rawhide Chew Stix Reg. 90¢ **55¢** ea. Limit 5 dozen with coupon		**ATC Digital Thermometer** with free sample digital Limit 4 dozen **58¢** ea.

NOTE: DATA BELOW WAS NOT ON ORIGINAL COPY.

	Normal Price	Cost	Sale Price
Golden Guide Books	$ 1.20	$ .878	$ .98
CD - Dish	.543	.27	.35
1" Air Stones	.135	.0855	.105
Maxi-Flo Power Filter	10.95	7.35	7.99
Lambert-Kay Shampoo	13.00	9.572	10.00
Rawhide Chew Stix	.90	.42	.55
Kitty Pottie	11.44	7.35	9.00
Geisler Corner Filter	.466	.293	.35
ATC Digital Thermometer	.715	.50	.58

EXHIBIT II
THOMPSON DISTRIBUTING COMPANY
ORGANIZATION CHART

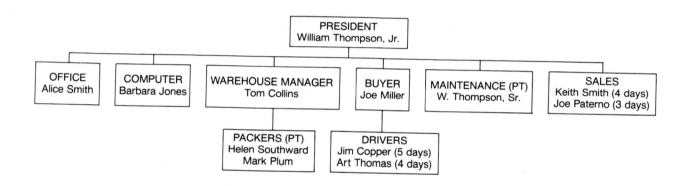

PRESIDENT
William Thompson, Jr.

OFFICE
Alice Smith

COMPUTER
Barbara Jones

WAREHOUSE MANAGER
Tom Collins

BUYER
Joe Miller

MAINTENANCE (PT)
W. Thompson, Sr.

SALES
Keith Smith (4 days)
Joe Paterno (3 days)

PACKERS (PT)
Helen Southward
Mark Plum

DRIVERS
Jim Copper (5 days)
Art Thomas (4 days)

EXHIBIT III
THOMPSON DISTRIBUTING COMPANY
INVOICE FORM

THOMPSON DISTRIBUTING COMPANY

650 Illinois Avenue
Tel: 419-429-5000

Maumee, Ohio

Wholesale Pet Supply Distributors'

INVOICE NO.

CUSTOMER NO.

1-GENERAL DISCOUNT
2-NET-NET
3-SPECIAL
4-O'DELL
5-SPECIAL NET-NET

DATE	ORDER NO.	SALESMAN	TERMS:	

QTY. ORDERED	QTY SHIPPED	DESCRIPTION	CODE	UNIT PRICE	AMOUNT

EXHIBIT IV

THOMPSON DISTRIBUTING COMPANY
INCOME STATEMENT
(In Dollars)

	6 months 3/31/76	9 months 6/30/76	3 months 9/30/76	6 months 12/31/76	9 months 3/31/77	12 months 6/30/77	3 months 9/30/77	6 months 12/31/77
REVENUE								
Sales	454,200	701,840	278,880	598,850	940,934	1,219.177	335,550	701,238
Less Ret. & Allow.			2,487	5,116	7,332	10,067	2,443	4,869
Net Sales	454,200	701,840	276,393	593,734	933,602	1,209,110	333,550	696,369
Rent Income		13,500	4,500	7,500	8,000	8,000	1,275	3,217
Total Revenue	454,200	715,340	280,893	601,234	941,602	1,217,110	334,382	699,586
COST OF GOODS SOLD	326,317	517,435	216,275	451,163	703,208	909,712	238,838	519,588
GROSS PROFIT	127,883	197,905	64,618	150,071	238,394	307,398	95,544	179,998
OPERATING EXPENSES								
Office Salaries	22,132	29,254	6,065	12,158	18,258	21,558	5,000	10.950
Salesmen Salaries	25,780	43,889	15,581	37,559	59,618	78,377	13,792	31,895
Warehouse Salaries	12,500	21,827	9,972	22,976	36,326	50,889	14,172	30,994
Total Salaries	60,412	94,970	31,618	72,693	114,202	150,824	32,964	73,839
Advertising	772	793	13	35	65	81	14	14
Accounting	225	820	440	875	1,985	2,585	940	2,055
Depreciation	2,161	13,296	3,044	6,128	9,212	266,881	6,765	13,530
Equipment Rental	295	499	208	369	505	612	220	566
Freight	4,120	8,216	2,856	7,848	10,173	12,058	3,732	8,590
Gas, Oil & Tires	6,622	8,598	1,359	5,467	8,833	11,386	1,634	5,131
Bad Debts		6,000				3,668		
Insurance - Emp.	2,506	3,729	724	2,004	3,009	4,119	1,109	2,517
Insurance - Gen.	1,846	2,212	713	2,750	7,697	7,441	7,376	9,671
Interest	3,554	17,172	6,893	12,872	18,898	25,561	6,114	12,664
Maint. & Repairs	2,069	4,956	963	2,810	3,928	5,434	1,492	2,945
Management Fee	3,249	5,749	2,000	5,000	8,000	11,000	2,000	5,000
Outside Services		15	248	376	376	519	93	1,069
Over & SHort	2,243	26	(644)	223	454	2,673	769	(1,877)
Rent	12,000						1,071	1,071
Sales Promotion		16		204	319	338	117	117
Salesmen Expenses					100	800	600	1,300
Supplies	1,145	2,529	1,409	3,696	5,150	6,232	2,954	4,548
Taxes - Payroll	4,799	7,372	2,534	4,420	8,695	11,534	2,141	4,669
Taxes - Real Est.	1,537	8,349			8,115	7,035		
Taxes - Other		1,455		621	1,474	2,901		
Travel		699	985	1,000	1,245	1,745	530	1,081
Telephone	4,307	5,739	1,972	3,331	4,600	5,348	197	1,568
Utilities	2,200	3,666	884	3,811	8,540	11,833	3,477	6,434
Miscellaneous	475	726	181	2,204	2,647	904	619	2,560
Total	116,537	197,602	58,400	138,737	228,222	313,512	76,928	159,062
NET PROFIT	11,346	303	6,218	11,334	10,172	(6,114)	18,616	20,936

EXHIBIT V
THOMPSON DISTRIBUTING COMPANY
BALANCE SHEET
(In Dollars)

	6 months 3/31/76	9 months 6/30/76	3 months 9/30/76	6 months 12/31/76	9 months 3/31/77	12 months 6/30/77	3 months 9/30/77	6 months 12/31/77
CURRENT ASSETS								
Cash	4,166	4,368	3,153	(1,124)	13,334	2,531	2,118	1,791
Net Accounts Rec.	31,219	36,986	51,108	41,076	46,721	29,987	46,106	39,696
Acc. Rec. - Other	34,375		4,028	5,759	6,874	7,297	8,499	11,249
Inventory	88,181	112,811	140,137	122,732	127,333	115,000	146,349	122,430
Total	157,941	154,165	198,426	168,443	194,262	154,815	203,072	175,166
FIXED ASSETS								
Land	26,000	26,000	26,000	26,000	26,000	26,000	26,000	26,000
Building	212,667	212,667	212,667	212,667	212,667	212,667	212,667	212,667
Bldg. Improvements			3,033	3,033	3,033	3,033	3,033	3,033
Computer	23,094	23,094	23,094	26,823	26,823	26,823	26,823	26,823
Machinery	6,423	6,668	6,818	7,274	7,274	7,413	7,413	7,413
Trucks	3,453	3,453	3,453	11,115	30,146	29,549	29,549	29,549
Office Equip.	2,232	2,232	2,722	6,164	6,164	6,164	6,164	6,164
Total	273,869	274,114	277,787	293,076	312,107	311,649	311,649	311,649
Less Depreciation	2,161	13,296	16,340	19,266	22,351	39,388	46,151	52,916
Net Fixed Assets	271,708	260,818	261,447	273,810	289,756	272,261	265,498	258,733
OTHER ASSETS								
Escrow	2,712	3,194	5,228	8,188	1,080	4,342	6,635	9,735
Prepaid Interest	10,241	9,792	9,343	10,263	8,446	7,997	7,548	7 098
Total	12,953	12,986	14,571	18,451	9,526	12,339	17,753	16,833
TOTAL ASSETS	442,602	427,969	474,444	460,704	493,544	439,415	482,753	450,732
CURRENT LIABILITIES								
Acc. Pay. - Trade	128,000	137,139	177,786	155,834	172,999	146,402	138 870	112,499
Acc. Pay. - Other		1,838				1,497		
Notes Payable	50,000	50,000	50,000	45,466	43,000	40,000	39,000	36,000
Accrued Taxes	4,450	6,294	6,035	4,691	7,902	6,015	3,081	3,308
Accrued Wages					4,320			
Total	182,450	195,271	233,821	205,991	228,221	193,914	180,951	151,807
LONG-TERM DEBT								
Auto Loan				14,116	26,571	25,686	18,293	16,572
Note Payable	30,641	29,038	28,000	26,365	24,226	22,623	21,019	19,415
Stockholder Loan	25,000	12,439	16,472	13,949	16,438	16,438	34,987	33,987
Mortgage Payable	182,165	180,918	179,933	178,949	177,916	176,868	205,000	204,129
Total	237,806	222,395	224,405	233,379	245,151	241,615	279,299	274,103
TOTAL LIABILITIES	420,256	417,666	458,226	439,370	473,372	435,529	460,250	425,910
EQUITY								
Common Stock	10,000	10,000	10,000	10,000	10,000	10,000	10,000	10,000
Retained Earnings	12,346	303	6,218	11,334	10,172	(6,114)	12,503	14,822
Total Equity	22,346	10,303	16,218	21,334	20,172	3,886	22,503	24,822
TOTAL LIAB. & EQUITY	442,602	427,969	474,444	460,704	493,544	439,415	482,753	450,732

228

EXHIBIT VI
THOMPSON DISTRIBUTING COMPANY

Month	Net Sales	Gross Margin
July, 1976	$79,995	5.0
August	91,779	39.6
September	104,619	23.2
October	93,344	25.0
November	105,799	23.2
December	118,198	31.0
January, 1977	99,460	29.5
February	108,371	23.9
March	132,037	25.0
April	98,495	36.0
May	82,529	11.6
June	94,484	25.3
July	90,110	35.8
August	114,922	24.0
September	128,075	2704.0
October	106,092	22.0
November	126,897	29.0
December	130,273	18.6

EXHIBIT VII
THOMPSON DISTRIBUTING COMPANY
28 HIGHEST SELLING PRODUCT LINES

Product Line	Sales	Six Months Weekly Average Cost	Markup	Inventory 1/3/78 Dollars	Weeks
875	$3,259	$2,507	130%	$16,729	6.7
280	2,840	2,103	135%	8,743	4.2
400	2,824	2,189	129%	9,230	4.2
725	1,224	921	133%	7,243	7.9
22	1,060	741	143%	11,568	15.6
640	1,042	695	150%	6,668	9.6
284	815	599	136%	765	1.3
270	797	531	150%	2,269	4.3
250	777	547	142%	4,972	9.1
303	725	525	138%	4,575	8.7
710	710	497	143%	1,026	2.1
630	546	382	143%	2,798	7.3
760	449	299	150%	1,417	4.7
845	437	262	167%	1,375	5.2
425	427	328	130%	543	1.7
260	370	259	143%	1,039	4.0
305	344	240	143%	1,220	5.1
730	325	195	167%	2,114	10.8
30	288	209	138%	721	3.4
135	287	172	167%	400	2.3
240	285	198	144%	1,310	6.6
650	276	184	150%	1,140	6.2
117	264	198	133%	1,433	7.2
800	236	166	142%	1,034	6.2
890	226	158	143%	1,093	6.9
287	214	150	143%	1,289	8.6
35	204	143	143%	129	0.9
835	203	133	153%	640	4.8
28 Lines	21,454	15,531	138%	93,483	6.0
Total Lines	26,780	19,984	134%	119,629	6.0

HOW DO YOU GET APPLES FROM AN ELM?

How do you get Apples from an ELM? During the 1981 through 1984 period in Michigan the answer to that question was to see the "Apple Lady," Elaine Moncur. Ms. Moncur was the President and owner of ELM Group, an Ann Arbor-based Michigan firm that was the manufacturing representative for Apple computers until September 30, 1984. She became known as the "Apple Lady" in Michigan because of the outstanding job she did in representing Apple to dealers in Michigan. As September, 1984, approached, she was occupied with determining a new strategy for her firm.

The Owner

Elaine Moncur did not have the background and training one would expect the president of an aggressive marketing organization to have. She was raised in a poor section of San Jose and was the only woman in her high school class to go on to college. She married and began studying humanities at Michigan State University where she had her first child. After a move back to California, she decided to study piano and within weeks began teaching piano. She later completed a Bachelor of Education degree in Special Education from Eastern Michigan University and a Master's degree in Learning Disabilities from the University of Michigan. She was interested in teaching the emotionally impaired, learning disabled and blind because she herself had polio at 12 and as a result she had a visual impairment that made it difficult for her to interpret words and numbers. To overcome this disability she developed a number recognition system that allowed her to learn math, which she had been unable to do in the past.

She taught music to the emotionally impaired in both public and private schools for a number of years but became unhappy with the violence she had to contend with. She decided it was time to make some money so she set out to find a new career. She researched the job market extensively in 1980. After some 32 job interviews, she determined that her skills best fit into the marketing and sales areas. The job she took was with Barrington International, who represented Texas Instruments computers. Ms. Moncur did not have experience in either sales or computers at the time but she did her homework and within four months was the top salesperson. Unfortunately, Barrington had financial problems and she was soon back looking for a job.

Apple Saleswoman

Ms. Moncur next tried to get a job with Apple Computer but they would not hire her initially because they thought she was not experienced enough nor did she have enough knowledge of computers. She interviewed a number of Apple dealers in Detroit and Toledo to find out about their current sales representatives and what the dealers needed and wanted from their representatives. After thoroughly researching Apple Computers as a company, she was able to get a job as a factory direct salesperson for the state of Michigan. At the final interview she told Apple that her findings showed that what dealers needed was information and training to help them sell and solve problems, which her background uniquely qualified her to provide. She became Apple's first saleswoman in May, 1981.

During the year in which she was a saleswoman for Apple she achieved some remarkable objectives. In spite of Michigan's depressed economy, she sold more Apple III's than any other sales representative in the country, and Apple's sales in the state quadrupled. She did this by attention to details using her organizational skills to handle paperwork, find lost orders and solve dealers' problems. Although she had never done advertising before she was able to put together an advertising seminar after being on the job for only two weeks. She did this by talking to advertising agencies, newspapers, radio and television stations, and other dealers outside Michigan about advertising. She also researched the local media in the hometown of each person attending the seminar. Needless to say the seminar was a success. Drawing upon her classroom experience as a teacher, she stressed hands-on participation in her seminar, following up with a test the following week to confirm what had been learned.

Her starting salary was $22,000 per year as compared to $40,000 per year for Apple's salesmen. She received a bonus after achieving 70 percent of her quota and a raise of 35 percent after a spectacular first six months. At Apple's annual sales meeting in Dallas, she was honored for her outstanding performance by receiving a prize cherished by salesmen, a ticket for a "topless shoe shine" at Billy Bob's Bar in Dallas. In order to accomplish all of this, she worked sixteen-hour days and regularly spent all night on Tuesdays learning new software. During this year period as a factory direct saleswoman, she heard that Apple was planning to change to manufacturer's representatives.

ELM Grows from an Apple Seed

Elaine Moncur promptly asked Apple to let her be the manufacturer's representative for Michigan but was turned down because she lacked experience and Apple's policy prohibited direct reps from becoming manufacturer's reps. She was offered the job of being a trainer for Apple Computer. She was not dissuaded and spent months researching and preparing a proposal with the aid of a professional proposal writer. Apple finally agreed, reluctantly, to her proposal provided she formed a joint venture with an established manufacturer's rep for the first year which she agreed to do. Thus ELM Group began in an apartment with her mother as an employee handling the accounting work. Three other employees were added quickly and $10 million in sales were handled from the apartment.

Within six months they outgrew their facilities and the number of employees rose to eleven. The final facilities move was made to 4,000 square feet of office space on the atrium level of the Burlington Office Building in Ann Arbor. The organization chart for ELM Group is shown in Exhibit I.

ELM Group grew to include Software Michigan, Inc., and ELM Indiana - Kentucky. All activities for the year ending in September, 1984, generated $40 million in sales on which ELM earned a 3 1/2 percent commission. The expenses incurred ran about $86,000 per month. A breakdown of these expenses is shown below.

Salaries	$48,000
Entertainment & Travel	10,000
Advertising Agency Fees	10,000
Car Allowance ($500/Mo./Person)	5,000
Rent	4,500
Telephone	4,000
Miscellaneous	5,500
Total	$86,000

Marketing

ELM Group's marketing strategy, as set by Elaine Moncur, began where her saleswoman's job left off. ELM's heavy focus was on education. Training was heavily stressed, and although it seemed too complicated at first it was smoothed out by asking "is it logical?" ELM trained the dealers in how to merchandise, how to do financial reports, and how to inventory merchandise. Elaine was the first to put training classrooms in individual stores which seemed "almost sinful" given the high cost of square footage in the stores. This concept is now accepted nationally. ELM set up distribution so that people were not competing with each other geographically.

ELM approved all Apple dealerships in Michigan and insisted that Apple would look professional. Anything would be done to help the dealers including loaning them money, supplying them with products from ELM's own supply, seeing them through divorces, renting a truck to bring in needed stock for Christmas from Chicago, running seminars and working booths at trade shows. ELM was always there, way beyond the normal expected for a rep firm. It is no wonder that ELM was in Apple's Excell Club for those reps who made more than 150 percent of their quota.

Research was done on compensation programs in order to establish one for ELM. Salespersons were paid a base salary plus a car allowance plus a performance bonus based upon total sales and training efforts carried out. Sales reps made about $25,000 per year base salary and total compensation was $40 -- 60,000 per year. It was hard for a salesperson to follow in Elaine's footsteps since she had developed so many of the dealer relations originally as a Apple rep. However, she gave her sales people a great deal of latitude.

In advertising ELM tried to present what was new for Apple products and software. Promotions were run with slogans such as "Buy an Apple and get an Apple tree." The "Twelve Apples of Christmas" promotion that was done for Inacomp is another example as is the Apple computer giveaway contest at the Detroit Lions games. Advertising agencies were sometimes used but, since ELM wished to maintain tight control, ads were often developed in-house. The need for clean-looking ads was stressed and all ad material was composed and evaluated very analytically. Elaine used her previous knowledge as a fashion designer to help with layouts.

ELM developed window displays for its dealers. Their use was discretionary. Participation was stressed with the concept that ELM provided the idea but the dealer was the one who carried it out.

Operations

The Operations function for ELM was handled by Leslie Christensen, Vice President of Operations. She initially came to work as Elaine's secretary with the understanding that she would learn the business and would have a larger role to play in the future. Her previous background included a degree in Political Science from the University of California at Berkeley with a minor in business as well as accounting and auditing experience with a newspaper in New Jersey and a large paper company in California. She also worked in Senator Alan Cranston's San Francisco office handling constituent case problems while she attended the University of California at Berkeley.

She found that Elaine thought in broad strategic terms and realized that one function she could provide was "to get clouds of Elaine's thoughts funneled down and implemented." She thought of herself as "being in the middle of an hourglass filtering ideas down to others." She found Elaine to be a true entrepreneur with incredible stamina, ideas and motivation. She also found there was little structure in the organization and few records kept. Leslie introduced more discipline and organization into ELM including the use of forms and records. Changes were often made quickly by Elaine without sufficient communication made to everyone. Leslie became the organizer and communicator. She made it a practice to debrief Elaine at the end of the day in order to find out what needed to be done administratively.

Operations, marketing and all areas of ELM worked long grueling hours. A normal day was ten to twelve hours and six and a half day weeks were the rule. But the atmosphere made it fun and rewarding. ELM prospered as did all of the employees. Money was not a problem.

Software Michigan, Inc.

Software Michigan, Inc., was established as a separate company because Apple's representation agreement prohibited the representative firm from representing anyone else even if the other manufacturer was not a competitor. ELM anticipated that Apple would someday do away with its manufacturer's reps because it would become too expensive for Apple to give up the commission to the reps once Apple became large and successful. Software Michigan was set up in May, 1983, with John Kolezar in charge. He had known Elaine for several years, having met her when she was a salesperson for Barrington and he was Data Systems Coordinator for Moore Business Forms. His job with ELM was to develop lines of products which were non-competitive to Apple which would serve as a nucleus for the day when ELM no longer would represent Apple.

Software lines such as Dow Jones, Electronic Arts, State of the Art, Think Tank and Software Publishing were acquired. Other peripheral items such as Maxell diskettes and disk storage units were added also. The commission rate on these kinds of items ran 7 to 10 percent.

Although ELM was limited to the state of Michigan, John Kolezar's strategy was to try to locate distribution firms whose headquarters were in Michigan but who distributed nationally. In this way he reasoned ELM could in effect achieve national distribution. He began to work with Michigan firms such as Handleman in Troy, who is the largest rack jobber in the world. At that time they were just beginning to handle software in their racks in such stores as Sears and Montgomery Ward. He also worked with Inacomp and other chains which specialized in computers and computer supplies. The business grew but in March, 1984, Apple found out about Software and insisted that ELM close it because of the distribution agreement with Apple. Apple insisted that this be done even though Apple knew at that time that they planned to terminate all manufacturer's representatives in May.

The Apple Stem Twists Again

Apple Computers' selling and distribution strategy had gone through a number of changes since the company's inception. From 1976 through 1978 distributors were used. From 1979 through 1981 factory direct salespersons were used. Finally, in 1982, manufacturer's reps were used. In 1984, Apple twisted again and announced in May, 1984, that it was going to return to factory direct sales. Although many thought the decision for this move had been made as early as December, the manufacturer's reps were led on that things would continue until a month before the announcement. For instance, ELM participated in the public introduction of the Apple IIC in San Francisco within 30 days of the cancellation notice and followed this up with an elaborate local product introduction day at The Fairlane Manor in Dearborn. This single day was very expensive, costing ELM $17,000 to put on a very professional program.

By its contracts Apple was only required to give one month's notice of termination of its manufacturer's reps, but it chose to give four months' notice with the termination date being September 30, 1984. Although this seemed fair but devastating for ELM at first, subsequent events called the fairness into question.

During the four-month hiatus period, ELM had to continue servicing its Apple dealers but was prohibited from acquiring any other lines of business. ELM could look for other lines but not begin representing them until after Apple's agreement ended. Apple made employment proposals to five of ELM's top employees, who accepted. ELM had to continue to pay these employees until September 30, but the employees soon began to relax their efforts since they were guaranteed their money. Apple consistently would not return phone calls from ELM after May. Relations deteriorated to the extent that, when the termination date arrived, Apple company representatives came in to remove anything that said Apple on it, even including coffee mugs. They began to remove memorabilia from the walls including a contrived facsimile newspaper advertisement in a cherry frame, which was presented to Elaine Moncur by her employees. Fortunately her lawyer had his office in the same building and came down to put a stop to the pettiness.

The ending of ELM's relationship was particularly distressing to Elaine Moncur because of her strong ethical values. She was raised as a Mormon. Her special education background showed her compassion. She understood that it was necessary to set up environments conducive to individuals. Then too she had been the recipient of some bad business practices once she entered the business world. Her working ethical policy had been, "What is good for the dealers and manufacturer is best for me." One of her early mentors and advisors, Don Chisholm of Ann Arbor Associates, influenced her with his value statement that "A good deal is good for everyone involved." No wonder the ending with Apple was disappointing when she considered the long hours and tremendous effort she put into the relationship.

She also had wondered about subsequent Apple policies such as severely discounting its products and selling through schools like the University of Michigan. Selling through the University of Michigan at deep discounts took 45 percent of the total Ann Arbor population and 89 percent of the total buying population away from the dealers. If a dealer were to sell competitively against the University, the salesperson would make $5 versus $120 if a comparable IBM-PC were sold. ELM found out about this move by Apple through a local dealer, who in turn found out from a U of M contact. Apple refused to have anyone come to explain things to the dealers. Apple also allowed multiple dealers in some areas as there was no allowance made for an exclusive location.

The Taste of Apple

What was Apple like? Apple had the reputation for being creative, wild and reckless. To ELM Apple was not an easy task master. "Code Red" was the standard operating signal, which meant decisions made at headquarters on April 15 got to ELM on May 10 and had to be implemented by the dealers on May 15. Apple was not known for tact. For instance, when ELM was phasing out as manufacturer's rep, a meeting was held at the Renaissance Center in Detroit by Bill Campbell, Vice President of Sales for Apple, attended by all the Apple dealers in Michigan and by Elaine Moncur and her key people. He proceeded to say that, although ELM had done a good job representing Apple, he and the Apple salesmen would do a much better job. It was hard to be "fired in public." Apple never gave pats on the back to ELM.

Leslie Christensen characterized Apple as "managing by intimidation." They were young, innovative and arrogant. They lived in an ivory tower that allowed them to think that there was no need to be IBM-compatible. They seemed to never know what their reps were doing and were not aware of the concept called "managing by wandering around." John Kolezar characterized Apple's regional sales management as "vanilla and bland, almost pompous."

Once the move to an Apple sales force was announced, a North American Manufacturer's Representatives Association of reps who were dumped by Apple was formed to help the reps get new lines, etc. This group proved to be helpful but it also made the reps aware of some of the inconsistencies and questionable practices Apple had used. For instance, there were different rates of commission given to various reps; some were paid for educational sales and some were not, as was the case with ELM. The rules of the game were not the same for all. Allocation of products that were in short supply, such as the Macintosh when it was introduced, were made at the sole discretion of the Area Sales Manager, which in turn was not done on a logical and fair basis.

Was there sex discrimination against ELM since it was owned by a female and employed predominantly females? Key employees at ELM believed Apple regional sales management took advantage of Elaine because they thought they could get away with it since she was the only female rep. She was advised by the Area Sales Manager not to get married, which would be unusual advice to give to a male rep. According to Elaine Moncur, tears were expected when the termination was officially given to her. ELM believed if women were to be successful they had to be twice as good as men.

Are female managers different? Both John Kolezar and Leslie Christensen agreed that there were differences. When asked if more intuitive would describe the difference, they both thought not. John saw women as being more sensitive toward employees, giving more attention to detail so that there were finer edges to a woman's sales presentation, a striving to make it perfect. He thought the decisions were more rational, but women were more sensitive, which may be mistaken for intuition. He sees them as to get married, which would be unusual advice to give to a male rep. According to Elaine Moncur, tears were expected when the termination was officially given to her. ELM believed if women were to be successful they had to be twice as good as men.

Are female managers different? Both John Kolezar and Leslie Christensen agreed that there were differences. When asked if more intuitive would describe the difference, they both thought not. John saw women as being more sensitive toward employees, giving more attention to detail so that there were finer edges to a woman's sales presentation, a striving to make it perfect. He thought the decisions were more rational, but women were more sensitive, which may be mistaken for intuition. He sees them as being more creative perhaps because they were not caught up in the "good old boy" syndrome which could be restricting and hard to break out of. Leslie also believed women were more attuned to the reactions of people and could read body language better. She thought there were fewer ego problems and therefore more flexibility and freedom to be creative.

The Future of ELM

As September approached brainstorming sessions were held to develop ideas for future strategy. At first everyone was included in these sessions, but, as employees began to make commitments to Apple, it became difficult to know who could be safely included in the sessions. Some of the ideas that surfaced in the sessions were to write a book, become a motivational speaker, become a consulting firm, continue as a manufacturer's rep for other firms (Software Michigan was still intact), become a distributor, or develop a chain of retail computer stores. Still another version of a retail chain was for ELM to organize the independent stores into a chain much like the IGA, Independent Grocers Association, which could achieve favorable buying terms, etc. This concept was investigated in some depth but eventually shelved because independents were in fact too independent and control became the real issue.

Elaine Moncur devoted much time to considering alternative strategies for ELM. The company had been highly successful and she had weathered many storms. She obviously was not one to give up easily and was highly motivated. Her employees were counting on her. To make matters worse her fortieth birthday was approaching and she "had to be something more than fat, forty and divorced." Although divorced, she certainly was not fat. To reward herself for a job well done, she decided to buy a white Corvette and then spent many nights out for a drive thinking about what her future strategy should be.

EXHIBIT I
ELM GROUP
ORGANIZATION CHART

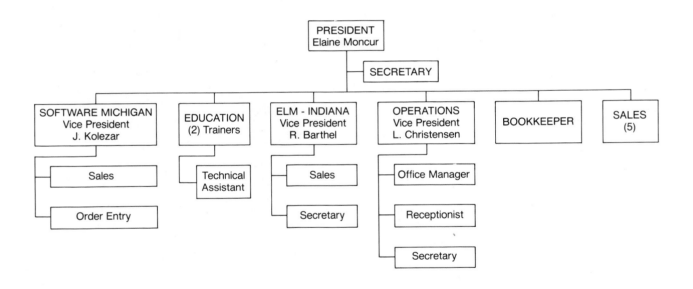

ENCORE

This case provides a sequel to the Miller Stamping & Die, Inc., case by describing what Peter decided to do. It should be used after the Miller case is discussed and a conclusion reached.

Taking a deep breath one evening Peter called Mr. Miller at home and began, "I don't know how much good this will do ..." When the story was completed a long pause ensued, and Mr. Miller then thanked him for his interest and information.

It was several days later that he received a luncheon invitation. "We're going to lunch and we'd like to have you join us," Peter's boss said. Over dessert and coffee the labor consultant making up the threesome spoke. "There is going to be some office reorganization and you're going to be on temporary layoff." Peter knew better. He was fired. On his way back to clean out his desk Peter reflected on how things could have been handled differently. Was he steamrollered by fate from the day the new secretary arrived, or was there anything that could have otherwise been done so the outcome would have been different. Or would the result have been the same no matter what he had done? Was there anything that could be done to help -- or even save -- the company, if only out of loyalty to fellow co-workers? He could undoubtedly act now without fear of retribution on his job. But what should he do now?